THE
COMPLETE GUIDE TO
WORD GAMES
- & -
WORD PLAY

THE
COMPLETE GUIDE TO
WORD GAMES
- & -
WORD PLAY

Ken Russell
and
Philip Carter

THE MENSA UK
PUZZLE EDITORS

foulsham
LONDON • NEW YORK • TORONTO • SYDNEY

foulsham
The Publishing House
Bennetts Close, Cippenham, Berks SL1 5AP

ISBN 0-572-01979-3

Typeset in Great Britain by Typesetting Solutions, Slough, Berks.
Printed in Great Britain by
St Edmundsbury Press Limited, Bury St Edmunds, Suffolk

CONTENTS

ABOUT MENSA

Mensa is a Social Club for which membership is accepted from all persons with an IQ (Intelligence Quotient) of 148 or above on the Cattell scale of intelligence. This represents the top two per cent of the population. Therefore one person in 50 is capable of passing the entrance test, which consists of a series of intelligence tests.

Mensa is the Latin word for 'table'. We are a round-table society where all persons are of equal standing. There are three aims: social contact amongst intelligent people; research in psychology; and the identification and fostering of intelligence.

Mensa is an International Society and has 110 000 members of all occupations: clerks, doctors, lawyers, policemen, industrial workers, teachers, nurses, etc.

Enquiries to: MENSA FREEPOST
Wolverhampton WV2 1BR,
England.

MENSA INTERNATIONAL
15 The Ivories,
6-8 Northampton Street,
London N1 2HV,
England.

ABOUT THE AUTHORS

Ken Russell is a London Surveyor and is Puzzle Editor of the *British Mensa Magazine,* a magazine which is sent to its 40 000 members monthly.

Philip Carter is a JP and an Estimator from Yorkshire. He is Puzzle Editor of *Enigmasig,* the monthly newsletter of the Mensa Puzzle Special Interest group.

INTRODUCTION

People delight in playing with words – pulling words apart, reconstructing them in different guises, arranging them in clever patterns and finding hidden meanings within them.

Playing with words is a universal activity. Word puzzles are probably the most popular and widely published of all puzzles. We all have to understand and speak the language to communicate, and the challenge of solving a word puzzle is one to which most of us like to respond.

We, the authors, are both word game addicts, whether it be creating novel crossword grids, decoding and devising ingenious cryptic crossword clues, or wrestling with chronograms, word squares, lipograms, palindromes, rebuses, heteronyms and homonyms. Our aim in this book has been to include every type of word game known to us.

We both are, however, conscious that any of you interested enough in word play to acquire this book, will also enjoy the task of solving puzzles. We have, therefore, throughout the text included puzzles which you can attempt. There are well over a hundred such puzzles, and the answers are given at the end of the book.

Our collaboration as compilers began ten years ago through our involvement with Enigmasig, a special interest group (SIG) within British Mensa, dedicated to the setting and solving of puzzles. Since then we have had more than 5000 puzzles published in book form, many of which are word based. The English language is, to us, a bottomless treasure chest of delight, and we take great pleasure in creating chaos, for that is what a puzzle compiler is - a creator of chaos.

This is not a puzzle book as such, but rather a catalogue of word play. We hope you derive much pleasure from it and enjoy the puzzles included for your additional entertainment. We hope also that you have the satisfaction of sorting out the chaos and arriving at many of the correct answers.

A1

ABBREVIATIONS

Puzzles based on the use of abbreviations have become very popular in recent years in newspapers and magazines and at parties. They can also be used as fund-raisers for charities. A sheet of 200 such questions, circulated recently in one of the author's home town, raised several hundreds of pounds for its chosen charity when contestants were charged 50 pence per entry with a prize on offer for the most correct answers.

The abbreviations can come in several categories. A few typical examples (a) to (e) are given for you to try.

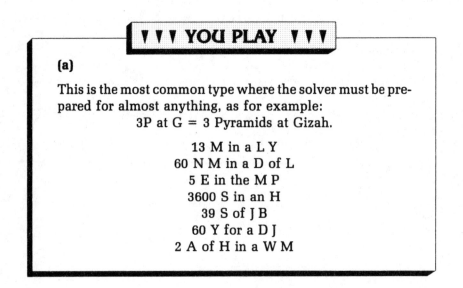

▼▼▼ YOU PLAY ▼▼▼

(a)

This is the most common type where the solver must be prepared for almost anything, as for example:

3P at G = 3 Pyramids at Gizah.

13 M in a L Y
60 N M in a D of L
5 E in the M P
3600 S in an H
39 S of J B
60 Y for a D J
2 A of H in a W M

(b)   **FAMOUS QUOTATIONS/SAYINGS**

For example: W A N A = We Are Not Amused (Queen Victoria).

T Q O M I N S

M L C

N T J

E M D W

(c)   **ALL CREATURES GREAT AND SMALL**

For example: P M F = Pigs Might Fly.

B O A F F T

C K T C

T F A D H

T R L A B

(d)   **AROUND THE WORLD**

For example: The G C in V = The Grand Canal in Venice.

The T M at A in I

The W W in J

S on S P

T M in C T

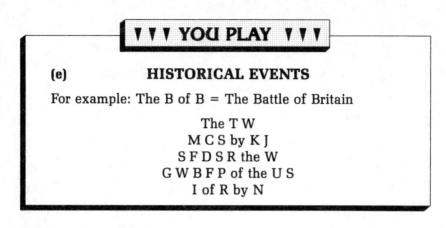
(e) **HISTORICAL EVENTS**

For example: The B of B = The Battle of Britain

The T W
M C S by K J
S F D S R the W
G W B F P of the U S
I of R by N

Non-communication

One of the problems with the use of abbreviations is that they are often only understood by the person who has used them and are, thus, not a very effective means of communication. Take, for instance, this extract from an article in *Integra,* the Journal of the High-IQ Society, Intertel.

> 'Sunday was also a holiday in the Army. If not selected for KP duty we were free to go to the chapel in the morning and to the PX or theatre in the after-noon. Everyone was restricted to the military base. I remember going to the theatre where a small girl sang, "I don't want to set the world on fire". I felt very lonely in a field of OD uniforms.'

No doubt the three abbreviations used will be instantly recognisable by anyone who has served in the US Army, but to others they are unlikely to be deciphered without some difficulty.

Plurals

One interesting curiosity worthy of mention is that of abbreviations which become pluralised by doubling a single letter, for example n/nn (note/notes) and v/vv (verse/verses).

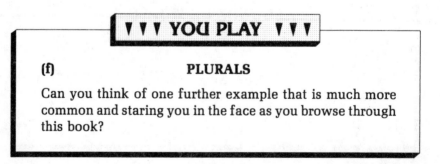

▼ ▼ ▼ **YOU PLAY** ▼ ▼ ▼

(f) **PLURALS**

Can you think of one further example that is much more common and staring you in the face as you browse through this book?

(Answers to A1 (a) to (f) on page 251)

ACRONYMS

An acronym is a word formed from the initial letter or letters of the words it represents, as in NATO (North Atlantic Treaty Organization). Examples of well-known acronyms are:

LASER   – Light Amplification by Stimulated Emission of Radiation

RADAR   – RAdio Detection And Ranging

SCUBA   – Self-Contained Underwater Breathing Apparatus

SONAR   – SOund NAvigation Ranging

ZIP   – Zone Improvement Plan

MODEM   – MOdulator + DEModulator

TELEX   – TELeprinter EXchange

MOPED   – MOtor + PEDal

WILCO   – WILl COmply

With the invention of more and more elaborate acronyms, such as CON-SCIENCE (Committee On National Student Citizenship In Every National Case of Emergency), acronyms have developed into a form of word play in their own right. They also lead to different kinds of word games and also quiz questions such as (a) and (b).

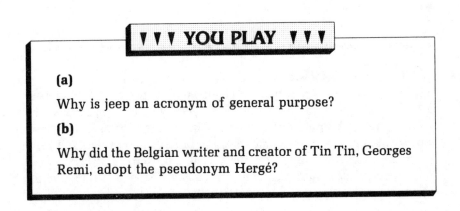

▼ ▼ ▼ YOU PLAY ▼ ▼ ▼

(a)

Why is jeep an acronym of general purpose?

(b)

Why did the Belgian writer and creator of Tin Tin, Georges Remi, adopt the pseudonym Hergé?

In one word game based on acronyms, players select a word and make a sentence from the initial letters of the word which is appropriate to that word; for example:

SLEDGE:	SNOW
	LOCOMOBILE
	EASILY
	DESCENDS
	GIANT
	ESCARPMENTS
MUSSEL:	MOLLUSC
	UNDER
	SEA
	SLITHERY
	EDIBLE
	LIMPET
FARMER:	FECUND
	AND
	RURAL
	MAN
	EARTHY
	RESOURCEFUL

▼▼▼ YOU PLAY ▼▼▼

(c)　　　　　　　　**MAKE A SENTENCE**

Now try this one:

K
N
I
F
E

'Yuppie' language

The late 1980s saw a new type of terminology that seemed to disappear just as quickly with the recession of the 1990s as it had appeared in the boom time of the mid-to-late-1980s. This was the 'Yuppie' language, where different groups of people were identified by appropriate and witty acronyms. The best known of these is, in fact, the term YUPPIE, a word now incorporated into the English language and meaning 'young upwardly-mobile (or urban) professional'.

(d)   **YUPPIES**

For how many of these 'Yuppie' examples can you remember, or work out, the meaning?

DEWKS, DIMPS, DROPPIES, DUMPIES, FRUMPIES, GRUMPIES, MAFFIES, MALLIES, MUPPIES, PREPPIES, PUPPIES, SKIPPIES, TICKS, WOOFIES, WOOPIES, YUFFIES.

Bacronyms

Another game, introduced in May 1992 *Word Ways* by David Morice, was called 'bacronyms'. The object was to work out acronyms from the final letters instead of the initial letters. That is, in the acronym Zone Improvement Plan (ZIP), the bacronym is ETN.

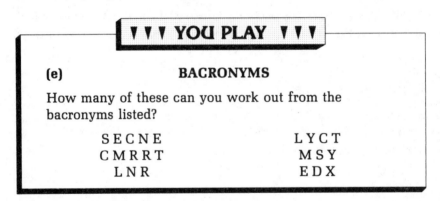

(e)   **BACRONYMS**

How many of these can you work out from the bacronyms listed?

S E C N E	L Y C T
C M R R T	M S Y
L N R	E D X

Future acronyms?

The use of acronyms continues to flourish and recently the authors have noted BRATS (a group of children belonging to the Be Really Active This Summer playscheme, founded in 1993) and NAFFOFF (the National Federation of Freedom Of the Fear of Flying). Perhaps one day the government might appoint a MAD officer in charge of a Media Acronym Department who could, in turn, form a CRAP (Committee to Resist Acronym Proliferation). They could then appoint a number of PRATS (employees forming the Public Regulation of Acronyms Team) who would then oversee anyone who wanted to be A THUG (Acronyms THink-Up a Good-one).

(Answers to A2 (a) to (e) on pages 251–2)

ACROSTICS

An acrostic is a composition, usually in the form of a poem, in which the initial letters of the lines taken in order spell out a word or short sentence. The pattern may also make use of letters from other parts of the lines or combination of letters, for example first and last, to produce a wide variety of puzzles and riddles.

Although most are written as puzzles, others make no attempt to conceal the answer, as in the case of the following by Intertel US High-IQ Society member, Ruth B. Altman, which appeared in the 'Sphinx Winks' column of the society's journal *Integra*, in August 1984.

> Play inspires a noteworthy ovation,
> If performer fulfils expectation.
> Any type gets a hand,
> Nine-foot ones are real grand.
> Out of tune, all key 'Liszt'ner's' frustration.

It will be noted that both the initial letters of the first line and the initial letters of the first word in each line spell out 'PIANO', and many musical terms are contained within the acrostic.

Using last letters

Sometimes the word is based on the last letter of a line (a telestitch) or a combination of first and last letters (a double-acrostic) as in example (a) compiled by the authors.

▼▼▼ YOU PLAY ▼▼▼

(a) DOUBLE-ACROSTIC

Each couplet provides the clue to a word. When the six words are listed, two more words are spelt out by the first and last letters of the six words.

> A tiny note, it's in quick time,
> All you need to solve this rhyme?
>
> Cry to Mark, it's so abrupt,
> Delight or horror will erupt.

Set a course to steer the ship,
Plot the route when off you trip.

Just a drop to come apart,
Joy perhaps, or sad at heart?

Describe a lad who now is striving,
One day his hopes may be arriving.

Sculpture of freedom and all is well,
Here's independence and the marching bell.

Triple acrostic

Next, is a rarely seen triple acrostic in which the solution is based on the initial, middle and final letters of the answer words.

▼ ▼ ▼ YOU PLAY ▼ ▼ ▼

(b) **TRIPLE ACROSTIC**

The first couplet gives a clue to the answer as a whole and the five numbered couplets provide the five answer words. This triple-acrostic is believed to date from around the middle of this century but, alas, the author is unknown.

Left, middle and right,
Give us a choice of light.

1 The kind of glance which he who's lost his heart,
   Bestows on her who wears the latter part.

2 Here is one,
   With a gun.

3 This is bound,
   To go round.

4 Simplify taste,
   And eliminate waste.

5 My meaning is plain,
   By my saying it again.

Acrostics in history

The word acrostic is derived from the Latin word 'acrostichis' which is a composite of two Greek words 'AKRON' (end) and 'STIKHOS' (line of verse). Acrostics are of ancient origin and examples appear throughout history.

One notable example is the Greek phrase 'Jesus Christ the Son of God, the Saviour' where, in the Greek original, the initial letters of the phrase form the Greek word 'ichthys' meaning fish. This is significant because the fish held mystical powers for the Ancient Greeks.

The Hebrews had what are known as ABECEDIAN hymns, which are sacred poems in which the first letter of each line, or stanza, runs in order through all 22 letters of the Hebrew alphabet. A famous example is King David's acrostic which is actually *Psalm 119*, also known as the *Abecedian Psalm*. In this, each eight-line stanza begins with words whose initials are the letters of the Hebrew alphabet in order, starting alpha, beth, etc.

Others who amused themselves and their audiences with acrostics include Plautus, who prefaced his comedies with an Argument, the first letters of each line spelling out the name of the play, and Sir John Davis, an Elizabethan poet whose 16 poems in praise of Queen Elizabeth I all contained 16 lines which spelled out ELISABETHA REGINA in a vertical line. These poems bore the collective title of *Hymns to Astraea*.

Word square acrostics

Many famous people from history, including Aristotle and Socrates, studied acrostics in the form of word squares. There is much evidence of the existence of such work in Great Britain during the Roman occupation.

THE SATOR ACROSTIC

The most famous example is, undoubtedly, the 'Sator acrostic' (see diagram) which has been discovered at Pompeii and, in 1868, at Cirencester, England, where it is now exhibited at the Corinium Museum. More recently it has been discovered during excavations at a site near Manchester in the north of England and no doubt will continue to be uncovered at sites of Roman occupation in different parts of the world.

The square is unique because the words read the same, not only across and down as with conventional magic squares which we feature later in this book, but also backwards and upwards.

The best translation of the words contained in the square (see diagram) is probably: 'Arepo the sower hold the wheels with force'. However, what is even more interesting is that 21 of the 25 letters of the acrostic can be

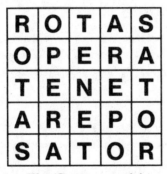

R	O	T	A	S
O	P	E	R	A
T	E	N	E	T
A	R	E	P	O
S	A	T	O	R

The 'Sator acrostic'

arranged in the form of a cross spelling out 'PATERNOSTER' in the horizontal and vertical. The paternoster is: the Lord's Prayer especially in Latin; every 11th bead of a rosary, indicating that the Lord's Prayer is to be repeated; and a fishing line with a weight at the end and short lines with hooks extending at intervals, again reinforcing the Ancient Greek preoccupation with fish. It should be noted that the remaining unused letters are 'AAOO', which could be said to represent Alpha and Omega, the first and last letters of the Greek alphabet.

A further remarkable feature is that all 25 letters can be arranged to spell out 'Oro Te, Pater; Oro Te Pater; Sanas', which, when translated, means 'I pray to Thee Father; I pray to Thee Father; Thou healest'.

There is no doubt that the 'Sator acrostic' is a remarkable work of genius, many centuries old, with a deep and meaningful significance which is unlikely ever to be matched.

The Stele of Moschion

A further example of an ancient acrostic is the Stele of Moschion, which is a 39 × 39 square found in Egypt. It is a clever symmetrical pattern of the symbols O, C, I, P, Δ, M, X, W, N, Y, Γ, A and Θ, which are so arranged whereby, starting at the centre O and reading right, left, up or down to the end and then turning at right-angles to the next corner, the same phrase: 'Moschion to Osiris, for the treatment which cured his foot', is repeated over and over. The acrostic was devised as a tribute to the god Osiris who had reputedly healed Moschion's foot.

Acrostic as a riddle

Other acrostics can be presented in the form of a riddle, as in example (c) –
which quotes the opening quatrain of the *Rubáiyát of Omar Khayyám*,
from the second edition of the famous translation by Edward Fitzgerald.

▼▼▼ YOU PLAY ▼▼▼

(c)   **ACROSTIC AS A RIDDLE**

What is the essence, or distinctive quality of this passage?

> 'Wake' for the sun behind yon Eastern height
> Has chased the Session of the Stars from Night:
> And, to the field of Heav'n ascending, strikes
> The Sultan's Turret with a Shaft of Light.

IT ISN'T A CODE,
IT'S MY LOTTERY TICKET !

Acrostic with clues

In modern times, acrostics have been presented in books and magazines as
puzzles with crossword-type clues. Example (d), compiled by the authors,
is typical.

(d) **ACROSTIC WITH CLUES**

In the Quotation Box are the first two lines of a quotation. Solve the clues, place the answers in the Answers Grid, then, transfer the letters to the Quotation Box. The first letter of each answer will spell out the initial and name of the Author of the Quotation.

Answers Grid
Author

Clues

Clue		No.
Together		1
Add sugar		2
60 minutes		3
They live in an abbey		4
Goes with kin		5
Think favourably of		6
Fire gun		7
Road workers		8
Without finish		9
Sum up		10
Circular		10
Heavenly		12

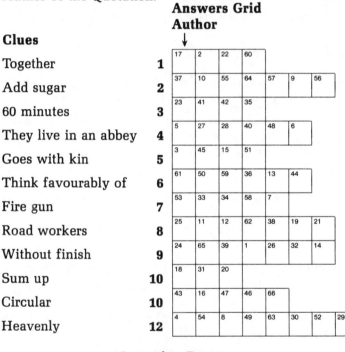

Quotation Box

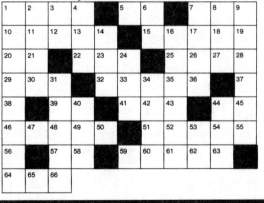

(Answers to A3 (a) to (d) on pages 252-3)

ALPHABET STORY

The object of this game is to compose a story of 26 words starting with a word beginning with the letter 'A' and then following with words beginning with each letter of the alphabet in sequence. For example:

Animals Being Caged Demand Every Favour. Good Husbandry In Jovial Kindly Loving Manner. Not One Person Quickly Repairs Sore Toe. Useful Vet Will X-ray Young Zebra.

Alphabet Telegrams

Another version of this game is called 'Telegrams', the object of which is to create a 26-word Telegram in a similar way. For example:

Always Be Cautious. Don't Encourage False Generosity. Hide Information. Just Keep Local Mail. Never Offer Postage Quickly. Remain Silent Too. Unless Vera Will Xerox Your Zip-code.

ALPHAMETICS

We deliberated whether or not to include alphametics in a book of word games as it is debatable whether they are, in fact, word or number puzzles. In the end we gave them the benefit of the doubt as the compiling of them is mainly a word puzzle, whereas the solving of them is purely a mathematical function.

This type of puzzle, in which the numerals of arithmetical calculations are replaced by letters, originated thousands of years ago in Ancient China where they were known as 'letter arithmetic'. Then, in the 1930s, the name 'cryptarithm' was proposed and, in 1955, the word 'alphametic' was coined by J. A. H. Hunter.

The best examples of this type of puzzle have unique answers and related words, as with:

GNOME + PIXIE = ELFIN   (14397 + 60807 = 75204)

Although it has related words, the example, SOLVE + TEST = GENIUS does not have a unique solution. There are, in fact, three possible answers: 74890 + 30737 = 105627, 34890 + 70373 = 105263 and 67590 + 40646 = 108236, the first two being closely related. Of course, the puzzle is not flawed if the number of possible solutions is pointed out to the solver at the outset. You may like to try examples (a) to (d).

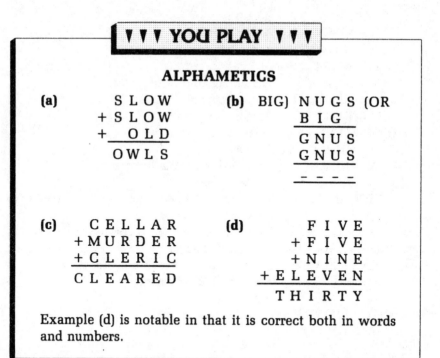

ALPHAMETICS

(a)
```
    S L O W
  + S L O W
  +   O L D
    O W L S
```

(b)
```
BIG) N U G S (OR
      B I G
     G N U S
     G N U S
     - - - -
```

(c)
```
    C E L L A R
  + M U R D E R
  + C L E R I C
    C L E A R E D
```

(d)
```
      F I V E
    + F I V E
    + N I N E
  + E L E V E N
    T H I R T Y
```

Example (d) is notable in that it is correct both in words and numbers.

(Answers to A5 (a) to (d) on page 253)

=======A6=======

ALTERNATIVE DICTIONARY

This is one of those addictive games where it is difficult to stop once you have started, the object being to find witty alternative definitions for words. For example:

WANTON : A Chinese weight.
EXTRAPOLATE : What one should be in genteel company.
ACCESS : A request to reduce the alphabet.
ELECTRON : A campaign slogan.
POLITICS : A bomb in a parrot.
DELICATE : An Indian household pet.
PLAINTIFF : A disagreement on board a transatlantic flight.
DIRECT : An exhausted Princess.
TARTRATE : A hooker's fee.
DIATRIBE : A bad bunch.

PROPAGATE	:	Keep the door ajar.
KINDRED	:	A fear of relations.
DEMONSTRATE	:	A devilish stretch of water.
THE RUBÁIYÁT OF OMAR KHAYYÁM	:	His inflatable pleasure craft.
PROGRAMME	:	An advocate of SI units.
CENTRIFUGAL	:	A guard singing Bach.
ORIENTEERING	:	Asian jewellery.
MINIMUM	:	A short parent.
ABUNDANCE	:	Aerobics for pregnant women.
ILLEGAL	:	A big sick bird.
CENTIMETRE	:	What you get when your wife's sister is due to arrive at the station.
GLADIATOR	:	How the cannibal felt about his mother-in-law.
MANUAL LABOUR	:	A Spanish builder.
SERGEANT MAJOR	:	A man who is rotten to the corps.
NOTE PAD	:	A musician's apartment.
COFFIN	:	A snuff box.
STONEHENGE	:	A heavy rock group.
FOOT BRAKE	:	A chiropodist's day off.

==A7==

ANAGRAMS

Do you find solving anagrams as 'INCOMPREHENSIBLE' as solving a 'PROBLEM IN CHINESE'? Do you know a 'ONE WORD' anagram for 'NEW DOOR'? 'NOR DO WE'!

Early anagrams

The origin of anagrams is ascribed to a Greek poet, Lycophron. He lived during the fourth century BC and was brought to Egypt by King Ptolomy where he amused the king's court by inventing flattering anagrams of their names. Originally, an anagram was simply a word which, when reversed, formed another word. For example: ROOM/MOOR or TIDE/EDIT. The word 'anagram' is derived from Greek. 'Ana' means 'backwards' and 'Gramma' means 'a letter'.

The best anagrams are those where the rearranged letters bear some relationship to the original word or name. For instance, the letters of the word 'SOFTHEARTEDNESS' can be arranged to form the phrase 'OFTEN SHEDS TEARS'.

One famous anagram dates back to the Middle Ages when an anagrammer devised a supposed dialogue between Pilate and Jesus. Pilate asks 'QUID EST VERITAS?' (What is truth?) and Jesus replies 'EST VIR QUI ADEST' (It is the man before you).

Anagrams of names

For hundreds of years compilers have tried to find hidden meanings in rearranging the names of famous people. Some of our favourites are: 'I'LL MAKE A WISE PHRASE' (William Shakespeare); 'ON THEN, O SAILOR' (Horatio Nelson); 'FLIT ON CHEERING ANGEL' (Florence Nightingale); and 'OUR BEST NOVELS IN STORE' (Robert Louis Stevenson). Politicians, too, inevitably found their names being re-arranged into appropriate phrases. Depending on your political leanings, Margaret Thatcher became either 'THAT GREAT CHARMER' or 'MEG THE ARCH TARTAR'; and 'I'M A WHIG WHO'LL BE A TRAITOR TO ENGLAND'S RULE' was an unkind 19th century anagram for 'Right Honourable William Ewart Gladstone', the four times British Prime Minister.

Anagrams have also been used by writers for pen names. CALVINUS was the pen name of Alcuinus (the U being converted to V). One of the authors of this book, an estimator by profession, has also experimented with the letters of his name. Thus, after doing the day-job 'The Estimating Philip Carter' becomes 'PEARL CHIRPIT THE ENIGMATIST' when he dons his puzzle-solving cap.

The ultimate anagram

In his book of 1903, *The Handy Book of Literary Curiosities*, Englishman William Walsh wrote, 'After centuries of endeavour, so few really good anagrams have been rolled down to us. One may assert that all the really superb anagrams now extant might be contained in a pillbox.'

Since then, however, the fascination for anagrams has never waned and one can be sure that whichever politician, entertainer or sportsman reaches star status, he or she will find the letters of his or her name being massaged into numerous permutations in the search for the perfect anagram. So what then is the ultimate anagram? Perhaps there is no better example than Melvin O. Wellman's classic of 1948:

ELEVEN + TWO = TWELVE + ONE

It is perfect in that it is completely transposed and grammatically correct and meets the purists' rule that an anagram should never contain more than three letters in the same sequence.

Helen Hovenic also noted in her 1941 book *The Puzzler's Paradise*, that 'Majolica' of the National Puzzlers' League defined the perfect anagram: 'The new word or phrase evolved shall be equivalent in meaning to that whence it was derived. Obviously this is a severe requirement; and a perfect anagram is, in consequence, a chef d'oeuvre of the puzzlistic art.'

Notable anagrams

The following is a fine example of an enigmatic poem culminating in a clever and appropriate anagram from an unknown compiler of many years ago:

> Can it be as legends say,
>   That this fête of friendly mirth –
> Cupid's gayest gala-day –
>   In a saintly brain had birth?
>   A quaint
>   Old saint
>   He was, I guess.
>   Who could
>   Have wooded
>   His sweet saintness
> With such vanities as these,
> Of tinsel, lace and fripperies!
>   Could a stern and monkish mind
> E'er have such a work designed –
> Such an airy, fairy bit?
> Nay, a lass invented it.

The answer to the riddle is, of course, in the final punch line – an anagram of 'Saint Valentine's Day'.

*   *   *

Here now, is a selection of anagrams which have all appeared in the *Journal of the National Puzzlers' League* during the past 100 years:

ANAGRAMS	– Ars magna
A BARTENDER	– Beer and art
THE DEATH OF WOLFE ON THE PLAINS OF ABRAHAM	– On a path to fame, both he and his war foe fell
DORMITORY	– Dirty room
FAMILIES	– Life's aim

THE LEANING TOWER OF PISA	– What a foreign stone pile
OLD MASTERS	– Art's models
ORCHESTRATE	– Score the art
PAYMENT RECEIVED	– Every cent paid me
SAINT ELMO'S FIRE	– Is lit for seamen
SHERMAN'S MARCH TO THE SEA	– The massacre on the marsh
THE LANDING OF THE PILGRIMS	– Slight-fed men hailing port
TEN COMMANDMENTS	– Can't mend most men
TO CAST PEARLS BEFORE SWINE	– One's labor is perfect waste
THE UPHOLSTERERS	– Restore the plush

Other notable anagrams are: UNO + CATORCE = CUATRO + ONCE and DOS + TRECE = TRES + DOCE, which in Spanish both total 15; THE GOOD SAMARITANS – Heart's go to man's aid (compiled by Loris B. Curtis in 1989); and CLINT EASTWOOD – Old West action.

More anagram games

Below are several other word games which are all on an anagram-based theme. Several of these are of the authors' own invention.

ANAGRAMMED PROVERBS

Word play, especially anagrams, became a very fashionable pastime during the second half of the 19th century. One popular game was to form sentences using the letters of well-known proverbs, as in these examples:

I DON'T ADMIT WOMEN ARE FAINT	– Time and tide wait for no man
IT ROCKS, THE BROAD FLAG OF THE FREE	– Birds of a feather flock together
STRONG LION'S SHARE ALMOST GONE	– A rolling stone gathers no moss

▼▼▼ YOU PLAY ▼▼▼

(a)   **ANAGRAM THEME**

Devised by the authors, the object is to find seven names on the same theme and anagram each name into two words. The 14 words are then listed in alphabetical order and the solver must then arrange the 14 words in pairs and find the original seven words. Look at these:

ARK, CAT, CURE, DOG, FIT, LEAN, LOAN, LOG, ME, SIR, SORE, STARE, RAGE, TEN

Can you pair up the words correctly and find seven names all on the same theme? (It is an extremely difficult puzzle to solve.)

▼▼▼ YOU PLAY ▼▼▼

(b)   **ANAGRAMMED SYNONYMS**

Another game devised by the authors. In each group of three words the task is to find the two of the three that can be paired to form an anagram of one word, which is a synonym of the remaining word.

Example: LEG-MEEK-NET. The words LEG and NET are an anagram of GENTLE, which is a synonym of the remaining word – MEEK.

Now try these:

CORE–ROD–ROT
GRAIN–NOVEL–OIL
LEAP–BAY–DUE
MOB–LAG–SKIP

ANIMALGRAMS
The object is to form anagrams from the names of animals. For example:

CORONA – RACOON
PAROLED – LEOPARD
ORCHESTRA – CARTHORSE

ANTIGRAMS

These are much rarer than ordinary appropriate anagrams. The object is to form a word or phrase which is opposite in meaning to the original. Perhaps the most famous is 'REAL FUN' which is an anagram, or antigram, of the word 'FUNERAL'. These all appeared in the *Journal of the National Puzzlers' League* during the past 100 years.

ADVERSARIES	–	Are advisers
ANARCHISTS	–	Arch saints
DESECRATION	–	Care is noted
DIPLOMACY	–	Mad policy
EARLIEST	–	Rise late
EPITAPHS	–	Happiest
FILLED	–	Ill-fed
FORTY-FIVE	–	Over fifty
HONESTLY	–	On the sly
MELODRAMATIC	–	A more mild act
ROOSEVELT	–	Vote loser
THOMAS A EDISON	–	Tom has no ideas
THE WINTER GALES	–	Sweltering heat

▼▼▼ YOU PLAY ▼▼▼

(c) BOOK TITLES

An invention of the authors. Each book title is the clue to a word and the name of the book's author is an anagram of that word.

As an example:
THE WRITER by A. ROUTH – Answer: AUTHOR.

HOLD SPELLBOUND by LEN HART

SHORT OF WIND by ALBERT HESS

RENEGADE by E N CARTER

SUGAR by GUS COLE

BEAMING WITH JOY by IAN DART

GEOGRAPHICAL ANAGRAMS

You might be surprised at the number of ordinary words whose letters can be rearranged to make place names. Here are a few.

AMINE	–	MAINE
NOMINATES	–	MINNESOTA
DIAGNOSE	–	SAN DIEGO
ANGRIEST	–	TANGIERS
ENEMY	–	YEMEN
TESTIER	–	TRIESTE
PENAL	–	NEPAL
LAITY	–	ITALY
ROMANCE	–	CREMONA
ERECT	–	CRETE
LOUSE	–	SEOUL
ORATION	–	ONTARIO
DOTTIER	–	DETROIT
SPRUCY	–	CYPRUS
PLANES	–	NAPLES
NERVED	–	DENVER
ANALOG	–	ANGOLA
TAXES	–	TEXAS
RUMBA	–	BURMA
PAINS	–	SPAIN
TANGERINE	–	ARGENTINE

However, the ultimate anagrammist's delight must be 'SACRAMENTO' which can be converted to: Actor's name; Scorn a mate; Escort a man; Same carton; Smart canoe; Coaster man; A master con; and, Not a scream; to give but a few. We could go on, but will not. You may wish to.

HIEROGRAMS

These are religious anagrams, normally in Latin. For example: 'O Mater Dei memento mei' (Oh Mother of God, remember me), which is an anagram of 'Amo Demeter enim timeo' (I love Demeter because I fear her). Demeter is the Goddess of Fruitful Earth and the Greek equivalent of Isis. The first sentence is written on the wall of the Tower of the Prisoners in the castle of Gisers in France.

▼▼▼ YOU PLAY ▼▼▼

(d)   **MARGANA**

This is an anagram in reverse. As an example, if presented with the words MAR, AM and FAR, and asked to find the smallest English word that contained all the letters from which these words could be produced, you would come up with the word FARM. Now here is a further list of words:

PROBE, OVEN, BRAIN, HOPE

What is the shortest English word from which all these words can be produced?

▼▼▼ YOU PLAY ▼▼▼

(e)   **NEWSPAPER HEADLINES**

This idea was proposed in 1992 by a publisher friend of ours, Tony Sharrock, who came up with the following examples. 'Newspaper headlines,' he said, 'have their own language, especially when it comes to crime. These could have been taken from any tabloid, but there is one curious thing about them. If you unscramble the letters in each headline, you will end up with the title of a popular television "whodunnit". Can you identify the programmes?'

LOVE MURDER SHOCK: HE SHOT ALF STEEN

THAI PIRATES HOIST CARGO

DAWN THIEVES STOLE A GIFT RING

DOLLIE INN CASE DRAMA

TRANSLINGUAL ANAGRAMS
These are words in English which can be anagrammed to give words in foreign languages, for example:

INCREMATIONS	=	RINASCIMENTO	(Italian – Renaissance)
LACERTION	=	TOLERANCIA	(Spanish – Tolerance)
ENHARMONIC	=	MONARCHIEN	(German – Monarchies)
LITHOMARGE	=	ALGORITHME	(French – Algorithm)

There is also one known trilingual synonym anagram:

MINE (English) – MIEN (French) – MEIN (German)

which, of course, has the same meaning in all three languages.

▼▼▼ YOU PLAY ▼▼▼

(f)   **UNIVERSAL ANAGRAMS**

A universal anagram is a word that can be anagrammed into a new word commencing with each letter in turn. For example:

STOP – TOPS – OPTS – POST

Can you find an example of such a six-letter word?

▼▼▼ YOU PLAY ▼▼▼

(g)   **NO NEIGHBOURS**

Devised by the authors, the idea is to scramble a word into interlocked shapes that have some connection with that word. To assist the solver, no two adjoining letters in the word must appear in the same shape. Can you solve this one?

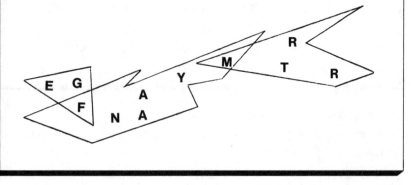

(Answers to A7 (a) to (g) on page 253)

THE AUSTRALIAN CROSSWORD CLUB

The existence of the Australian Crossword Club was brought to our attention by a friend of one of the authors, Audrey Austin, who lives in New South Wales and is, herself, a prolific compiler of puzzles. The club publishes all kinds of crossword-related puzzles in its monthly newsletter, all submitted by members. These puzzles include: alphabetical jigsaws, which are cryptically-clued and the solutions fitted into the grid until they all match up; standard cryptic crosswords; and thematic crosswords. (a) *Choose your weapon*, is a typical puzzle, from the November 1993 newsletter.

We are grateful to the Australian Crossword Club for allowing us to reproduce this puzzle.

Anyone interested in membership of the club should write to:

> Mr Alan Walter,
> 7 Allunga Close,
> Mona Vale,
> NSW 2103,
> Australia

(a) **CHOOSE YOUR WEAPON**
by Coming and Going

All answers are eight-letter words which go around the clue number in either direction, beginning at any point. Touching letters in neighbouring hexagons are the same. The 22 letters against the heavy boundary lines spell out the name of a Shakespearian play, and, in the same direction, the name of the hero's friend, who died following a sword fight. The names go around one way or the other, beginning at a certain point.

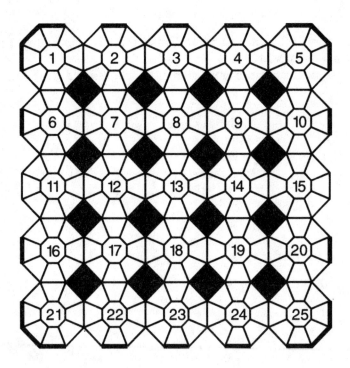

1 Ere crumb was crumbled he got in the way

2 Pasted or attacked by artillery

3 Deposit excavation for explosive dropped by parachute (4–4)

4 Artillery once over a muddled mended hole

5 Mud in greater quantity for heavy two-edged sword?

6 Is armed man sane running around with pram?

7 Swimming exhibition brings water to pet lamb

8 Old-time hand-gun sounds to have come out of the ark with a vehicle

9 Cult about a valve is good for launching aeroplanes

10 Amazing; she quietly went and smartened up the powder-room

11 Angry rod strung with horse-hair for shooting arrows

12 Spitfire has aura and cunning

13 No charge decree is voluntary (4–4)

14 Small protuberance inside the diamond is crossed

15 Nile mite irritated the explosive

16 Liquefy undulating land and achieve overheating

17 Building our dream-like kind of car?

18 Ruffians in untidy slum after falcon cover

19 If Mum or Roger's starting unevenly with cells arranged like bricks in a wall

20 A lone fact about old field-gun

21 To offer in sacrifice I ate without my mixture of lollies initially

22 Limit ray-gun without pistol re-ordered for the armed forces

23 A dollar projected – not passed – it's used on big game

24 Shake a processed Eastern toddy and open slightly for a venomous snake

25 Grab back curious left/right poem . . . it trims lance

(Answers to A8 (a) on page 254)

BATTLESHIPS

The game of battleships played by children can be adapted into an excellent word game for two players. Each player has two 10 × 10 grids numbered 1 to 10 at the top and lettered A to J down the side. One grid is the player's own; the other is a grid on which he can mark the hits he achieves.

How to play

Each player first places eight ships in his own grid, without letting his opponent see where, as follows:

◯	One battleship, comprising four squares in a straight line. (1 ship – 4 squares)
▲	Two cruisers, each comprising three squares in a straight line. (2 ships – 6 squares)
◆	Two destroyers, each comprising two adjoining squares. (2 ships – 4 squares)
⬤	Three submarines, placed at random. (3 ships – 3 squares)

Table of symbols for ships

The game commences by Player 1 firing a two-letter word anywhere in the grid hoping to hit one of his opponent's ships. For example, he may choose the word 'AT' and nominate squares F8 and G8 (Move 1). Both players then write the word 'AT' in the appropriate position in their grids. If Player 1 had scored a hit, then Player 2 would call out 'hit' and would name the ship but not the square.

It is then the turn of Player 2, whose task is to turn the two-letter word 'AT' into a three-letter word, crossword style. If this is not possible he selects, instead, a new two-letter word and fires it into his opponent's

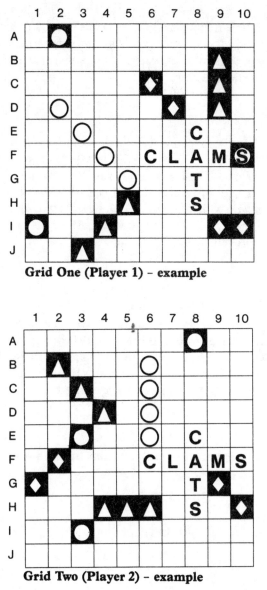

Move 2
Player 2 makes 'AT' into 'CAT' by firing C.

Move 4
Player 2 makes 'CLAMS' by firing C, L, M, S and sinks a submarine of Player 1.

Grid One (Player 1) – example

Move 1
Player 1 fires 'AT'.

Move 3
Player 1 makes 'CAT' into 'CATS' by firing 'S'.

Grid Two (Player 2) – example

grid. Assuming, however, that he makes 'AT' into 'CAT', he calls out 'Letter C on E8' (Move 2) and both players add this to their grid.

It is now the turn of Player 1 and he must make a four-letter word, crossword style. In the example shown, he transforms 'CAT' into 'CATS', calling out 'Letter S on H8' (Move 3).

Player 2 now has to make a five-letter word, and, by using 'A' in 'CATS', calls out 'CLAMS', nominating C, L, M and S on squares F6, F7, F9, F10 (Move 4). By doing this he scores the first kill by sinking one of the submarines of Player 1.

The game continues in this way until one player sinks all his opponent's ships, wins by default, or a stalemate is reached whereby it is not possible to place further words into the grid. Note that, except for the submarines (each 1 square), a 'hit' does not constitute a sinking. All the squares comprising a ship must be hit to sink the ship.

DEFAULTING

It is possible to lose by default in the following way: In the example game, it is now the turn of Player 1 to make a six-letter word. If he says 'Not possible' and Player 2 agrees, he starts again with a two-letter word. If, however, Player 2 says 'Challenge' and comes up with a six-letter word, for example, 'ASSESS' joining up with 'S' in 'CLAMS', he will have successfully challenged and will win the game through default. All words can be verified if necessary in a previously-agreed dictionary.

STALEMATE

If during the later stages of the game a stalemate is reached whereby not even a two-letter word can be placed and not all ships have been sunk, then the player who has sunk the most ships is the winner. If, however, no ships have been sunk, the winners is the player with the highest score for 'hits' using a previously agreed points system (say, 2 points for each 'hit' on the battleship and 1 point for each hit on a cruiser or destroyer).

FURTHER GUIDANCE

All three-letter, four-letter, five-letter, etc. words must link up crossword style. For example the following is permitted:

		C		A
C	L	A	M	S
		T		S
		S		E
				S
				S

However, the following is **not** permitted:

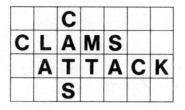

Any new two-letter word can be placed anywhere in the grid but must **not** link up with previously placed words.

Subsequent three-letter, four-letter, five-letter, etc. words may, however, link up with previously placed words if this is possible, for example:

						A
				C		S
M		C	L	A	M	S
A				T		E
S		W		S		S
S	E	E				S

This could produce:

						A
				C		S
M		C	L	A	M	S
A				T		E
S		W	A	S	P	S
S	E	E				S

The five-letter word 'WASPS' has utilised the 'S' from 'CATS' and the 'S' from 'ASSESS' from the previous group of words.

BIGRAMS

A bigram is any sequence of two letters occurring consecutively in a word, such as 'IG' in the word bigram. A double bigram is such a sequence which occurs twice in succession, such as 'IGIG' in whirligig. A triple bigram, a rare phenomenen, is a sequence which occures three times. Such a rarity occurs only in unusual or obscure words. For example: logogogue, feminining or sheheheyanu. There is also one known quadruple bigram, kukukuku, to be found in *Webster's New International Dictionary*.

In all there are 676 possible bigrams in the English alphabet, including double letters, and the master of word play, the late Dmitri Borgman, reputedly found words beginning with all but 47 of these possible ways. Obviously, he had to delve deep into libraries of obscure words and dialects to do so.

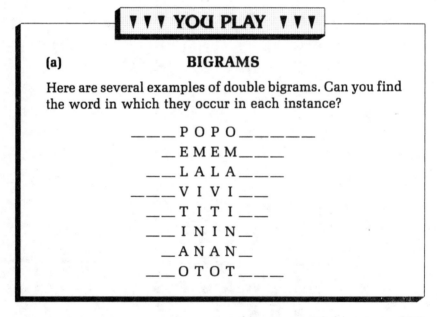

▼ ▼ ▼ YOU PLAY ▼ ▼ ▼

(a)   **BIGRAMS**

Here are several examples of double bigrams. Can you find the word in which they occur in each instance?

```
____ P O P O _____
  _ E M E M ____
 __ L A L A ____
____ V I V I __
 __ T I T I __
 __ I N I N _
 _ A N A N _
 __ O T O T ____
```

(Answers to B2 (a) on page 254)

BLANK CROSSWORDS

This game, based on the crossword puzzle, was invented by the authors.

Any crossword puzzle is taken from a newspaper, magazine or book. A non-playing adjudicator is elected, who holds the completed crossword puzzle. Two players then compete against each other to solve the puzzle.

Player 1 studies the blank grid which has been lettered across the top and numbered down the side. An example is shown in the diagram.

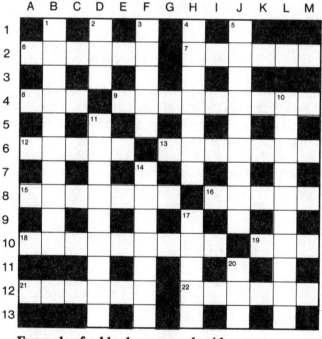

Example of a blank crossword grid

Player 1 then calls out a letter and a grid position. For example, letter E, in position F2. If this is correct, E is written in by the adjudicator and player 1 scores one point and has another turn. If his next guess is incorrect then it becomes the turn of player 2. The game continues thus. When a word is completed by a player, then that player scores an extra point for each of the letters in the word.

BOGGLES

Boggle is now a popular marketed word game, along with such as *Lexicon*, *Kan-U-Go* and *Scrabble*. In *Boggle*, sixteen lettered dice are shaken on to a tray and then shaped into a square. The diagram shows a possible example. Players have to make words by moving from letter to letter, horizontally, vertically or diagonally.

T	F	E	L
W	R	C	P
I	K	A	D
N	X	O	J

Example of a boggle square

The idea of the game is based on the popular word search principle, the major difference being that words in conventional word search puzzles are found in straight lines only but 'boggles' can move from square to adjoining square in any direction.

The authors have devised several types of puzzle based on the 'boggle' movement. Two examples, (a) and (b) are given.

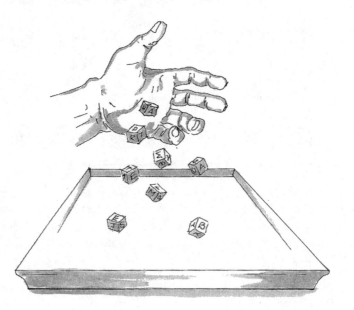

(a) **BIRDS**

By moving from square to square horizontally, vertically or diagonally it is possible to find the names of 32 birds in this grid. Squares may be used more than once but not in the same name.

N	I	O	L	N	I	W	I
I	O	R	C	E	D	R	N
B	K	U	E	G	R	T	G
O	C	T	N	W	A	R	O
R	R	J	N	I	P	K	W
O	M	A	L	A	R	S	A
E	Y	G	L	D	O	E	N
I	P	A	R	V	E	V	E

(b) **NO REPEAT LETTERS**

This grid contains 25 different letters of the alphabet. What is the longest word that can be found by starting anywhere and working from square to square horizontally, vertically or diagonally, and not repeating a letter?

K	M	Q	O	L
F	C	U	A	R
W	H	S	V	B
Y	T	I	E	G
X	P	D	J	N

(Answers to B4 (a) and (b) on page 254)

BOOK CRICKET

Book cricket was very popular in the 1930s and was played by many schoolboys on wet afternoons when their game was rained off, a frequent event in British summers. It proved to be a good apprenticeship for budding cricket scorers as the game was played using an authentic cricket score book.

The letters of the alphabet represent different events in the game of cricket, for instance 4 runs or stumped, etc. The full code is shown in the table.

A	0	N	1 bye
B	CAUGHT	O	0
C	2	P	4
D	2	Q	HIT WICKET
E	0	R	1
F	3	S	1
G	4 byes	T	1
H	3	U	0
I	0	V	STUMPED
J	BOWLED	W	2 byes
K	6	X	RUN OUT
L	2	Y	1 leg bye
M	2	Z	LBW

Table showing code for Book cricket

Each player selects a team, say England or Australia. Then a book is selected at random and a passage chosen, also at random. One player bats first and each letter of the chosen passage is taken in order and the player's score entered in the batsman's section. The other player is the bowler and the scores against him are entered in the bowler's figures. The cricket match could be played under normal cricket rules.

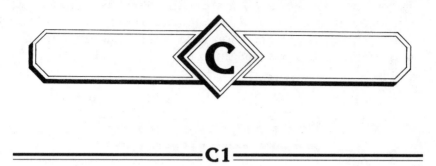

CARROLLIAN WORD PLAY

Lewis Carroll was the pen-name of Charles Lutwidge Dodgson, who was born at Daresbury, Cheshire in 1832. He was educated at Rugby and Oxford, took orders in 1861, and was a lecturer in mathematics at Christ Church College, Oxford, from 1855 until 1881, when he resigned to devote his life to writing under his pen-name. As a boy he was fascinated by the craft of conjuring and this, together with ideas for games, puzzles, anagrams, riddles, chess problems, mathematical recreation and logic, occupied his mind throughout his life. He was responsible for many original puzzles and new innovations including Doublets, Mischmasch and Syzygies, all of which are featured in greater detail later in this book.

The extent of his obsession with puzzles can be appreciated by considering that almost all 72 of his so-called 'Pillow Problems', many having complicated mathematical solutions, were compiled while he was lying awake at night. He would commit nothing to paper until the morning, when he would first of all write down the answer, followed by the question, and then the detailed solution.

The children's classic, *Alice's Adventures in Wonderland* (1865), was written for the young Alice Liddell, the daughter of the Dean of his Oxford College. Along with its sequel, *Through the Looking-Glass* (1872), it combines elements of fantasy, logic and nonsense. He also wrote nonsense verse, notably *The Hunting of the Snark* (1876).

Although he was primarily a mathematician, Carroll was also a master wordsmith of the highest order and was a prolific compiler of rebuses, riddles, anagrams, acrostics and conundrums. The scale and quality of his work can be gauged from the few examples we now give.

Anagrams

In June 1892, he wrote in his diary: 'Invented what I think is a new kind of riddle: A Russian had three sons. The first, named Rab, became a lawyer. The second, Ymra, became a soldier. The third became a sailor; what was his name?

The answer, of course, is based on the earliest form of anagram, a word simply reversed, and is Yvan, a reversal of the word Navy.

Some years ago this very puzzle inspired one of the authors to compile the puzzle (a), which was published in their 1987 book, *Take the IQ Challenge 2*.

▼▼▼ YOU PLAY ▼▼▼

(a) If the man who always transgressed against divine or moral law was named Dennis, the girl who always felt unwell was named Delia, and the lady who had a thing of value was named Tessa, what was the name of the man who carried a bag of letters?

(Answer to C1 (a) on page 255)

Carroll also left us with some classic anagrams, notably two which he compiled from the name 'William Ewart Gladstone': 'A wild man will go at trees', and 'Wild agitator means well'. He was also responsible for one of our favourite anagrams: 'Flit on cheering angel' (Florence Nightingale).

Acrostics

This double acrostic was composed by Lewis Carroll in 1869, on a train journey between Torquay and Guildford. It was dedicated to a Miss E. M. Argles, who was presumably, the Edith referred to in the final verse, and who must have been his Editor. It was published in 1932 on the centenary of his birth. The first two verses are clues to the vertical words in the solution.

> I sing a place wherein agree,
> All things on land that fairest be,
> All that is sweetest of the sea.
>
> Nor can I break the silken knot
> That binds my memory to the spot,
> And friends too dear to be forgot.
>
> . . . . . .
>
> On rocky brow we loved to stand,
> And watch in silence hand in hand,
> The shadows veiling sea and land.

Then dropped the breeze: no vessel passed:
So silent stood each taper mast,
You would have deemed it chained and fast.

Above the blue and fleecy sky;
Below, the waves that quivering lie,
Like crispéd curls of greenery.

'A sail!' resounds from every lip,
Mizen, no square-sail – ah, you trip!
Edith, it cannot be a ship!

So home again from sea and breach,
One nameless feeling thrilling each,
A sense of beauty passing speech.

Let lens and tripod be unslung!
'Dolly!'s the word on every tongue;
Dolly must sit, for she is young.

Photography shall change her face,
Distort it with uncouth grimace –
Make her bloodthirsty, fierce and base.

I end my song while scarce begun;
For I should want, ere all was done
Four weeks to tell the tale of one.

And I should need as large a hand
To paint a scene so wild and grand,
As he who traversed Egypt's land.

What say you, Edith? Will it suit ye?
Reject it, if it falls in beauty:
You know your literary duty!

The solution is:

B	luf	F
A	ncho	R
B	roccol	I
B	arqu	E
A	ppreciatio	N
C	lou	D
O	diou	S
M	ont	H
B	elzon	I
E	ditorshi	P

Riddles

Lewis Carroll composed many riddles, including this one, which was written for a friend, Mary Watson:

> Dreaming of apples on a wall,
> And dreaming often, dear,
> I dreamed that, if I counted all,
> How many would appear?

The answer to the question posed is 'Ten', which is revealed in the second line 'dreaming often' (or 'dreaming of ten').

. . . . .

The riddle which follows was the first he ever published and was included by him, without a solution, in his own family magazine *Mischmasch*. Almost a year after his death in December 1898, his nephew and biographer, Stuart Dodgson Collingwood, used the riddle in his article, *Before 'Alice': The Boyhood of Lewis Carroll*, published in the *Strand Magazine*.

> A monument – men all agree –
> Am I in all sincerity,
> Half cat, half hinderance made,
> If head and tail removed should be,
> Then most of all you strengthen me;
> Replace my head, the stand you see
> On which my tail is laid.

It is a measure of Carroll's ingenuity that no answer to this riddle was provided until 31 years after the Collingwood article appeared, when the six-letter word 'Tablet' was proposed. This is undoubtedly the solution that Carroll intended.

CATEGORIES

This is a word association puzzle invented by the authors in 1984 and first introduced in their 1986 book *Take the IQ Challenge*. In the puzzle, twelve words are listed and the solver has to arrange them into four groups, with three words in each group. The words in a particular group must have some connecting link, but the problem is to find these connecting links, avoiding all the pitfalls that have been set.

As an example, take the 12 words:

ABODE, BAR, BICYCLE, HOME, LEVER, MACMILLAN,

PEDAL RESIDENCE, ROD, ROOF, STRAW, THATCHER

The immediate temptation is to group together HOME, MACMILLAN and THATCHER, all names of Conservative Party British Prime Ministers. However, this will not lead to the correct solution, which is:

MACMILLAN, PEDAL, BICYCLE (The connection is bicycle; Kirkpatrick Macmillan being the inventor of the world's first pedal cycle.)

LEVER, BAR, ROD (All levers.)

THATCHER, STRAW, ROOF (All words connected with thatching.)

HOME, RESIDENCE, ABODE (Where people live.)

▼▼▼ YOU PLAY ▼▼▼

(a) **CATEGORIES**

You may like to try these:

AMITY, ASTRONOMY, CONCORD, CHEMISTRY,

SHACKLETON, HARMONY, HARRIER, PEACE,

PLANET, PHYSICS, STAR

(Answer to C2 (a) on page 255)

CENTOS

This is a type of poetry in which a poem is constructed using each separate line from a different poet.

The name 'centos' comes from the Latin word for patchwork quilt. Originating in ancient Greece, it was very popular with Roman poets but died out in the late 19th century and is now rarely seen. Here is an example:

> As shallow streams run dimpling all the way,
> Delicate filmed as new spun silk, will the neighbours say,
> Turned upward to the sky she lay, her head on a heap of hay,
> Welcome the coming of the longed for month of May.

The poets are:

> Line 1 – Alexander Pope (1688-1744)
> Line 2 – Thomas Hardy (1840-1928)
> Line 3 – William Morris (1834-1896)
> Line 4 – Thomas Carew (1595-1639)

CHANDLERISMS

Raymond Thornton Chandler (1888-1959) was an American writer, born in Chicago and educated in England, France and Germany. During the Depression he began to write short stories and later specialised in 'private eye' novels such as *The Big Sleep* (1939) and *Farewell, My Lovely* (1940). He was the creator of the cynical detective Philip Marlowe.

In one of his stories Chandler wrote, 'She was the kind of blonde that could make a bishop kick a hole through a stained-glass window'. This prompted David Morice, in his column 'Kickshaws' for *Word Ways* magazine, in 1989, to coin the word 'Chandlerism' for the composition of similar statements, several examples of which are suggested here. You may like to compile a list of your own.

> He was the kind of guy who could make a nun kick the habit.

> She was the kind of gal who could make an angler throw back a 90 lb salmon.

> She was the kind of girl who would drive a life member of a temperance society to drink.

CHARADES

It is believed that the charade was invented in the 19th century. The word 'charade' is a derivative of the Italian 'schiarare', meaning to disentangle or clear up. In such puzzles a word is broken down into its syllables (as in CAR-PEN-TRY). Each of these syllables must be guessed from clues provided before combining them to arrive at the answer as a whole. Charades can be written in prose or verse, as in these two examples:

> My first is bashful, my second is fastening and my whole is a Shakespearian character.
>
> *(Answer:* Shylock)

or:

> My first is a sailor.
>   My second's to gain.
> My whole, though oft shot at,
>   Has never been slain.
>
> *(Answer:* Target)

A 19th century charade

One of the most famous charades was compiled during the 19th century by Winthorpe Mackworth Praed, an English author who is best remembered for his humorous verse. He tried his hand at puzzle compiling, composing the following charade but without ever revealing his intended solution:

> Sir Hilary charged at Agincourt;
>   Sooth, 'twas an awful day!
> And though in that old age of sport
> The rufflers of the camp and court
>   Had little time to pray,
> 'Tis said Sir Hilary muttered there
> Two syllables by way of prayer:
>   My First to all the brave and proud
>   Who see tomorrow's sun;
> My Next with her cold and quiet cloud,
> To those who find their dewy shroud
>   Before today's be done.
> And both together to all blue eyes
> That weep when a warrior nobly dies.

Although puzzle historians have reluctantly accepted 'good night' as the best answer, the charade nevertheless became quite controversial because none could really agree. In the hope that one day a more feasible solution than 'good night' might be put forward, we included the charade in a section of Unsolved Puzzles in one of our 1993 books, *The Ultimate IQ Book*. This brought a response from one of our good friends, Mitzi Christiansen Kuehl, a retired teacher and resident of Bakersfield, USA. We quote from her letter:

> 'I'm especially intrigued by the unsolved charade on page 94. "Good night" seems as good a guess as any, but might not the answer also be "Well done"? Prayer: ("I pray our mission will prove to have been) well done." To the survivors: "Well! Well!" As in "Good to see you this morning," as well as, "You are well this morning." "Done," as in "It's finished. I'm done." This is a very poignant charade.'

Who can say that Mitzi has not hit on the correct solution to this unsolved puzzle?

Line by line

A development of the charade is a favourite children's puzzle in which each line of a verse produces a single letter. These letters, read down in order, form a word, which is indicated by the final line of the verse. Example (a) was compiled by the authors in 1989. You may like to try it.

▼▼▼ YOU PLAY ▼▼▼

(a)   **LINE BY LINE**

My first is in bacon but not in egg,
My second's in slipper but not in leg,
My third is in sunshine but not in day,
My fourth is in heavy but not in weigh,
My fifth is in kitten but not in cat,
My sixth is in funny but not in hat,
My seventh's in orange but not in juice,
My eighth is in solve but not in deduce,
My ninth is in tiger but not in bay,
My whole you'll enjoy almost every day.

(Answer to C5 (a) on page 255)

Visual charades

There is a popular game of visual charades which, usually, is played by two teams. Each team in turn chooses the title of a film or a book, or a well known saying, etc. and then acts out each part of it (words or syllable) in mime until the whole is guessed by the other team. Here are some words which would be excellent to include when playing visual charades: Nightingale, Bluebottle, Tenterhook, Landingstrip, Leapfrog, Shortsighted.

Some years ago there was a television programme of visual charades called *Give Us A Clue*. In this, the questionmaster gave a team member a card which showed the film title, or whatever. The team member had to act this out in mime to the other members of his or her team who had two minutes to come up with the solution. If they failed, the opposing team could offer the solution for an extra point. The contestants developed a useful system of visual codes to indicate things such as: 'one word', 'first syllable', 'sounds like', 'short two-letter word' and different letters of the alphabet, etc. to aid their team members.

═══════════════ **C6** ═══════════════

CHRONOGRAMS

A chronogram is the practice of hiding a date within a series of words by using appropriate letters of the word for Roman numerals:

I (1), V (5), X (10), L (50), C (100), D (500), M (1000)

Sometimes, use is made of the letter U for 5, the letter J for 1 and two VV to form a W (10).

The significant letters are usually written in capitals as opposed to the rest of the text so that they stand out in the line. Chronograms have been used throughout history on medals, tombstones, foundation stones and books to mark the date of the event, but are a comparative rarity nowadays.

The earliest chronograms were found written in Hebrew in the early 13th century. The prefix 'chrono' is from the Greek 'chronos' meaning 'time'; hence chronogram, meaning the indicating of a date.

Historical examples

The following are examples from the past several hundred years. It will be seen that different compilers have put different interpretations on the rules of how chronograms should be devised.

In the example 'My Day Closed Is In Immortaility', it is the intial letters only of the words which form the chronogram and all other Roman numerals in the text are ignored. The initial letters are extracted to form the number MDCIII = 1603, the year of the death of Queen Elizabeth I.

In the chronogram used in the tower vaulting of Winchester Cathedral, the verse of scripture reads: 'sInt DoMVs hVIVs pII reges nVtrItII, regInae nVtrICes pIae' (*Isaiah* 49:23, 'Kings shall be the nursing fathers and queens the nursing mother of thy house'). In this chronogram the numerals are extracted and listed in descending order of value: MDCVVVVVIIIIIIIIII, and then totalled up individually to arrive at 1635, the date of completion of the roof.

The same method was used in the chronogram: 'GeorgIVs DVX BVCkIngaMIae'; giving MDCXVVVIII = 1000 + 500 + 100 + 10 + 5 + 5 + 5 + 1 + 1 + 1 = 1628, the date when the Duke of Buckingham was murdered by Felton.

It should be noted that, in the above examples, the letters are taken individually and then totalled; that is, in GeorIVs', the IV is taken as I + V = 6 and **not** IV = 4.

In another, perhaps less elegant, example, the letter V is again used for U: 'LorD haVe MerCIe Vpon Vs'; giving MDCLVVVI = 1000 + 500 + 100 + 50 + 5 + 5 + 5 + 1 = 1666, the year of the Great Fire of London.

Spin-off games and puzzles

There are several spin-off games and puzzles using the idea of chronograms, some of which are now given.

WORD PLAY

For example, the word MESEMBRYANTHEMUM repeats four M numerals and is believed to be the highest scoring Roman numeral word in the English language.

Another challenge is to find words containing specified Roman numerals such as 1 = It (I), 7 = Vitrify (VII), 13 = Exhibition (XIII), 44 = Expletive (XLIV), 55 = Love (LV), 90 = Except (XC). These are typical examples for each number and there are, of course, alternatives.

(a) **WORD PLAY**

Can you find words for the numbers 42, 59, 62, 52 and 97?

Note that in this game the numerals are presented in true Roman numeral fashion, for example, XC = 90 and not X + C = 110.

(b) **PUZZLE**

This puzzle was compiled by the authors in 1993. Which is the odd one out?

50YN10
100E500AR
E50AN500
100AME50
5050A1000A
BU5050

(c) **THE HIDDEN CHRONOGRAM**

This word puzzle was invented by the authors in 1992 and is difficult to compile but even more difficult to solve.

L	H	E	U	H	M
U	N	S	X	O	T
N	N	I	A	O	Y
D	D	N	W	T	M
D	R	N	D	T	R
E	A	C	F	O	M

Find the correct starting point and work from square to square, horizontally, vertically and diagonally (that is boggle-style – see page 44), to spell out a number.

Each letter may be used only once. The letters that are not used can be arranged to form the Roman numeral value of the number spelled out.

(Answers to C6 (a) to (c) on page 255)

CLERIHEWS

The Clerihew was invented by Edmund Clerihew Bentley (1875-1956). It is a satirical or humorous poem consisting of two couplets, usually biographical, and with the name of the subject comprising the first line. This is the most famous example:

> Said Sir Christopher Wren
> I'm having lunch with some men,
> If anyone calls,
> Say I'm designing St Paul's.

This one is also worthy of note:

> The digestion of Milton
> Was unequal to Stilton.
> He was only feeling so-so,
> When he wrote *Il Penseroso*.

Double-dactyls

Similar to a Clerihew, but much more challenging to compile, is the double-dactyl, or higgledy-piggledy as it is known in America. This consists of a verse form of two quatrains where the last line of the first rhymes with the last line of the second. The first line is a nonsense line (thus the name higgledy-piggledy); the second line is a proper name (as with the first line of the Clerihew); and at least one of the lines is a single word. This is a perfect example:

> Tweedledum Tweedledee
> Alice in Wonderland
> First she was tiny and
> Then she was tall
>
> Argued with animals
> Anthropomorphical,
> Didn't accept their
> Conclusions at all.

COLLECTIVE NOUNS

Collective nouns were first used in a book published in 1486 *The Boke of St Albans* written by Dame Juliana Berners, the prioress of a nunnery near St Albans. In the book can be found these examples:

A pace of asses
A dule of doves
A herd of cattle
A kindle of kittens
A pride of lions
A nye of pheasants
A rout of wolves

Since then, several hundred collective terms have been devised for all manner of things. We list just a few here.

knob   (of pochards, teal, toads or widgeon)
rope   (of onions or pearls)
blush   (of boys)
doylt   (of tame swine)
troop   (of boy scouts, brownies, cavalry, kangaroos, lions or monkeys)
covert   (of coots)
sleuth   (of bears)
clouder   (of cats)
dopping   (of sheldrakes)
richesse   (of martens)
morbidity   (of majors)
chattering   (of choughs)
exhaltation   (of larks)
observance   (of hermits)
simplicity   (of subalterns)
convocation   (of clergy or university authorities)
murmuration   (of starlings)

One interesting curiousity is that a group of geese is called a gaggle, except when in flight – in which case the collective noun is skein.

(a) **COLLECTIVE NOUNS**

In this puzzle, 28 collective nouns are hidden in three paragraphs. How many can you correctly identify?

In the cove near Hove rafters tend to rake and span and slot home on buildings.

In the same cove your outer charm will be the downfall of a gang of husky gamblers.

You can hear the snide remarks of a wisp of blushing kennel maids as they drift and clamour and mingle and hover and cry at the observance of a dray full of troops.

(Answers to C8 (a) on page 255)

=========================== **C9** ===========================

COLOURFUL LANGUAGE

All colours will agree in the dark – Francis Bacon

Items of picturesque speech can be found sprinkled around the pages of many newspapers and magazines, often as space fillers. These are some typically colourful examples.

I would not have given it for a wilderness of monkeys. – Shakespeare (*The Merchant of Venice* III, i, 130)

Snowy, Flowy, Blowy, Showery, Flowery, Bowery, Hoppy, Croppy, Droppy, Breezy, Sneezy, Freezy. – George Ellis (*The Twelve Months*)

The man's silence is wonderful to listen to. – Thomas Hardy

Mad, bad and dangerous to know. – Lady Caroline Lamb (of Byron)

Lost, yesterday, sometime between Sunrise and Sunset, two golden hours, each set with sixty diamond minutes. No reward is offered, for they are gone for ever. – Horace Mann

Thus the whirligig of time brings in his revenges. – Shakespeare (*Twelfth Night* V, i, 388)

Every drop of ink in my pen ran cold. – Horace Walpole

The pen is the tongue of the hand – a silent utterer of words for the eye. – Henry Ward Beecher

Contentment is natural wealth; luxury artificial poverty. – Socrates

. . . . . .

In his book *Family Words* (1988), Paul Dickson explores words coined within a family group and used only by its members, such as, for example, 'ghost poo' for white styrofoam packing pieces. He goes on to claim that almost all family units have such words or terms. Here are a few that we have come across:

Spung – The debris left in the sink plug-hole when the washing-up water is emptied.

An Owdamn – The breaking of a valued piece of household china or glass.

Scribbles – Any small furry animals in the wild.

Mullocks – Children's toys left strewn about the house.

Great hairy monster – Any arachnid (larger than a money-spider) that appears in the bath.

In her August 1984 'Sphinx Winks' column in *Integra* (see page 221), Mitzi Christiansen Kuehl explored the creation of words to describe things which do not already have a name. The following suggestions were among those submitted by readers:

Twirlex – The little twirled peak of ice cream on a machine-made ice cream cone.

Noles – The little round pieces of paper produced by a paper punch.

. . . . . .

Many areas of the world produce their own particular brands of colourful language, not least of which are the inhabitants of the Deep South of the United States of America, with such descriptions as 'hopping like peas on a hot shovel' and 'mad as a pig on ice with his tail froze in'.

. . . . . .

The creation of such colourful language can be a great challenge and has led to the compilation of several types of puzzles. In our 1989 book *Junior Mensa Puzzle Book*, we included several very familiar proverbs which had been disguised by the use of flowery language. In fact, the type of language that many people will remember being used by the chairman, Leonard Sachs, when introducing Acts on the BBC television show *The Good Old Days*. You may like to try examples (a) to (g).

COLOURFUL LANGUAGE

How many of these proverbs can you recognise?

(a) Whither there is a gaseous product of burning material there is combusion.

(b) A feathered creature in the extremity of the arm is equal to the value of a brace in a densely branched shrub.

(c) A revolving piece of rock fails to accumulate lichenous growth.

(d) Don't procrastinate as far as the day after the present that which can be accomplished now.

(e) A loop made by a needle at the proper moment prevents the occurrence of a cardinal number just below ten.

(f) Retiring before it is late, and getting up soon, causes a person to become vigorous, affluent and sagacious.

(g) Accurate optical observation is advisable before putting into voluntary effect vehement motion of the locomotory muscles.

Puzzle (h) was compiled by the authors in 1992.

(h) My pleasant journey commences when I briefly meet a familiar character marking a pitch in front of a wooden strip. I then pass several apartments with many whimsical fancies among a fine array of glossary. Often feeling a tremble, I find many keen edges between several siestas. I visit several places of refreshment before my journey ends. Where has my journey taken me?

(Answers to C9 (a) to (h) on pages 255-6)

CONCRETE POETRY

In the 1950s a creative form of poetry was invented. This was more artistic, and used words to form shapes and pictures to emphasise the theme of the poem. This is one such example:

My first unless the vintage
Smiles, and plenteous crops appear,
Can ne'er be had to fill my next,
With bright and sparkling cheer.
My second is a compound made
By man's ingenious art,
Which can reflect the human form,
Or liquid good impart.
My whole enables many
a one convivial
joys to
know
with
wishes
kind
salutes
the
friend,
confusion
to the foe.
Allegorical lozenges
1812

The answer is, of course, a wineglass.

CONFESSIONS

This is an old party game and was described in *Foulsham's Fun Book of 1933* as follows:

'The players sit round a table and each is given a strip of paper and a pencil. The High Priest then commands everybody to write his or her name on the top line and, that done, the paper is folded over two or three times so that the name will not be revealed.

Next, the H.P. commands everybody to pass his paper around the circle of players in a left-hand direction. After they have travelled a good way round he cries "Halt" and they stop. Each player, then, has a paper and he should not be able to guess who was the original owner.

The H.P. now commands everyone to write a confession, in short, the worst thing he has ever done. This is written below the portion which has been folded over.

A second time the papers are folded and passed on, and, when they are halted, the thing is to write "why he did it".

A third time the papers continue their journey and, when the H.P. calls a final halt, each person unfolds the paper in his possession and in turn, reads aloud the three sections. Naturally, some of them are screamingly funny. Such entries as this are obtained: "Ann Winterton – stole a motor car – because I didn't care two hoots."'

CONSEQUENCES

This is another old party game, very similar in fact to 'Confessions'. As before, each person has a sheet of paper and the game is played to these set rules. Each person first writes down an adjective suitable for describing a girl. The paper is passed round after being folded over and the next person writes a girl's name, folds it over and passes it on again. At the third stage the participants write the word MET followed by an adjective to describe a man then, at the next stage, the man's name. The game proceeds thus through twelve stages, the remaining eight stages being: (5) at location, (6) time, (7) he said to her, (8) she said to him, (9) what he did (10) what she did (11) what the consequence was, (12) and what the world said about it.

The results are then read out and, as with Confessions, the results can be quite hilarious. The game can be played by children or at adult parties when the result could be some rather risqué suggestions.

The authors also remember the game being played to a less set pattern when a single sheet of paper is passed round the room and each player in turn writes whatever comment he wishes and then, after folding the paper over, passes the paper to the next player. Again it is surprising how many of the comments are suitably linked.

．　　．　　．　　．　　．

A similar sort of game, 'Verses while you wait', was also described in *Foulsham's Fun Book of 1933*. In it the players are seated round a table, and each is given a sheet of paper and a pencil. The host exhibits a card on which is written the first line of a verse of poetry, together with the last rhyming words of the subsequent four lines, thus:

I could not see for the wind and rain,
>   (train)
>   (caught)
>   (sought)
>   (wane)

Each player writes on his or her paper the line supplied and then adds a second line according to fancy. The paper is then folded and it passes to the next person on the left who adds the next line. This continues until the complete five line verse is composed.

═══════════════ C13 ═══════════════

CONUNDRUMS

Many conundrums have their origin deep in folklore and are, we believe, so ingenious as to be worthy of much greater recognition. Basically, they are punning jokes that make the listener groan when he or she hears the answer, but the descriptions propounded and clever play on words are a true test of wit and provide many an unexpected, and often very amusing, solution. These give a typical cross-section:

What is often brought to the table, often cut, but never eaten?
Answer:　A pack of cards.

Why is B like a hot fire?
Answer:　Because it makes oil boil.

What is the largest word in the English language yet is only five letters long?
Answer: Smiles, because it has a mile between the first and last 'S'.

Why is 'S' like a sewing machine?
Answer: Because it makes needles needless.

Did Boxing Day ever fall on Good Friday?
Answer: Yes, at Kempton Park in the 1.30.

Why can't you place a kangaroo in a pen?
Answer: Because the kangaroo knows no bounds.

Why did the sausage roll?
Answer: Because it saw the jam turn-over.

When did London begin with an 'L' and end with an 'E'?
Answer: Always. 'London' begins with L, and 'End' with E.

▼▼▼ YOU PLAY ▼▼▼

(a)   **CONUNDRUM**

Perhaps the most famous and controversial conundrum is this one, where a man, looking at a photograph, says:

'Brothers and sisters have I none,
But that man's father is my father's son.'

Do you know whose photograph he is looking at?

(Answer to C13 (a) is on page 256)

C14

CRAMBO

Crambo is a game in which one player selects a word which has to be guessed by rhymes. Dumb crambo is a variation in which the rhymes are expressed in mime, rather like a game of charades. The word 'crambo' is from the Latin 'crambe' in reference to Juvenal's 'crambe repetita' ('cabbage served up again').

Crambo is a very old game and reference was made to it in Samuel Pepys' diary of 1660.

The method of play is that one player leaves the room and the rest select a word. The player returns and is told another word which rhymes with the chosen word. The game might progress like this:

Say the chosen word is CLAMP and the rhyming clue given is DAMP.

Guesser:	'Is it an inclined slope?'
Room:	'No, it is not ramp.'
Guesser:	'Is it a bivouac area?'
Room:	'No, it is not a camp.'
Guesser:	'Is it placing your foot down sharply?'
Room:	'No, it is not stamp.'
Guesser:	'Is it a source of light?'
Room:	'No, it is not a lamp.'

And the game continues accordingly, until the chosen word is guessed.

═══════════════ C15 ═══════════════

THE CROSSWORD CLUB

The Crossword Club, based in Hampshire, England, was formed by, and for, people who are devotees of the true art of the crossword. Members appreciate the finer points of clue-writing and diagram construction. They enjoy tackling really challenging crosswords and are prepared to spend time unravelling subtle cryptic clues.

By means of its monthly Prize Crossword Competitions, the club aims to promote the setting and solving of puzzles of a high standard. It offers two puzzles each time. The first is a difficult *Listener*-type crossword, invariably involving some kind of gimmick. The second – sometimes plain, sometimes with a gimmick – should prove easier to solve.

The club also has a bimonthly Clue-Writing Contest and the quarterly Any Answers Clue-Solving Contest. A handbook is also provided which gives much useful information on different types of clues.

The club's monthly magazine *Crossword* is sent free to members and this publication contains also articles, news and opinions on all aspects of crosswords, especially the construction and solution of the esoteric type of puzzles used in the competitions.

Anyone interested in membership of the club should write to:

Mr Brian Head, Coombe Farm, Awbridge,
Romsey, Hants, SO51 0HN

The puzzle (a), by 'Pidghins', is reproduced from issue number 181 of *Crossword* and is dated May 1993.

(a)　　　　　**PUZZLE BY 'PIDGHINS'**

All Across clues contain a redundant word. The initial letters of these words, in clue order, give an instruction. Hidden within the grid is a phrase of five words (running together). Its source, acting as a suggestion, together with the instruction, give the metal and purity of the ring. Enter both inside the ring. The phrase may be shaded.

Across

1　Hard drink, cut back bitter ale (7)
6　Judge leaves old wig with Dutch island natives (6)
12　Dealer fixed established firm (9)
13　A great number run in to attend work (5)
16　Meeting corner. Number ten regroup (9)
17　Church elder leaves shore marker-buoy for boat (6)
18　Seize with pistol – xenophobe in captivity (7)
19　Heartless dog enters tough race for the border (6)
21　Recruit runs in water without a wash (5)
22　Hart disturbed arch serow (4)
23　Destitute footman's stateless galleries (5)
25　Oyster! Put it beside river fish (4)
27　Mostly timid Northern Zulu dance (5)
29　Caffeine in the coffee. Espresso finally blended (6)
30　Indian greeting servant. Returning East upset? Never (7)
31　Cold beer with no head – start to serve notice for tenant (6)
33　Criminal inside, almost finishes businesses (9)
36　Burning ambition's rousing primary passion (5)
37　Labour's leader goes absent – No 1 replaced. Major's beginning new doctrine (9)
38　Traders mining licence – not for Scottish lead sulphide (6)
39　They stop speakers swearing. About time (7)

Down

1　Wild ant drew a sting, bringing tears to the eyes (13, hypen)
2　Snub mixed salon (5)
3　She keeps going to tidy up under old plot (7)
4　Earthenware vessel – line with stone (5)
5　Girl embraces river bird (4)
7　Name turned up in a hollow caution (8)
8　Punch boxer's head – not counted out! (3)
9　God's hairy appendage trimmed for cult members (6)

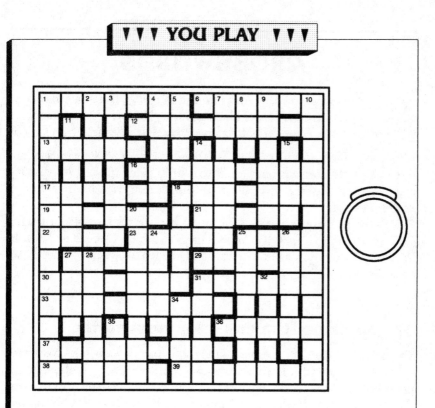

10   One of their orders? "Prevent topless woman entering prostitution" (13, hyphen)

11   Surf runs into lake shore (6)

14   A bird flew up nibbling the top fruit (5)

15   Important books taken off press (4)

18   Vessel losing line – not ready (5)

20   Runner-up left missing Irishman without a badge (8)

24   Cave in! Caveman treated (5)

25   Goldsmith's pot – run check for safety (8, hyphen)

26   Cut and run. Saves face showing grins (6)

27   Cat litter's ending in path (4)

28   Clay sheds weight – absorbs punch. Explosive stuff (6)

31   Smallest man taking active part finally (5)

32   Exhaust tail removed hazard for driver (5)

34   No hearts for passion-flower (4)

35   Rubber erased top of dash (3)

(Answers to C15 (a) on page 257)

CROSSWORDS

'All I did was to take an idea as old as language and modernise it by the introduction of black squares. No one is more surprised at its amazing popularity.' (Arthur Wynne)

Although some claim its origins date back to China 8000 years ago, and there was a children's game similar to it in England in the 19th century, it is accepted that the modern crossword puzzle was the invention of Arthur Wynne.

Wynne was British, born in Liverpool, and was responsible for the fun section of the *New York World* and, on Sunday, 21 December 1913, he introduced a new innovation, a diamond-shaped 'word cross puzzle' (see example (a)).

The spread of the craze for crosswords

Wynne's idea caught on immediately and the passion for crosswords swept America with the Baltimore and Ohio railroads supplying all its main-line trains with dictionaries for its addicts. Crosswords were a perfect escape as an intellectual stimulant or a diverting time-filler, and began to appear more and more in newspapers.

In 1924 the idea eventually came to Britain when the first British crossword, by C. W. Shepard, appeared in the *Sunday Express* and it could be said that the crossword had finally 'arrived' when *The Times* began its own up-market version in 1930.

The crossword era had started and the first book of crosswords was published by the American publisher, Simon and Schuster, in 1924. In 1925 a Broadway revue, *Puzzles of 1925*, included a scene set in a 'Crossword Puzzle Sanatorium' for people who had been driven insane by their infatuation and obsession with this new craze.

Hardly surprising, then, that a few of the pseudonyms of some of the great crossword compilers of this century are Torquemada, Ximenes and Azed (Deza in reverse), all names of leaders of the Spanish Inquisition!

(a)   CROSSWORD

The grid shown is to the exact design of that used by Arthur Wynne, but the clues and answers are entirely different, and are of the authors' own compilation.

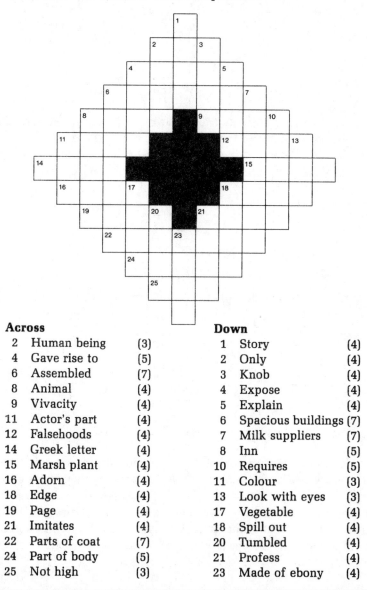

Across

2	Human being	(3)
4	Gave rise to	(5)
6	Assembled	(7)
8	Animal	(4)
9	Vivacity	(4)
11	Actor's part	(4)
12	Falsehoods	(4)
14	Greek letter	(4)
15	Marsh plant	(4)
16	Adorn	(4)
18	Edge	(4)
19	Page	(4)
21	Imitates	(4)
22	Parts of coat	(7)
24	Part of body	(5)
25	Not high	(3)

Down

1	Story	(4)
2	Only	(4)
3	Knob	(4)
4	Expose	(4)
5	Explain	(4)
6	Spacious buildings	(7)
7	Milk suppliers	(7)
8	Inn	(5)
10	Requires	(5)
11	Colour	(3)
13	Look with eyes	(3)
17	Vegetable	(4)
18	Spill out	(4)
20	Tumbled	(4)
21	Profess	(4)
23	Made of ebony	(4)

The evolution of crosswords

Crossword puzzles evolved from 19th century puzzles called 'word forms', in which words are interlocked in geometric shapes. The first form published in America was a square and appeared in a sporting paper, *Wilkes' Spirit of the Times*, on 24 September 1859:

```
C  I  R  C  L  E
I  C  A  R  U  S
R  A  R  E  S  T
C  R  E  A  T  E
L  U  S  T  R  E
E  S  T  E  E  M
```

By the 1870s, some puzzle contributors were producing what were termed 'double-forms', where different words read across and down. The puzzle shown, in the shape of a diamond, was compiled by someone using the pseudonym 'Hyperion' for *St Nicholas Magazine* of September 1875.

'Hyperion's' double-form of 1875

The 'Hyperion' puzzle is actually cited as the world's first crossword by the *Guinness Book of Records*. However, most experts would disagree and would call the diamond a form rather than a crossword – which should be free from the constraints of simple geometric shape. Crosswords should be more complex, but at the same time symmetrical, constructions with more than one word in some rows and columns – a condition that is met in every way by the Wynne 'word-cross' puzzle of 1913.

Basic types of crossword

There are two basic crossword puzzle types, one having synonym-type clues and one having cryptic clues. The synonym-type clue is a straightforward description of the answer, for example: 'White ball in bowls' (Jack). The cryptic clue type is a puzzle in its own right and can come in many forms; for example: 'Dispel misspelt and badly pronounced' (Lisped, an anagram of dispel). Synonym crosswords invariably have a small number of black squares and cryptic crosswords a much larger number. A typical cryptic crossword (13 × 13) would have 40 black squares and 129 white squares. A typical synonym-type of the same size would have 28 black squares and 141 white squares.

Around 1930, the *London Evening News* published a synonym-type crossword each evening, submitted by readers. To get their puzzles published, the contributors would vie with one another to produce a crossword with the least number of black squares. The lowest number ever achieved was 16 black squares – a remarkable feat. During the decade 1960 to 1970, one of the authors had more than 30 published. One of these is shown, (b), which had just 21 black squares. You may like to solve it.

. . . . . .

The year 1988 saw the 75th anniversary of the publication of the first-ever crossword puzzle. It was also the year in which a milestone was reached for one of the authors of this book, being the 50th year after the young Kenneth Russell began his interest in compiling crosswords. As a pupil of the Strand Grammar School in Tulse Hill, South London, he had been among a small group of boys who assisted the headmaster, Mr L. S. Dawe, in compiling the *Daily Telegraph* crossword.

Some years after this, in 1944, Mr Dawe was still compiling the *Telegraph* crossword, with another group of boys, when, shortly before the D-Day invasion of France by the Allies in the Second World War, he received a visit from MI5. He was detained for questioning because one edition of the newspaper contained the crossword answers: Fido, Pluto, Omaha and Overlord. All were key code names used in the invasion plans. Mr Dawe somehow convinced MI5 that this was just coincidence. However, it was not until 1980 that the mystery was finally unravelled when a letter appeared in the *Sunday Times* from an old boy of the school who had been a member of the crossword team. He confessed to having been the culprit. It appeared that his mother had been evacuated to Lincolnshire during the war and had found work in an American Air Force base. He frequently visited her at weekends and moved freely about the camp where the secret code names were often bandied about. The names had stuck with him and he had, as a result, fed them into the crossword grid.

(b) ## CROSSWORD

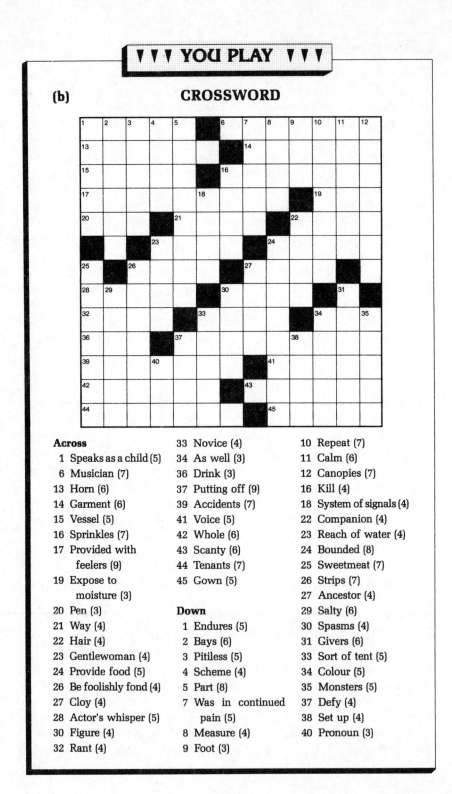

Across

1 Speaks as a child (5)
6 Musician (7)
13 Horn (6)
14 Garment (6)
15 Vessel (5)
16 Sprinkles (7)
17 Provided with feelers (9)
19 Expose to moisture (3)
20 Pen (3)
21 Way (4)
22 Hair (4)
23 Gentlewoman (4)
24 Provide food (5)
26 Be foolishly fond (4)
27 Cloy (4)
28 Actor's whisper (5)
30 Figure (4)
32 Rant (4)
33 Novice (4)
34 As well (3)
36 Drink (3)
37 Putting off (9)
39 Accidents (7)
41 Voice (5)
42 Whole (6)
43 Scanty (6)
44 Tenants (7)
45 Gown (5)

Down

1 Endures (5)
2 Bays (6)
3 Pitiless (5)
4 Scheme (4)
5 Part (8)
7 Was in continued pain (5)
8 Measure (4)
9 Foot (3)
10 Repeat (7)
11 Calm (6)
12 Canopies (7)
16 Kill (4)
18 System of signals (4)
22 Companion (4)
23 Reach of water (4)
24 Bounded (8)
25 Sweetmeat (7)
26 Strips (7)
27 Ancestor (4)
29 Salty (6)
30 Spasms (4)
31 Givers (6)
33 Sort of tent (5)
34 Colour (5)
35 Monsters (5)
37 Defy (4)
38 Set up (4)
40 Pronoun (3)

Cryptic clues

The more difficult type of crossword makes use of cryptic clues. These require the solver to understand the different forms in which these clues can be presented, for example, as a play on words, an anagram, an abbreviation or a key word. Several books have attempted to explain the use of such clues and these can, initially, be very useful. But the real learning is 'hands on' experience. Here is a selection of typical cryptic clues which have been compiled by the authors:

A large glass for the acrobat (7) – TUMBLER

Mother's sister processed tuna (4) – AUNT

Offering a present of French wine in carriage (6) – GIVING

Find me in the up lane and give me a coat! (6) – ENAMEL

Sounds as though it's a ring for the young swan (6) – CYGNET

A bad dose may be found to come in a hot flush (3) – FLU

Popular pet fractured the arms! (7) – HAMSTER

Food for the bird table and money, crikey! (11) – BREADCRUMBS

Fifty-one in a party of soldiers, very sordid! (7) – SQUALID

Some beastly direction (4) – EAST

Motor-bike had low spirits (5) – MOPED

Men tug around to find a spice (6) – NUTMEG

Big disagreement over nuclear deposits (4, 3) – FALL OUT

Aries Rodney will make a strict disciplinarian (6) – RAMROD

Halls around for a moral obligation in future tense (5) – SHALL

Sounds as though the vet has a sore throat (5-6) – HORSE-DOCTOR

Champ's coil unravelled to perform (10) – ACCOMPLISH

Urban quarter, the home of cups and saucers? (9) – CHINATOWN

Mere star ruined a flag (8) – STREAMER

Do these sea journeys take a long time in the end? (7) – VOYAGES

Change animals feet about (4) – SWAP

Ancient clock may have seen it all before (3-5) – OLD-TIMER

Study computer data in the garden (4-3) – READ-OUT

Sea eagle seen in Sheerness (4) – ERNE

My French span will reach the king (7) – MONARCH

Initially some old damp lump of turf (3) – SOD

A gentleman is around the Princess Royal with a certain style (6)
                                              – MANNER

The above examples are ideal simple cryptic clues for beginners. They will provide good practice before progressing to the simpler newspaper crosswords and then to the more difficult newspapers such as the *Daily Telegraph* and *The Times*.

Thematic crosswords

Another popular type of crossword has general knowledge type clues and a good example appears daily in the *Daily Mirror*. Also popular, nowadays, are 'theme' crosswords, of which example (c) is one of 80, all on a Crime theme, which one of the authors compiled for a crime-puzzle magazine, *Whodunnit*, during 1992.

▼▼▼ YOU PLAY ▼▼▼

(c) THEMATIC CROSSWORD

THEMATIC CROSSWORD CLUES

Across

1 The freeing of a prisoner before his sentence has expired on condition of his good behaviour (6)

3 Sham (5)

6 These remains may be found after an arson attack (7)

9 Set at liberty (5)

10 A dangerous explosive (abb 5)

11 Geoffrey, British traitor and Russian spy sentenced to 38 years imprisonment November 1982 (5)

12 Al Capone had facial ones known as Von Stonheim's scalp or Durante's nose (5)

14 Pilfer (5)

19 Magistrates collectively (5)

20 Police call sign for 'R' (5)

21 Escape capture (5)

22 Conspirator (7)

23 Chinese gangsters who ran first large scale protection rackets in USA (5)

24 Someone who lends at an unlawfully high rate of interest (6)

Down

1 Film star, Al, who played in The Godfather (6)

2 In the movie Key ———, gang boss Edward G Robinson holds Bogart, Bacall and Barrymore hostage in Florida Keys hotel (5)

3 1968 movie which had Steve McQueen as a cop doing his own driving in an 11 minute car chase through San Francisco (7)

4 Worn by criminals so as not to leave fingerprints (5)

5 A detective (6)

7 Room in the house which could reveal nasty secrets (5)

8 Cheat (4)

13 Armed troops who police state or district in USA (7)

15 Confess (5)

16 Concealed and deceptive activity or operation (6)

17 Slang term for informing to police (4)

18 Extreme fear and apprehension (6)

19 Slang term for 'hit hard on the head' (5)

20 Where thieves may strip lead from (5)

Crossword trivia

For trivia buffs, here is a selection of crossword puzzle miscellanea.

- A crossword constructor is called a cruciverbalist.

- The largest crossword ever published has 2631 clues across and 2922 clues down. It was compiled by Hank Koval (USA) between 22 February 1974 and 1 October 1975.

- On 1 May 1970 *The Times* Crossword Editor, Edward Akenhead, succeeded in including the word HONORIFICABILITUDINITATIBUS in one of his crosswords.

- Ximenes (Derrick Macnutt) was responsible for laying down much of the 'ethical' basis of clue-writing and grid construction in his book, *Ximenes on the Art of the Crossword*.

- Noel Coward loved crosswords and said 'When I can make 1 across fit with 1 down, my day is made.'

- The person credited with most of the innovation now incorporated in the modern crossword, including symmetry, is the late Margaret Farrar. She was the first person to compile crosswords exclusively for *The Times* and one of her pupils, Maura Jacobsen, who graduated to puzzles editor at *New York Magazine*, says of her: 'Right from the beginning she raised the level of the language in crosswords. The early puzzles were pedantic.'

- Merle Reagle of the *San Francisco Examiner Magazine* created a puzzle that had S-E-X buried in each answer. Thus, 'Expensive job for Jimmy Durante' turned out to be 'nose x-ray'.

- The Provost of Eton College claimed he timed his breakfast egg by the time it took him to complete *The Times* crossword. To which one cynic remarked 'He must like them hard boiled.'

- The record for completing *The Times* crossword under test conditions is 3 minutes 45 seconds by Roy Dean of Bromley, Kent in 1970.

- HRH Princess Margaret entered a *Sunday Times* competition, but forgot to complete a clue.

- Michael Mates MP, once held a party in The House of Commons to celebrate having won his first *Times* crossword competition after 25 years.

- Colin Dexter, creator of Inspector Morse, is a crossword addict who believes that every word in the English language has, waiting to be compiled, its own perfect clue.

- The longest time taken to complete a *Times* crossword was 34 years when, in May 1966, a Mrs D. T. Lloyd sent in her completed version of Puzzle 673, which had been set in 1932.

- Dr John Sykes has won *The Times* crossword a record ten times. He is a former astrophysicist who gave up his job to work for the Oxford University Press, compiling dictionaries.

(Answers to C16 (a) to (c) on pages 257-8)

=C17=

CROSSWORD VARIATIONS

There are many puzzles which are a variation on the traditional crossword puzzle, several of which have been devised by the authors. The following, (a) to (i), are a few examples:

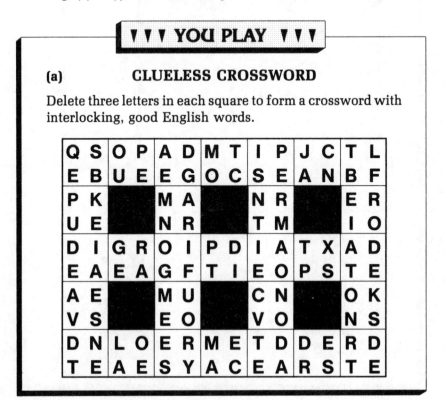

▼▼▼ YOU PLAY ▼▼▼

(a)   **CLUELESS CROSSWORD**

Delete three letters in each square to form a crossword with interlocking, good English words.

Q S	O P	A D	M T	I P	J C	T L
E B	U E	E G	O C	S E	A N	B F
P K	■	M A	■	N R	■	E R
U E	■	N R	■	T M	■	I O
D I	G R	O I	P D	I A	T X	A D
E A	E A	G F	T I	E O	P S	T E
A E	■	M U	■	C N	■	O K
V S	■	E O	■	V O	■	N S
D N	L O	E R	M E	T D	D E	R D
T E	A E	S Y	A C	E A	R S	T E

(b)   **HEXAGON**

Fit each of the listed words into the six spaces encircling the appropriate number on the diagram, so that each word correctly interlinks with the two words on either side (you will see that each word has two consecutive letters in common with the word on its side). (Note: to arrive at the correct solution some words will have to be entered clockwise and some anticlockwise.)

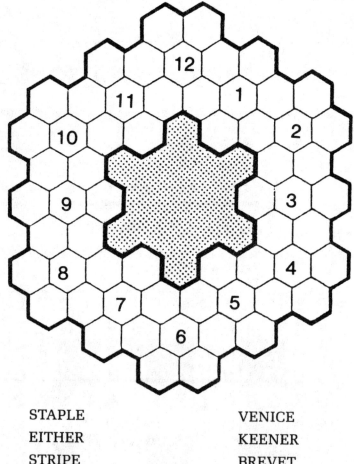

STAPLE	VENICE
EITHER	KEENER
STRIPE	BREVET
DEBRIS	RENEWS
PLIERS	NICKED

(c)   **WORD POWER**

This puzzle was invented by the authors several years ago. The answers are all 9-letter words and will be found in the grid, one letter on each line, in order. Each letter is used only once.

P	P	T	M	H	T	P	S	N
O	E	E	A	R	O	R	H	E
Q	X	D	I	N	V	R	L	O
I	U	E	E	M	M	I	M	E
T	N	N	A	M	E	Y	I	E
N	A	C	E	S	N	E	N	S
I	T	T	O	E	T	T	T	I
E	N	E	I	A	M	E	E	S
M	C	D	R	T	R	L	B	R

1 Bee's store

2 Fare meter

3 Frenzy

4 Occurring every ninth year

5 To set aside

6 Standing out

7 Three months

8 Contemplated

9 A card game

(d) **TARGET**

This puzzle was also invented by the authors. Find sixteen 6-letter words by pairing up the thirty-two 3-letter bits.

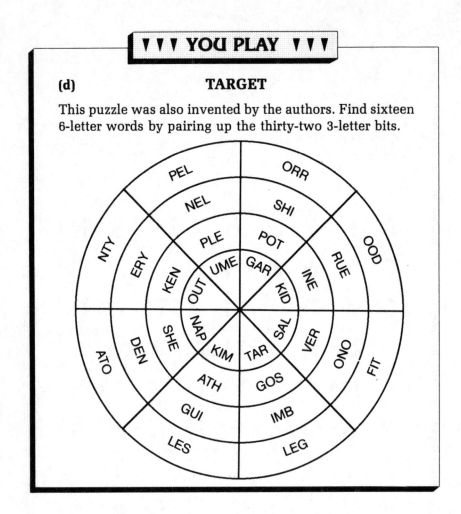

(e)   **QUOTATION PYRAMID**

This was devised by the authors, in the late 1980s. The most
difficult part of compiling such puzzles is finding a quotation having a pyramid number of letters, that is 15, 21, 28,
36, 45 or 54 letters long.

> 'I is the most popular letter in the alphabet'
> (Oliver Hereford)

Using all 36 letters of the above quotation, complete the
pyramid. Across clues are given, but in no particular order.

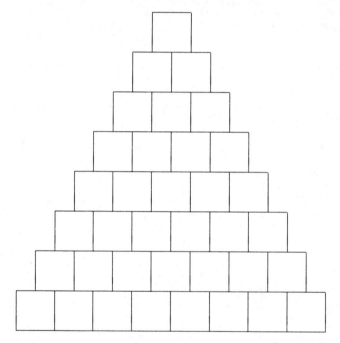

Clues

1 Put to the proof
2 Clothing
3 Circular letter!
4 Boundary
5 Money to be allotted

6 Wager
7 Slab under base
  of column
8 Third person
  masculine pronoun

(f)   DIRECTIONAL CROSSWORD

Again, this was devised by the authors. Answers run horizontally, vertically, or diagonally, either to right or left, down or up. Each solution starts on the lower number and finishes on the next higher number, i.e. 1 to 2, 2 to 3, etc. Finish at square 18.

Grid							
1 / 5							4
10		13		12			7
17					15		
18				14			
		16					
11	8			9		6	
3						2	

1 Seasoning
2 Shopkeepers
3 Loudness
4 Illegal importer/exporter
5 Turnabout
6 Madman
7 Bravery
8 Poems
9 Parts of flowers
10 Small stones
11 Electric fire bar
12 Tour
13 Concerning punishment
14 Boy
15 Woman
16 Detect
17 Tree

(g) **NO BLANKS**

This is an unusual crossword in that it has no blanks. Place the 20 words in the grid, so that each horizontal and vertical line forms a word. Some words have to be entered horizontally and some vertically.

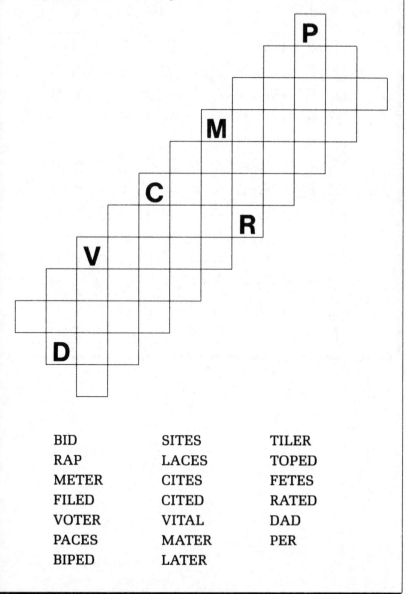

BID	SITES	TILER
RAP	LACES	TOPED
METER	CITES	FETES
FILED	CITED	RATED
VOTER	VITAL	DAD
PACES	MATER	PER
BIPED	LATER	

(h)   **BLANK OUT CROSSWORD**

In this crossword all the blanks have been replaced by spurious letters. The solver has to work out which are these spurious letters and blank them out to recreate the crossword. The answer is a conventional symmetrical crossword.

P	E	R	M	I	T	D	O	R	A	N	G	E
E	R	E	A	R	R	I	V	A	L	E	A	N
A	R	A	R	I	A	D	E	N	I	T	I	G
R	E	D	S	S	P	E	N	T	H	E	R	A
L	A	Z	E	S	C	C	R	E	B	R	I	G
S	T	E	M	M	A	L	E	S	O	N	C	E
S	A	T	B	O	N	A	N	Z	A	N	K	S
A	B	L	E	A	D	I	D	I	R	E	E	D
B	L	U	R	E	R	R	E	D	A	T	E
L	E	T	S	C	A	S	T	E	A	R	Y	E
A	T	E	W	E	R	S	U	P	O	N	O	M
Z	O	N	E	R	U	P	T	E	D	I	N	E
E	S	T	E	E	M	S	S	E	E	D	E	D

(i)   **NINERS**

This unusual use of a crossword grid was devised in recent years by the authors.

Place the 3-letter bits in the grid to make eight 9-letter words which go in the directions of the arrows. Clues to the words are given, in no particular order.

Four letters are duplicated; four letters are triplicated; one letter is quadruplicated.

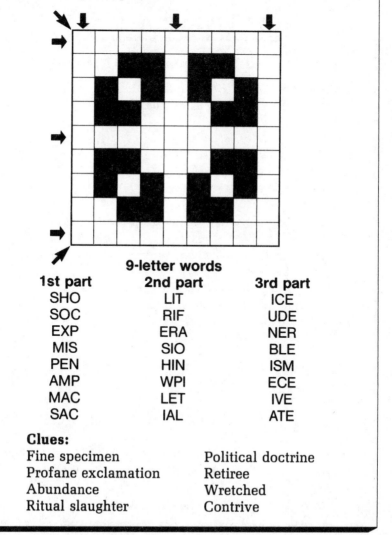

9-letter words

1st part	2nd part	3rd part
SHO	LIT	ICE
SOC	RIF	UDE
EXP	ERA	NER
MIS	SIO	BLE
PEN	HIN	ISM
AMP	WPI	ECE
MAC	LET	IVE
SAC	IAL	ATE

Clues:

Fine specimen   Political doctrine

Profane exclamation   Retiree

Abundance   Wretched

Ritual slaughter   Contrive

(Answers to C17 (a) to (i) on pages 258 to 260)

CRYPTIC ELIMINATION

The authors were once commissioned to compile 200 cryptic crosswords, all of which had to be completed in two months to meet the publisher's deadline. By burning the midnight oil the task was completed on time, but the problem was that they could not then stop compiling cryptic clues and, as a result, devised this game, (a), with the left-over clues.

▼▼▼ YOU PLAY ▼▼▼

(a)   **CRYPTIC ELIMINATION**

Each clue is solved by joining together two words from the 25 listed. You will use 24 words. Find the odd word left over.

A   Does this recluse use a gin in his grounds?
B   Thigh-slapping transvestite.
C   In charge of the road works.
D   12 makeshift people who are biased.
E   Does this marauder of the deep like the sun?
F   Charge for the cutlery and get the bird.
G   Difficult to get Jackson out unless the bowler is Hadrian.
H   Hire the knight, the price looks good.
I   This bird will do well in the marathon.
J   Sounds like an irritable monster.
K   Russian sea-faring lepidopterist.
L   Put the government away for the duration.

1 Admiral	10 Jury	19 Shark
2 Basking	11 Lance	20 Snap
3 Bill	12 Monk	21 Spoon
4 Boy	13 Principal	22 Squash
5 Cabinet	14 Red	23 Stone
6 Dragon	15 Rigged	24 Trappist
7 Drill	16 Road	25 Wall
8 Filing	17 Runner	
9 Free	18 Sergeant	

(Answers to C18 (a) on page 260)

CRYPTICS

This is a spin-off game from Cryptic Crosswords and is very popular as a fund-raiser for charities and organisations. A large number of cryptic clues is compiled on a certain theme: food, places, boys' names, girls' names, etc. and these clues are printed on a single sheet.

The sheets are then offered to the public who must complete as many of the answers as possible within a set time limit, say two or three weeks, and then hand in their entry with a fee of, say, £1. After the closing date the entries are marked and a prize given to the person with most correct, with the balance of the entry fees being donated to the specified charity or organisation.

A typical example, (a), was compiled by Enigmasig member, Jo Kennington. The answer to each cryptic clue is a London underground station.

▼▼▼ YOU PLAY ▼▼▼

(a) LONDON UNDERGROUND STATIONS QUIZ

1 She is not amused.
2 Heavenly messenger.
3 Ellipse.
4 A well known Teddy Bear.
5 Napoleon met his in 1815.
6 He wrote to the Corinthians.
7 Minister's jealous.
8 Sir's crossing road.
9 007 road.
10 Large animal and large building.
11 Monks' enclosure, then market, now operaland.
12 Detective at 221B.
13 Penultimate resting place of Queen Eleanor.
14 Carbonised wood.
15 A little boy stands ready here with bow and arrow.
16 Old Lady of Threadneedle Street

17 $CaCO_3$ to cultivate the land.
18 Reasonable cut.
19 Royal palace, original site of games.
20 Death's map in shreds.
21 Earnings related supplement initially between two colours.
22 Low Country stopping place.
23 White roll crumbled on the block.
24 Youth smashed plantation.
25 A fortress
26 Dower gone to pieces.
27 Take us to nearby hiding place.
28 'A jealous male and maid of sweet sixteen'.
29 Scorning casts sparks confusion.

Continued ▶

89

(a) *continued*

30 A regular enclosure for the Duke of Bedford's family.
31 ... and a similar one for the Rangers ...
32 Get long thin tail agitated.
33 Nothing comes after 3.142 + 1000 + 51 +100.
34 Ruin costs sage's wit.
35 Bore holes, then put on.
36 Groom reversed and spilt tea.
37 Applaud meat, not unusual.
38 Bewildered Pete gathers one thousand and fifty to form large church.
39 Did the PM steer his boat in a middle course?
40 United Nations shortly back into a brief time span.
41 Octans rennet curdled.
42 Make dim in the third month.
43 Men set wrist that is broken.
44 Noblemen make amorous approaches.
45 Chip at wheel irregularly.
46 It 'hath three thousand, Sire,' in disarray.
47 Residence of the Lord Mayor.
48 Keep Gran or lose nothing in exchange.
49 Guides former US president.
50 Ten cross between two rings.

(Answers to C19 (a) on pages 260-1)

C20

CRYPTOGRAPHY

Cryptography is the alteration of the form of a message by codes and ciphers to conceal its meaning. A cryptogram is the coded message, and cryptoanalysis is the breaking of the codes or cipher without the key.

What are cryptograms?

The simplest cryptograms are those in which each letter of the alphabet from A to Z (the plain text) is substituted for another in the coded text –for instance F for H or B for T.

Another method is to substitute randomly chosen numbers for each letter – for example, 156 may stand for E or 29 for K. In even more complicated versions of such ciphers, one letter may have more than one number equivalent, for example, the letter E may be 29 the first time it appears, 36 the second time and 21 the third time. These alternative numbers are known as 'homophones'. Without the key such messages, and even more complicated variations of them, would be virtually impossible to decode except by intelligence departments with sophisticated equipment.

Decoding simple cryptograms

Cryptoanalysts have at their disposal a great deal of information on such things as letter- and word-frequency. The order in which letters appear most frequently in English today is ETAOINSRHLDCUMFPG WYBVKXJQZ; the order in which they appear most often at the beginning of a word is TAOSIWHCB; and at the end ESDTNRYO.

So, armed with such information, how does one go about decoding a simple substitution cryptogram, that is, one is which each letter of the alphabet has been substituted for another?

The easiest types to deal with are those that contain a four-letter word which begins and ends with the same letter; for example, 'FGHF'. There is a very good chance this is the word 'THAT', which should enable you to discover the word 'THE', and now you are well on your way to solving the cryptogram. If, however, the word 'THAT' does not appear, then try to work out what might be the letter 'E'. Then look for single letter words – usually 'A' or 'I', and a repeated three-letter word ending, usually 'ING' (the most common three-letter ending in English). Also look for other obvious words such as 'AND', and the most common two-letter word in English – 'OF'. Double letters (EE, FF, LL, OO, RR and SS are the most common) and four-letter endings such as 'LESS' and 'NESS', can also be identified.

Keywords

Although the majority of cryptograms are straightforward simple types, what if the sender of the message wishes to convey a further message in the same cryptogram? This is done by the addition of keywords, which may be hidden in the plain or the keyed text. We can illustrate how these are uncovered by means of the following comment from Oliver Hardy, which he made to explain why he thought people found the Laurel and Hardy partnership so funny. (There is a further quotation, keyed 5-2-4-8, by Henry Ward Beecher.)

G LZOKK GI BRK SOPRZKO BO BOHO KM PMFXWOIOWD
ZQWGVO GQ OAOHD BRD. SZI, WGVO SRPMQ RQN OLLK,
BO KOOFON IM SO RSMZI XOHTOPI IMLOIJOH – SZI QMI
KM LMMN RXRHI.

This is a simple substitution cryptogram, which when deciphered reads:

I guess it was because we were so completely unlike in every way. But, like bacon and eggs, we seemed to be about perfect together – but not so good apart.

THE KEYED QUOTATION

To find the keyed quotation, place the code text, above, in juxtaposition to the plain text, thus:

Plain text: A B C D E F G H I J K L M N O P Q R S T U V W X Y Z
Code text: R S P N O T L J G V W F Q M X H K I Z A B D

As nothing appears yet which might look like a message, arrange the code text alphabetically in juxtaposition to the plain text:

Code text: A B C D E F G H I J K L M N O P Q R S T U V W X Y Z
Plain text: V W Y M I R T H S G O D E C N A B F K L P U

Usually the keyword or, in this case, the keyed quotation, contains the only letters which do not appear in alphabetical order. By inspecting the plain text you may usually easily pick out where the alphabet appears in orderly succession and thus isolate the keyword letters.

Above, we see A to Y in order, thus suggesting the keyed quotation is contained in the letters MIRTHSGODECN.

Because letters cannot be repeated in simple cryptograms, the fun now begins if the keyed quotation repeats letters. It is then necessary to use your imagination to make sense of the message. In the case the quotation is: MIRTH IS GOD'S MEDICINE.

You may now like to try deciphering the cryptogram in example (a).

▼ ▼ ▼ YOU PLAY ▼ ▼ ▼

(a)   **CRYPTOGRAM**

In this simple cryptogram, there is a message, keyed 4-3-4.

ME MR SQAHQ EA ZPQJ ELPE HO QOON RAYMEFNO
EA VMQN AFDROYGOR. BODLPBR ME MR QAE RA
HOYY SQAHQ ELPE HO QOON RAYMEFNO EA VMQN
AFD   VOYYAHR. OGOQ   ELO   RPGMAFD   MR
NORUDMTON PR DOPULMQW ZPQSMQN ELDAFWL
ELO HMYNODQORR.

LPGOYAUS OYYMR

Different types of cryptograms

The following is a selection of different types of cryptograms, several of which have been developed throughout history, including one unsolved mystery.

THE POLYBIUS CIPHER

This code was invented by a Greek writer, Polybius, in the 2nd century BC. Read the numbers down and across to find the number by which each letter is represented in the coded message. For example, the letter C = 13, G = 22, O = 34, Z = 55, etc.

	1	2	3	4	5
1	A	B	C	D	E
2	F	G	H	IJ	K
3	L	M	N	O	P
4	Q	R	S	T	U
5	V	W	X	Y	Z

THE CAESAR ALPHABET

This was a very simple system devised by Julius Caesar that proved surprisingly effective. In it he moved each letter two places up in the alphabet, that is:

A B C D E F G H I J K L M N O P Q R S T U V W X Y Z

Y Z A B C D E F G H I J K L M N O P Q R S T U V W X

THE LINCOLN SYSTEM

Abraham Lincoln had a simple cipher that he used frequently. To make the true message audible, all you had to do was read it aloud rapidly from the last word to the first word while paying attention to the sounds of the words instead of their meanings. One such actual message ended:

... AUNT CONFIDE IS ANDY EVACUATE PETERSBURG REPORTS GRANT MORNING THIS WASHINGTON SEC'Y WAR.

This reads:

WAR SECRETARY
WASHINGTON

THIS MORNING GRANT REPORTS PETERSBURG EVACUATED AND HE IS CONFIDENT.

Simple enough to decode. Perhaps, but the message in example (b) was sent to the Aquia Creek Headquarters of Major General Burnside on 25 November 1862. It was intercepted by a confederate operator but was not deciphered by him.

Can you decipher the message? Note that 'flesh' was a word commonly used in those days instead of meat.

Burnside replied in a similar cipher which also got through unbroken. At the subsequent meeting, held on the steamer *Baltimore*, a plan was developed which cost Lee thousands of lives three weeks later.

(b)   **THE LINCOLN SYSTEM**

Washington DC
November 25, 1862

Burnside, Falmouth, Virginia: Cann Inn Ale me withe 2 oar
our ann pass me flesh ends N.V. corn inn out with U cud inn
heaven day nest wed roe moore tom darkey hat greek why
hawk of abbot inn B chewed I if. Bates.

(Answers to C20 (a) and (b) on page 261).

THE BEALE CIPHERS

Since 1845, in America, many people have devoted a great deal of their
time trying to break what is known as the Beale Ciphers in an attempt to
find the whereabouts of several tons of gold, silver and jewels supposedly
buried near the town of Montvale (formerly Bufords), Virginia.

It was a Virginian, Thomas J. Beale, who set out with a party of men in
1817 on a hunting trip which eventually took them towards the Colorado
mountains. Here they discovered gold and stayed on to mine both gold
and silver for 18 months. Then, in November 1819, fearing for their safety
and their vast fortune, they returned to Virginia to hide their treasure in a
secret excavation six feet below ground. Two years later they again
returned to the site with some $13 000 in jewels, which they had
purchased in St Louis.

During the time, Tom Beale had become acquainted with Robert
Morriss, the proprietor of a hotel where Beale had stayed. Beale entrusted
to Morriss a strong iron box for safe keeping. Later he wrote to Morriss,
asking him to keep the box for 10 years, telling him that if he had not by
then called to collect it, he should open it up.

Beale was never heard of again but, to be on the safe side, Morriss
waited for almost 25 years before opening the box, in 1845. Inside he found
several sheets of paper and letters telling the story of the treasure, together
with three cryptograms giving details of the location of the treasure, its
contents and Beale's next of kin. One letter promised that the three
ciphers could easily be cracked using a key which would be sent to
Morriss, but it never arrived.

Since Morriss could not crack the ciphers he enlisted the help of a friend who became obsessed with them and, after 20 years, was finally able to crack one of the ciphers – the one giving the contents of the vault of treasure.

He discovered the method that Beale had used was to take the *Declaration of Independence* and allocate each word a number, from WHEN = 1 to HONOR = 1322. Then, taking the first letter of the word which corresponded to each number of the cipher, the message was spelt out, starting: 115 (I), 73 (H), 24 (A), 807 (V), 37 (E), 52 (D), 49 (E), 17 (P), 31 (O), 62 (S), 647 (I), 22 (T) . . .

Since then, the remaining two ciphers have remained a mystery, despite many thousands of hours of research and effort, and no treasure has been found. Research, however, still continues, especially by the members of the Beale Cypher Association in Pennsylvania. The complete Beale Ciphers are reproduced on pages 96 to 98.

ACTUALLY, IT SAYS 'APRIL FOOL!'

CIPHER NO.1 : LOCALITY

```
    71,   194,  38,   1701,  89,  76,  11,  83,   1629,
48,  94,  63,  132,  16,  111,  95,  84,  341,  975,  14,
40,  64,  27,  81,  139,  213,  63,  90,   1120,  8,  15,
3,  126,  2018,   40,  74,  758,  485,  604,  230,  436,
664,  582,  150,  251,  284,   308,   231,   124,  211,
486,  225,  401,  370,  11,  101,  305,  139,  189,  17,
33,  88,  208,   193,  145,   1,  94,  73,  416,  918,
263,  28,  500,  538,  356,  117,  136,  219,  27,  176,
130,   10,  460,   25,  485,  18,  436,   65,  84,  200,
283,  118,  320,  138,   36,  416,  280,  15,  71,  224,
961,  44,  16,  401,  39,  88,  61,  304,   12,  21,  24,
283,  134,  92,  63,  246,   486,   682,  7,  219,  184,
360,  780,   18,  64,  463,  474,  131,  160,  79,  73,
440,  95,  18,  64,  581,   34,  69,  128,   367,   460,
17,  81,  12,  103,  880,   62,   116,  97,  103,  862,
70,  60,  1317,  471,  540,  208,  121,  890,  346,  36,
150,  59,  568,  614,  13,  120,  63,  219,  812,  2160,
1780,  99,  35,  18,  21,  136,   872,   15,  28,   170,
88,   4,  30,  44,  112,  18,  147,  436,  195,  320,  37,
122,  113,  6,  140,  8,  120,  305,  42,  58,  461,  44,
106,   301,  13,  408,   680,  93,  86,  116,  530,  82,
568,   9,  102,  38,  416,  89,  71,  216,   728,  965,
818,   2,  38,  121,   195,   14,  326,  148,  234,  18,
55,  131,   234,   361,   824,  5,  81,  623,  48,  961,
19,  26,  33,  10,   1101,  365,   92,  88,  181,  275,
346,   201,  206,  86,  36,  219,  324,  829,  840,  64,
326,  19,  48,  122,  85,  216,   284,  919,  861,  326,
985,  233,  64,  68,  232,   431,  960,  50,  29,  81,
216,  321,  603,   14,  612,  81,  360,  36,  51,  62,
194,  78,  60,  200,  314,  676,  112,  4,  28,  18,  61,
136,  247,  819,  921,  1060,  464,  895,  10,  6,  66,
119,  38,  41,  49;  602,  423,  962,  302,  294,  875,
78,  14,  23,  111,  109,  62,  31,  501,  823,  216,
280,  34,  24,  150,   1000,  162,  286,  19,  21,  17,
340,  19,  242,  31,  86,  234,  140,  607,  115,  33,
191,  67,  104,  86,  52,  88,  16,  80,  121,  67,  95,
122,  216,  548,  96,  11,  201,  77,  364,  218,  65,
667,  890,  236,  154,  211,  10,  98,  34,  119,  56,
216,  119,  71,  218,  1164,  1496,  1817,  51,  39,
210,  36,  3,  19,  540,  232,  22,  141,  617,  84,
290,  80,  46,  207,  411,  150,  29,  38,  46,  172,
85,  194,  39,  261,  543,  897,  624,  18,  212,  416,
127,  931,  19,  4,  63,  96,  12,  101,  418,  16,  140,
230,  460,  538,  19,  27,  88,  612,  1431,  90,  716,
275,  74,  83,  11,  426,  89,  72,  84,  1300,  1706,
814,  221,  132,  40,  102,  34,  868,  975,  1101,  84,
16,  79,  23,  16,  81,  403,  912,  227,  936,  447,
55,  86,  34,  43,  212,  107,  96,  314,  264,  1065,
323,  428,  601,  203,  124,  95,  216,  814,  2906,
654,  820,  2,  301,  112,  176,  213,  71,  87,  96,
202,  95,  10,  2,  41,  17,  84,  221,  736,  826,  214,
11,  60,  760.
```

CIPHER NO.2: CONTENTS

115, 73, 24, 807, 37, 52, 49, 17, 31, 62,
647, 22, 7, 15, 140, 47, 29, 107, 79, 84, 56,
239, 10, 26, 811, 5, 196, 308, 85, 52, 160,
136, 59, 211, 36, 9, 46, 316, 554, 122, 106,
96, 53, 58, 2, 42, 7, 35, 122, 53, 31, 82, 77,
250, 196, 56, 96, 118, 71, 140, 287, 28, 353,
37, 1005, 65, 147, 807, 24, 3, 8, 12, 47, 43,
59, 807, 45, 316, 101, 41, 78, 154, 1005, 122,
138, 191, 16, 77, 49, 102, 57, 72, 34, 73, 85,
35, 371, 59, 196, 81, 92, 191, 106, 273, 60,
394, 620, 270, 220, 106, 388, 287, 63, 3, 6,
191, 122, 43, 234, 400, 106, 290, 314, 47, 48,
81, 96, 26, 115, 92, 158, 191, 110, 77, 85,
197, 46, 10, 113, 140, 353, 48, 120, 106, 2,
607, 61, 420, 811, 29, 125, 14, 20, 37, 105,
28, 248, 16, 159, 7, 35, 19, 301, 125, 110,
486, 287, 98, 117, 511, 62, 51, 220, 37, 113,
140, 807, 138, 540, 8, 44, 287, 388, 117, 18,
79, 344, 34, 20, 59, 511, 548, 107, 603, 220,
7, 66, 154, 41, 20, 50, 6, 575, 122, 154, 248,
110, 61, 52, 33, 30, 5, 38, 8, 14, 84, 57, 540,
217, 115, 71, 29, 85, 63, 43, 131, 29, 138, 47,
73, 239, 540, 52, 53, 79, 118, 51, 44, 63, 196,
12, 239, 112, 3, 49, 79, 353, 105, 56, 371,
557, 211, 505, 125, 360, 133, 143, 101, 15,
284, 540, 252, 14, 205, 140, 344, 26, 811, 138,
115, 48, 73, 34, 205, 316, 607, 63, 220, 7, 52,
150, 44, 52, 16, 40, 37, 158, 807, 37, 121, 12,
96, 10, 15, 35, 12, 131, 62, 115, 102, 807, 49,
53, 135, 138, 30, 31, 62, 67, 41, 85, 63, 10,
106, 807, 138, 8, 113, 20, 32, 33, 7, 353, 287,
140, 47, 85, 50, 7, 49, 47, 64, 6, 7, 71, 33,
4, 43, 47, 63, 1, 27, 600, 208, 230, 15, 191,
246, 85, 94, 511, 2, 270, 20, 39, 7, 33, 44,
22, 40, 7, 10, 3, 811, 106, 44, 486, 230, 353,
211, 200, 31, 10, 38, 140, 297, 61, 603, 320,
302, 666, 287, 2, 44, 32, 511, 548, 10, 6,
250, 557, 246, 53, 7, 52, 83, 47, 320, 38, 33,
807, 7, 44, 30, 31, 250, 10, 15, 35, 106, 160,
113, 31, 102, 406, 230, 540, 320, 29, 66, 33,
101, 807, 138, 301, 316, 353, 320, 220, 7, 52,
28, 540, 320, 33, 8, 48, 107, 50, 811, 7, 2,
113, 73, 16, 125, 11, 110, 67, 102, 807, 33,
59, 81, 158, 38, 43, 581, 138, 19, 85, 400, 38,
43, 77, 14, 27, 8, 47, 138, 63, 140, 44, 35,
22, 176, 106, 250, 314, 217, 2, 10, 7, 1005, 4,
20, 25, 44, 48, 7, 26, 46, 110, 230, 807, 191,
34, 112, 147, 44, 110, 121, 125, 96, 41, 51,
50, 140, 56, 47, 152, 540, 63, 807, 28, 42,
250, 138, 582, 98, 643, 32, 107, 140, 112, 26,
85, 138, 540, 53, 20, 125, 371, 38, 36, 10, 52,
118, 136, 102, 420, 150, 112, 71, 14, 20, 7,
24, 18, 12, 807, 37, 67, 110, 62, 33, 21, 96,
220, 511, 102, 811, 30, 83, 84, 305, 620, 15,
2, 10, 8, 220, 106, 353, 105, 106, 60, 275, 72,
8, 50, 205, 185, 112, 125, 540, 65, 106, 807,
191, 96, 110, 16, 73, 33, 807, 150, 409, 400,
50, 154, 285, 96, 106, 316, 270, 205, 101, 811,
400, 8, 44, 7, 52, 40, 241, 34, 205, 38, 16,
46, 47, 85, 24, 44, 15, 64, 73, 138, 807, 85,
78, 110, 33, 420, 505, 53, 37, 38, 22, 31, 10,
110, 106, 101, 140, 15, 38, 3, 5, 44, 7, 98,
287, 135, 150, 96, 33, 84, 125, 807, 191, 96,
511, 118, 440, 370, 643, 466, 106, 41, 107,
603, 220, 275, 30, 150, 105, 49, 53, 287, 250,
208, 134, 7, 53, 12, 47, 85, 63, 138, 110, 21,
112, 140, 485, 486, 505, 14, 73, 84, 575, 1005,
150, 200, 16, 42, 5, 4, 25, 42, 8, 16, 811,
125, 160, 32, 205, 603, 807, 81, 96, 405, 41,
600, 136, 14, 20, 28, 26, 353, 302, 246, 8,
131, 160, 140, 84, 440, 42, 16, 811, 40, 67,
101, 102, 194, 138, 205, 51, 63, 241, 540, 122,
8, 10, 63, 140, 47, 48, 140, 288.

317, 8, 92, 73, 112, 89, 67, 318, 28, 96,
107, 41, 631, 78, 146, 397, 118, 98, 114, 246,
348, 116, 74, 88, 12, 65, 32, 14, 81, 18, 76,
121, 216, 85, 33, 66, 15, 108, 68, 77, 43, 24,
122, 96, 117, 36, 211, 301, 15, 44, 11, 46, 89,
18, 136, 68, 317, 28, 90, 82, 304, 71, 43, 221,
198, 176, 310, 319, 81, 99, 264, 380, 56, 37,
319, 2, 44, 53, 28, 44, 75, 98, 102, 37, 85,
107, 117, 64, 88, 136, 48, 154, 99, 175, 89,
315, 326, 78, 96, 214, 218, 311, 43, 89, 51,
90, 75, 128, 96, 33, 28, 103, 84, 65, 26, 41,
246, 84, 270, 98, 116, 32, 59, 74, 66, 69, 240,
15, 8, 121, 20, 77, 89, 31, 11, 106, 81, 191,
224, 328, 18, 75, 52, 82, 117, 201, 39, 23,
217, 27, 21, 84, 35, 54, 109, 128, 49, 77, 88,
1, 81, 217, 64, 55, 83, 116, 251, 269, 311, 96,
54, 32, 120, 18, 132, 102, 219, 211, 84, 150,
219, 275, 312, 64, 10, 106, 87, 75, 47, 21, 29,
37, 81, 44, 18, 126, 115, 132, 160, 181, 97,
318, 238, 106, 24, 93, 3, 19, 17, 26, 203, 76,
81, 299, 314, 337, 351, 96, 11, 28, 60, 73, 88,
14, 126, 138, 234, 286, 297, 321, 365, 264, 19,
22, 84, 56, 107, 98, 123, 111, 214, 136, 7, 33,
45, 40, 13, 28, 46, 42, 107, 196, 227, 344,
198, 203, 247, 116, 19, 8, 212, 230, 31, 6,
328, 65, 48, 52, 59, 41, 122, 33, 117, 11, 18,
25, 71, 36, 45, 83, 76, 89, 92, 31, 65, 70, 83,
96, 27, 33, 44, 50, 61, 24, 112, 136, 149, 176,
180, 194, 143, 171, 205, 296, 87, 12, 44, 51,
89, 98, 34, 41, 208, 173, 66, 9, 35, 16, 95, 8,
113, 175, 90, 56, 203, 19, 177, 183, 206, 157,
200, 218, 260, 291, 305, 618, 951, 320, 18,
124, 78, 65, 19, 32, 124, 48, 53, 57, 84, 96,
207, 244, 66, 82, 119, 71, 11, 86, 77, 213, 54,
82, 316, 245, 303, 86, 97, 106, 212, 18, 37,
15, 81, 89, 16, 7, 81, 39, 96, 14, 43, 216,
118, 29, 55, 109, 136, 172, 213, 64, 8, 227,
304, 611, 221, 364, 819, 375, 128, 296, 1, 18,
53, 76, 10, 15, 23, 19, 71, 84, 120, 134, 66,
73, 89, 96, 230, 48, 77, 26, 101, 127, 936,
218, 439, 178, 171, 61, 226, 313, 215, 102, 18,
167, 262, 114, 218, 66, 59, 48, 27, 19, 13, 82,
48, 162, 119, 34, 127, 139, 34, 128, 129, 74,
63, 120, 11, 54, 61, 73, 92, 180, 66, 75, 101,
124, 265, 89, 96, 126, 274, 896, 917, 434, 461,
235, 890, 312, 413, 328, 381, 96, 105, 217, 66,
118, 22, 77, 64, 42, 12, 7, 55, 24, 83, 67, 97,
109, 121, 135, 181, 203, 219, 228, 256, 21, 34,
77, 319, 374, 382, 675, 684, 717, 864, 203, 4,
18, 92, 16, 63, 82, 22, 46, 55, 69, 74, 112,
134, 186, 175, 119, 213, 416, 312, 343, 264,
119, 186, 218, 343, 417, 845, 951, 124, 209,
49, 617, 856, 924, 936, 72, 19, 28, 11, 35, 42,
40, 66, 85, 94, 112, 65, 82, 115, 119, 236,
244, 186, 172, 112, 85, 6, 56, 38, 44, 85, 72,
32, 47, 63, 96, 124, 217, 314, 319, 221, 644,
817, 821, 934, 922, 416, 975, 10, 22, 18, 46,
137, 181, 101, 39, 86, 103, 116, 138, 164, 212,
218, 296, 815, 380, 412, 460, 495, 675, 820,
952.

CYCLICYCLES

In a cyclic transposal a letter is moved from the end of a word to the beginning, or vice-versa, to form a new word. For instance, 'end' becomes 'den' and 'start' becomes 'tarts'. Put these together and an amusing transposal is created whereby 'START END' becomes 'TART'S DEN'.

In a Cyclicycle, such sets of cyclic transposals are used in sequence, for example, 'I evolved to devolve'.

The following examples are taken from Dmitri Borgmann's book *Language on Vacation* and are all triple cyclicycles.

Eat? I ate tea.

Levi was evil, vile.

I rave: 'Aver Vera!'.

The stable had tables – the ablest.

A stripe on the tripes indicates the ripest.

D1

DECEPTIONS

The sign shown is outside *The Plough* public house at East Hendred, Oxfordshire. Such signs can become word games in their own right and the altering of word boundaries can lead to, initially, confusing results.

HERESTO PANDS PEN D ASOCI
AL HOU R INHAR M (LES SMIRT)
HA ND FUNLET FRIENDS ♦
HIPRE IGN BE JUSTAN DK
INDAN DEVIL SPEAKOF NO NE

Public house sign

Consider also these famous examples:

1 A sign on a post in Peru:

TOTI EMU LESTO

2 A sign on a door in Cornwall, England.

TOOP
ENDO
ORPU
SH

At first glance these are written in some strange language but close inspection reveals the messages **1** To tie mules to; and **2** To open door push.

The following appears to be a cryptogram: 'M ISC HIEV OUSO FM ETOT RYTOTR ICKY OU' but again it has simply had its word boundaries altered to disguise its original meaning: 'Mischievous of me to try to trick you'.

A further example is this headstone:

```
              BENE
        AT . HTH . IS ST
        ONERE . POS . ET              Beneath
   H . CLAUD . COS . TERT            this stone
            R . I . P                reposeth
        ES . ELLE . RO            Claud Coster
            F . IMP                 tripe seller
     ING . TONAS . DO            of Impington
        TH . HISCO                 as doth his
          N SORT J               consort Jane
          A . N . E
```

Note the 'pièce de resistance' which is the central and appropriate use of
the letters R.I.P. It is a both sad and amusing example of word play.

A further favourite type of deception is the Latin-type verse, which in
fact is not Latin at all. This is perhaps the best known example:

O SIBILI SI EMGO	O see Billy, see 'em go
FORTIBUSES I NARO	Forty buses in a row
O NOBILI DEMIS TRUX	O no Billy 'dem is trucks
VATIS INEM? CAUS AN DUX	What is in 'em? Cows and ducks

And, much more difficult to decipher:

O, Tome, isa eres ago	O, Tommy, I saw years ago
Fortibus es in aro	Forty buses in a row
Nobile, Nobile	No, Billy, no, Billy
Themstrux, Yusile	Thems trucks, you silly
Sewat Sinem – Ivst Gvano	So what's in 'em? Just guano

Note that this version uses the Roman V for U (as in CLAVDIVS =
CLAUDIUS) and includes the difficult word 'guano' (manure).

================ D2 ================

DEVILRY

Printer's devilry is the kind of thing we very frequently come across in
newspapers, magazines and books. They are the gremlins of the printing
industry and are a type of what is more commonly known as a 'printer's
error'. They are also used in some crosswords as a type of cryptic clue and
are described in the handbook of 'The Crossword Club' (see page 67)
as follows.

'Such a clue consists of a passage from which the printer has removed a hidden answer, closing the gap, taking liberties with punctuation and/or spacing sometimes, but not disturbing the order of the remaining letters. Each passage, when complete, makes sense.

'Example: "Mum wanted to sack the au pair. She tried to. Sad! (6)"
Solution: EDUCED
Undevilled version: "Mum wanted to sack the au pair. She tried to SEDUCE Dad!"

'Lack of a definition makes a normal PD clue unsatisfactory. A more elegant variation is Printer's Devilry with Definition (PDD):

'Example: "Will Socialists hound capitalists and curs? (6)"
Solution: BASSET
Definition: HOUND
Undevilled version: "Will Socialists hound capitalists and curB ASSETs?"'

Devilry can also be a fine game or puzzle in its own right, as illustrated by the following examples by Enigmasig member, Bob Newman. Such are very difficult to compile and equally difficult to solve. Puzzle (a) is introduced in Bob Newman's own words.

▼▼▼ YOU PLAY ▼▼▼

(a)   DEVILRY

Recipe: For each clue, choose a word to split, and insert the fruit of your choice. Rearrange spacing and punctuation to taste (though you may not alter the order of the letters) to give something that still makes sense – usually more sense than the original. For example: 'The praises of a glorious egg, low in gin: the dark ages like a beacon' yields 'The praises of a glorious eRA I SINg, glowing in the dark ages like a beacon.'

Some of the fruit are a little more exotic or obscure than those of the first helping.

1 In India they charge snakes with musical trickery.

2 Whatever the regent does, make a profit.

3 I must pay off the loans – harsh interest rates were not always so high.

(a) *continued*

4 Tweedledum said he'd hidden the rattle in the jar, said Tweedledee.

5 The freight company sped coal to Tyneside.

6 Tonight I am wearing my slim dressing for warmth.

7 We can see in the design of the airship with the extractor fan.

8 As I left the casino for my hotel room I was offered a dice; cup of cocoa was what I wanted.

9 Look at the goddess in the beautiful woollen cloak! Isn't that Hera?

10 The sports master wanted to publish a school magazine at the parents' expense, but he couldn't make any one sprinter.

11 Hog ate date ton as we boys grew weary of school food.

12 Councillors shunted by vice scandal.

13 'Don't spend all that money on prisons, Neil Smith!' wailed miser. Abrupt, he left by demolishing some.

14 Holmes composed a violin piece: *The Mystery of the Red Sea.* Sing to excite him.

15 I'd heard so much about Alvaro Mendoza the football coach that while in Central America I simply had to visit the man – and Al's team.

16 Despite having a figure like a large – hi, pa! – shop, which was popular with slimmers, she was a real character, my Aunt Margaret.

17 The boat with the lateen sailed down the river towards Yarmouth.

18 And behold, as he poured the water into the glass, each of them saw that had turned to wine.

19 Bees find, according to exhaustive research by diligent Mendel, 'weiss' flowers more easily than coloured flowers.

20 Switzerland and Holland, countries as different as chalk and cheese, are both celebrating the Emmentaler centenary this year.

(Answers to D2 (a) on page 261)

DONKEY

In this game the object is to select an animal and then each player invents rhyming pairs. For example:

What do you call a crude donkey?

A crass ass.

What is an old donkey called?

A grayer brayer.

What is a prolific donkey called?

A critter emitter.

What is the name for a sleeping donkey?

A supine equine.

What is a donkey's burden?

A jack's pack.

What do you call a donkey's cry?

A hinny whinny.

What do you call a donkey banquet?

A beast feast.

DOUBLETS

Invented in 1879 by Lewis Carroll, the puzzle which he named Doublets, but which is now probably better known as Word Ladders, has remained popular to this day. Over the years it has also been referred to as Laddergrams, Stepwords, Transitions, Transformation, Changelings, Passes, Word Chains, Word Ping-Pong and Word Golf.

In this extract from a letter to the magazine *Vanity Fair* in March 1879, Carroll himself describes the object of his puzzle:

'The rules of the puzzle are simple enough. Two words are proposed, of the same length, and the puzzle consists in linking these together by interposing other words, each of which shall differ from the next word in one letter only. That is to say, one letter may be changed in one of the given words, then one letter in the word so obtained, and so on, till we arrive at the other given word. The letters must not be interchanged among themselves, but each must keep to its own place. As an example, the word "head" may be changed into "tail" by interposing the words "heal, teal, tell, tall". I call the two given words a "Doublet", he interposed words "Links" and the entire series "a Chain".'

Again, Carroll writes to a friend:

'My dear Edith, You will find this puzzle very soothing: what doctors call "an alternative" i.e. if you happen to have a headache, it will charm it away; but if you haven't one, it will probably give you one.'

Here are a few of the doublets which Carroll had published in *Vanity Fair* between April and July 1879.

1 Change TEARS into SMILE in 5 links:
   Tears, sears, stars, stare, stale, stile, smile

2 Get WOOD from TREE in 7 links:
   Tree, free, flee, fled, feed, weed, weld, wold, wood

3 Make TEA HOT in 3 links:
   Tea, sea, set, sot, hot

4 Make WINTER SUMMER in 13 links:
   Winter, winner, wanner, wander, warder, harder, harper, hamper, damper, damped, dammed, dimmed, dimmer, simmer, summer

Recently, computers have generated shorter solutions to many of Carroll's puzzles although many use obscure words and do not have the charm of the Carroll original.

It is a fact that the more obscure words one uses, the shorter the chain. For example, in an American radio contest in 1992, listeners were invited to form a ladder from WHITE to HOUSE using all common words and no plurals. The winning entry was: White, while, whole, whose, chose, chase, cease, lease, least, beast, boast, roast, roust, rouse, house. But, by delving into the realms of rare and obscure words the following much shortened version with just three links can be produced: White, whute, woute, houte, house, all words appearing in the official *Scrabble Players' Dictionary*.

However, the fun to us seems to be to solve a puzzle using common words with which everyone is familiar. Once rare and obscure words are used, then all general interest in the puzzle is killed off immediately.

(a)   **DOUBLETS**

Now try this one for yourselves.

Change SMITH to JONES in 10 links.

(Answer to D4 (a) on page 261)

=====D5=====

DUTCH AUCTION

This is a game for two people or teams. Firstly, person or team 1 selects a word.

Team 1 says: The word has 4 letters and begins with R. Guess the word for 6 points.

                     Definition: To draw off (wine, etc.) from the lees.

                     Team 2 cannot answer.

Team 1 says: Definition: The neck and spine of a forequarter of veal or mutton, for 5 points.

                     Team 2 cannot answer.

Team 1 says: Definition: Light vapoury clouds, for 4 points.

                     Team 2 cannot answer.

Team 1 says: Definition: A type of horse's movement, for 3 points.

                     Team 2 cannot answer.

Team 1 says: Definition: An open framework of bars, for 2 points.

                     Team 2 cannot answer.

Team 1 says: Definition: To stretch or strain, for 1 point.

                     Team 2 answers RACK and scores one point.

Now it is the turn of team 2 to select a word, and so on.

The number of points available at the start of each round is determined by the number of definitions that the team presenting the word has available. For example, if the team can only find three definitions for a word, then three points are available at the first guess. If a team fails to guess a word, then all points are gained by the team selecting the word. For example, had team 2 failed to guess RACK at the sixth attempt, then 6 points would have been awarded to team 1, instead of one point to team 2.

It is, of course, good tactics for the team selecting the word to start off with the most difficult clue and leave the easiest until last.

AND WE USE THIS BOOK OF
WORD GAMES FOR INSPIRATION
WHEN WE'RE WRITING UP
THE HOUSE DETAILS .....

ENIGMAGRAMS

This puzzle was invented by the authors, who recently published 100 of them in book form *The Book of Enigmagrams* (Futura). The puzzle can be made very difficult by using more unusual words. The example, (a), is typical of a fairly easy to solve enigmagram.

▼▼▼ YOU PLAY ▼▼▼

(a) **ENIGMAGRAM**

The four six-letter words have each been jumbled. Solve the four anagrams of Birds and then transfer the arrowed letters to the key anagram to find a fifth Bird. The Birds read from left to right, or top to bottom.

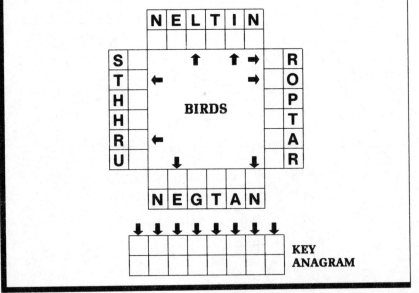

(Answers to E1 (a) on page 261)

ENIGMAS

'It may well be doubted whether human ingenuity can construct an enigma of the kind which human ingenuity may not, by proper application, resolve.'

Edgar Allan Poe

The word 'enigma' comes from the Greek verb signifying 'to darken and hide' and in verse form is a puzzle in which the answer to be guessed is hidden in cryptic fashion.

Enigmas are tantalising puzzles, often very difficult to solve, and many have remained unanswered for many years. They have been compiled as diversions by many famous people during the past few hundred years. Take (a) for example, which was by George Canning (1770-1827), who was Foreign Secretary (1807-9 and 1822-27) and Tory Prime Minister (1827).

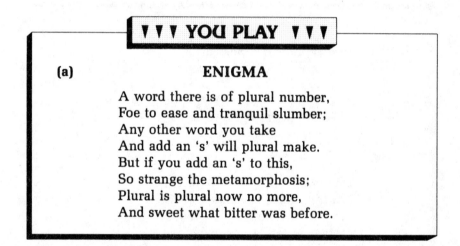

▼▼▼ YOU PLAY ▼▼▼

(a)   ENIGMA

A word there is of plural number,
Foe to ease and tranquil slumber;
Any other word you take
And add an 's' will plural make.
But if you add an 's' to this,
So strange the metamorphosis;
Plural is plural now no more,
And sweet what bitter was before.

The Irish satirist and author of *Gulliver's Travels*, Jonathan Swift, was also fond of compiling Enigmas. In the two examples, (b) and (c), the answer you are looking for in each case has three letters.

▼ ▼ ▼ YOU PLAY ▼ ▼ ▼

(b)   **ENIGMA**

From India's burning climes I'm brought,
With cooling gales like Zephyrs fraught.
Not Iris, when she paints the sky,
Can show more different hues than I;
Nor can she change her form so fast:
I'm now a sail and now a mast.
I here am red, and there am green,
A beggar there and here a queen;
I sometime live in house of hair,
And oft in hand of lady fair.
I please the young, I grace the old,
And am at once both hot and cold.
Say what I am then, if you can,
And find the rhyme, and you're the man.

And (c) is the second of Swift's Enigmas.

▼ ▼ ▼ YOU PLAY ▼ ▼ ▼

(c)   **ENIGMA**

In Youth exalted high in Air,
Or bathing in the Waters fair;
Nature to form me took Delight,
And clad my Body all in White:
My Person tall, and slender Waist,
On either Side with Fringes grac'd;
Till me that Tyrant Man espy'd,
And drag'd me from my Mother's Side:
No Wonder now I look so thin;
The Tyrant strip't me to the Skin:
My Skin he flay'd, my Hair he cropt;
At Head and Foot my Body lopt:
And then, with Heart more hard than Stone,
He pick't my Marrow from the Bone.
To vex me more, he took a Freak,

(c) *continued*

To slit my Tongue, and made me speak:
But, that which wonderful appears,
I speak to eyes and not to Ears.
He oft employs me in Disguise,
And makes me tell a Thousand Lyes
To me he chiefly gives in Trust
To please his Malice, or his Lust.
From me no Secret he can hide;
I see his Vanity and Pride:
And my Delight is to expose
His Follies to his greatest Foes.

All Languages can I command,
Yet not a Word I understand.
Without my Aid, the best Divine
In Learning would not know a Line:
The Lawyer must forget his Pleading,
The Scholar could not shew his Reading.
Nay; Man, my Master, is my Slave:
I give Command to kill or save.
Can grant ten Thousand Pounds a Year,
And make a Beggar's Brat a Peer.

But, while I thus my Life relate,
I only hasten on my Fate.
My Tongue is black, my Mouth is furr'd,
I hardly now can force a Word.
I dye unpity'd and forgot;
And on some Dunghill left to rot.

The enigma in (d) was compiled by Horace Walpole (1717-97), the fourth son of Sir Robert Walpole – the first British Prime Minister. Horace Walpole was a man of letters and writer of the popular gothic novel *The Castle of Otranto* (1765).

(d)   ENIGMA

Before my birth I had a name,
But soon as born I chang'd the same;
And when I'm laid within the tomb,
I shall my father's name assume.
I change my name three days together,
Yet live but one in any weather.

(Answers to E2 (a) to (d) on page 262)

(Answers to E2 (a) to (d) on page 262)

E3

ENIGMASIG

Enigmasig is the name of the Special Interest Group (SIG) within British Mensa which is run jointly by we two authors and is devoted to the setting, solving and invention of all types of puzzles. It is in fact a puzzle club and, although the majority of members live in the UK, there are also members from many parts of the world. We also assist members by giving advice on how to get their work published and at least three other members, apart from ourselves, have been successful in getting puzzle books published within the past few years.

We also run various competitions. One popular feature is 'What's in the Box?' where, in each edition of the monthly newsletter, we provide a cryptic clue, and members must guess what is in the box. This could be anything from a small object to a building, person or place. Usually we find that this is guessed extremely quickly. For example, one clue was '6th June'. Within a day we had a postcard with the correct answer, 'Doris Day', the 6th June being D-Day. Another time, the clue was 'The Netherlands' and immediately the correct answer, 'An orange', was guessed, the ruling house of the Netherlands being the House of Orange.

Mensa, itself, is a society where the sole qualification for membership is to have attained a score in any supervised test of general intelligence which puts the applicant in the top two per cent of the general population.

It is perhaps best described as a social club, where members may communicate with other members through correspondence, meetings, think-ins, dinners, special interest groups, lectures and international gatherings, and it provides members with the opportunity to exchange, and try out, new ideas and opinions.

Now, (a) and (b) are a couple of typically challenging word puzzles from the pages of the monthly newsletter of Enigmasig.

▼▼▼ YOU PLAY ▼▼▼

(a)   **RELICS RETURN**

(by Bob Newman)

Each of the words listed, originally contained four consecutive letters of the alphabet, in order, but not necessarily occurring consecutively within the word. Those four letters have been removed.

An example is INSTRUCTIVE, which would become INRCTIE after the STUV had been removed. Can you find the words which yielded these fragments?

aced	lasp	roa
asueflowe	latin	son
eptoaia	ooly	spaclit
faig	orm	suae

▼▼▼ YOU PLAY ▼▼▼

(b)   **NEXT IN LINE**

(by Lloyd King)

Find the next word.

Embark, Cotton, Ochre, Calm, Frost, ?

Choose from:

Dell, Flute, Globule, Orange, Plume

(Answers to E3 (a) and (b) on page 262)

EQUIVOQUES

An equivoque is an ambiguous term or phrase; an equivocation or a pun or other play upon words.

The form of word play called equivoques originated in France (*c.*1500). It involves verses whose lines can be reordered so that they can be read in two or more different ways. Take, for example, this extract from a famous equivoque by C. C. Bombaugh.

> I love my country – but the king
> Above all men his praise I sing.
> Destruction to his odious reign,
> That plague of Princes, Thomas Paine.

That quite clearly shows allegiance to the king. But, suppose the lines are changed around:

> I love my country – but the king
> Destruction to his odious reign.
> Above all men his praise I sing,
> That plague of Princes, Thomas Paine.

It is then quite a different matter; allegiance has clearly switched to Thomas Paine.

EVERYBODY'S DOING IT

This is a word game where the object is to invent an amusing one liner on the theme 'Everybody's doing it'. It is left to the imagination to guess what 'it' is exactly.

> Palindromists do it backwards.
> Hang gliders do it floating on air.
> Australians do it upside down.
> The Swiss do it with a yodel.
> Trampolinists do it bouncing up and down.
> Crossword puzzlers do it horizontally and vertically.
> Swimmers do it with a breast stroke.

Much of this sort of thing finds itself made into car rear window stickers, of which the following are a few other different types that we have noted.

> Follow me. I know where I am going.
> Promote wildlife. Throw a party!
> Happiness is yelling Bingo.
> I owe, I owe, it's off to work I go.
> See me for a date. I sell calendars.
> A fool and his money are soon partying.
> Reach out and touch someone's.
> To all you virgins, thanks for nothing.
> Stop tailgating or I'll flush.
>   (on a 27-foot motor home in America)
> Bram Stoker for coroner.
>   (on a large black car with darkly tinted windows)

YOUNG DOCTORS DO IT IN UNDER THREE MINUTES.

FEGHOOTS

Feghoots are a form of punning game and have been described as a long shaggy dog story with a ridiculous punch line. They are an American version of Spoonerisms, the word 'feghoots' being derived from an anagram of 'the goofs'. The original feghoots were one-pagers in *The Magazine of Fantasy and Science Fiction* by Grendel Briarton, and concerned the adventures of his creation, Ferdinand Feghoot.

You will soon get the drift from these examples.

> Have you heard about the swami who went to the butcher's shop to buy some liver? The butcher, seeking to cheat the swami, beckoned his assistant and said 'Weigh down upon the swami's liver'.

> The King caught the Count stealing from the treasury. The Count wouldn't tell where he had hidden the treasure. The King ordered him to be beheaded. The Count at the last moment started to tell, but the Executioner couldn't stop his axe. That will teach the King 'not to hatchet his Counts before they chicken'.

> Eskimos hunt their prey in thin-skinned boats called kayaks. Since the water is very cold, they frequently freeze their nether regions. However, they resist any form of relief because, as they say, 'You can't have your kayak and heat it too'.

> A snail bought a racing car and had a big 'S' painted on the side of it. As it sped down the street, people remarked, 'Look at that S-car-go'.

> An awkward and poorly-coordinated bumble bee became ill while gathering pollen but continued his work and infected all the flowers with his virus. The disease, of course, was called 'the blight of the fumble bee'.

I heard of a drama critic for a major newspaper who insisted that he always praised the first show of a new season. He explained that he was reluctant to 'stone the first cast'.

There was a rich American Indian whose sons joined the exclusive yacht club and said, 'At last I see red sons in the sail set.'

Two fishermen on the Riviera were digging for worms. One held up a nightcrawler. The other said, 'Well, I guess that's another worm of Cannes.'

Perhaps we had better end on that one!

=========== F2 ===========

FIGURES OF SPEECH AND RHETORICAL DEVICES

Rhetoric, in its broadest sense, is the theory and practice of eloquence, whether spoken or written. In this book we have given several figures of speech and rhetorical devices (such as MALAPROPISMS, OXY-MORONS and TAUTOLOGY) sections in their own right. But there are many more which seem to cause people endless confusion. Below is a list of some of these which, from time to time, you may encounter. Many lead to ingenious forms of word play in theire own right.

Note that we have included EPIGRAMS, EPONYMS, HAPLO-GRAPHY and TOPONYMS in this list for the reader's interest, although they are not strictly figures of speech or rhetorical devices.

Alliteration   Use of words starting with or containing the same letter or sound:
Awaiting the sensation of short sharp shock,
From a cheap and chippy chopper on a big black block.
W. S. Gilbert (The Mikado)

Anacoluthon   A grammatically inconsistent sentence with a shift in constrution mid-way: *My advice is, since time is running out, shouldn't you get started at once.*

Anadiplosis   Repetition of words at the end of one phrase and at the beginning of another, for rhetorical effect: *He waited for tomorrow – the tomorrow that would never come.*

Anastrophe   Inversion of the natural order of the words in a sentence or clause: *Full many a glorious morning have I seen.*

Anticlimax A sequence of ideas abruptly diminishing in dignity or importance at the end of a sentence or passage, generally for satirical effect: *Among the great achievements of Benito Mussolini's regime were the revival of a strong national consciousness, the expansion of the Italian Empire and the running of trains on time.*

Antiphrasis Ironic use of words in an opposite sense to the accepted sense: *Seventy years young.*

Antithesis: Sharp opposition; carefully balanced contrast between words: *More haste, less speed.*

Antonomasia The substitution of an epithet for a proper name, as: *The Corsican* for *Napoleon;* or the use of a proper name to describe one of a class, as: *a Cicero,* for *an orator.*

Aposiopesis or Ellipsis A stopping short for rhetorical effect: *The window was flung open, and . . .*

Apostrophe A direct address to an absent or dead person or thing: *O Freedom! Hear my call!*

Assonance A repetition of vowel sounds, a word or syllable answering to another in sound, producing a half-rhymed effect: *Slow progress across the cold plateau.*

Asyndeton A rhetorical figure by which a conjunction is omitted, as: *I came, I saw, I conquered.*

Climax An arrangement of words, clauses or sentences in the order of their importance, the least forcible first and rising in power to the last: *It is an outrage to bind a Roman citizen; it is a crime to scourge him; it is almost parricide to kill him; but to crucify him – What shall I say of this?*

Conceit An elaborate, often extravagant metaphor which makes an analogy between totally dissimilar things. Its use is characteristic of 17th century English metaphysical poetry. An example appears in John Donne's poem *A Valediction Forbidding Mourning* in which the *human soul* is compared to *a compass.*

Epigram Originally, an inscription; hence, any short, pithy poem. Coleridge's definition is also an example: *What is an epigram? A dwarfish whole, its body brevity, and wit its soul.*

Eponym A name given to a people, place or institution, after some person. As with *Platonic* (after the Greek philosopher Plato).

Euphemisms The use of a soft or pleasing term or phrase for one that is harsh or offensive: *Passed away* for *died.* The Greek Furies were called *The Kindly Ones* in an attempt to divert attention away from their fierceness.

Exclamation   Sudden outcry or interjection expressing violent emotion, for example, grief, fear or hatred: *O villain, villain, smiling damned villain,* from Shakespeare's *Hamlet.*

Haplography   Inadvertent writing of a word, syllable or letter once which should be written twice, as: *superogatory* for *supererogatory.*

Hendiadys   Use of two nouns joined by, and to express an idea that would normally be expressed by, an adjective and noun; or a similarly expanded phrase: *Through storm and weather* instead of *Through stormy weather.*

Hyperbole   Exaggeration for emphasis, as: *I could drink a well dry.*

Irony   An expression intended to convey the opposite to the literal meaning. An instance of irony is the suggestion put forward with apparent seriousness by satirist Jonathan Swift in his *Modest Proposal*, to the effect that the poor people of Ireland should rid themselves of poverty by selling their children to the rich to eat.

Litotes (or Meiosis)   An understatement by which an affirmative is expressed by negation of its contrary, or a weaker expression is used to suggest a stronger one: *He's not exactly sober,* or *Something has happened to him* (meaning he is dead).

Metaphor   A figure of speech by which a word is transferred from one object to another and related by analogy: *She sailed across the room.*

Metonymy   use of a term to refer to some wider idea that it characterises: *The Crown* for *The Monarchy,* or *The Bench* for *Magistrates.*

Onomatopoeia   The imitation of a natural sound in language: *screech, babble, tick-tock, sizzle, splash, ping-pong.* Also heard in poetry, where, as Pope said, 'The sound must give an echo to the sense': *The slithering and grumble as the mason mixed his mortar.* (Seamus Heaney).

Paradox   Statement or sentiment that appears contradictory in the usual sense but is in fact true: *Mobilization for peace; Well-known secret agent.*

Pathetic Fallacy   The assigning of human feelings to inanimate objects, as: *The trees groaned.*

Personification (or Prosopopoeia)   A rhetorical figure by which abstract things are represented as persons, or absent persons as speaking: *The jovial Moon smiling down at us.*

Pleonasm   Very similar to Tautology (see page 228). Otherwise known as a 'redundancy', it is the use of more words than is necessary to denote mere sense: *The man he said.*

Polysyndeton   Repetition of conjunctions for rhetorical effect: *I went to the butchers and the grocers and the doctors and the chemists.*

Rhetorical Question (or Erotema)   A question asked to convey information: *Isn't it snowing heavily today?*

Simile   A comparison of two things which have some strong point of resemblance: *Lips like rosebuds*, or *Kisses like wine.*

Syllepsis   Use of a single word to apply to two others, in different ways: *He held his tongue and my hand.* The difference between a Syllepsis and a Zeugma is that a syllepsis is grammatically correct but a zeugma is not. Other humorous examples of syllepsis include: *On his fishing trip, he caught three trout and a cold; Wearing a see-through negligee she turned on the light and her boyfriend; The flirtatious pickpocket pinched her purse and her bottom; The dinner guest stained the linen and his reputation.*

Synecdoche   Use of the name for a part to refer to the whole, or vice versa, as: *fifty sail* to refer to *fifty ships.*

Tmesis   Separation of word parts by insertion of another word: *Abso-blooming-lutely.*

Toponym   A place named after a person or based on the name of a person: *St Peter's Port.*

Transferred Epithet (or Hypallage)   Deliberate misuse of an adjective to a noun for a compact or dramatic effect: *He spent a sleepless night*, or *The prisoner in the condemned cell.*

Zeugma   Also known as a FAULTY SYLLEPSIS, the use of a word to modify or govern two or more words, usually in such a manner that it applies to each in a different sense or makes sense with only one: *She opened the door and her heart to the homeless boy.*

Also worthy of mention in this section are GOLDWYNISMS. Sam Goldwyn, whose original name was, almost unbelievably, Samuel Goldfish, founded the film company Goldwyn Pictures Corporation in 1917 and, in 1925, Metro-Goldwyn-Mayer Company. He was a giant of the film industry but has also left wordsmiths a legacy of verbal howlers, a few examples of which are:

We shall have to get some new clichés.

In two words im – possible.

A verbal contract ain't worth the paper it's written on.

FORGOTTEN WORDS

These are words which are never used, although they are real words in their own right. The reason is because they have a negative form which is a popular and well used word.

Here are some examples. The game is to find more, and there are many of them.

Rarely used positive form	(Meaning)	Negative form
ADVERTENT	(Heedful)	INADVERTENT
ALGESIA	(Sensitiveness to pain)	ANALGESIA
BIOTIC	(Relating to life)	ANTIBIOTIC
CANNY	(Free from weird qualities)	UNCANNY
CONSCIONABLE	(Conscientious)	UNCONSCIONABLE
CONSOLATE	(Comforted)	DISCONSOLATE
CORRIGIBLE	(Correctable)	INCORRIGIBLE
COUTH	(Marked by finesse)	UNCOUTH
DELIBLE	(Capable of being deleted)	INDELIBLE
DESCRIPT	(Described)	NONDESCRIPT
DOMITABLE	(Tamable)	INDOMITABLE
EFFABLE	(Capable of being expressed)	INEFFABLE
EVITABLE	(Avoidable)	INEVITABLE
FECKFUL	(Powerful)	FECKLESS
GRUNTLE	(Put in good humour)	DISGRUNTLE
GUST	(Liking)	DISGUST
INFECTANT	(Agent of infection)	DISINFECTANT
KEMPT	(Trim)	UNKEMPT
LICIT	(Allowable)	ILLICIT
MACULATE	(Besmirched)	IMMACULATE
NOCUOUS	(Harmful)	INNOCUOUS
ODORANT	(An odorous substance)	DEODORANT
PECCABLE	(Prone to sin)	IMPECCABLE
PERVIOUS	(Substance that can be penetrated)	IMPERVIOUS
PLACABLE	(Tolerant)	IMPLACABLE
SIPID	(Savoury)	INSIPID
SPEAKABLE	(Capable of being spoken)	UNSPEAKABLE
WIELDY	(Strong)	UNWIELDY

FRACTURED ENGLISH

Most seasoned travellers will have encountered the type of tortured English listed below. We wonder, sometimes, if these are genuine howlers or deliberate errors for amusement purposes. If the latter, then they are certainly, in our view, very successful in achieving their intent.

Hotel notice, Cairo:	On September 30, winter timing will start. As of 12.00 midnight all clocks will be forward one hour back.
Barber's shop, Bombay:	Hair cutter and clean shaver. Gentlemen's throats cut with very sharp razors with great care and skill. No irritating feeling afterwards.
Hotel brochure, Italy:	Suggestive views from every window.
Hotel lift, Leipzig:	Do not enter lift backwards, and only when lit up.
Tailor's shop, Athens:	Order your summer suit. Because is big rush we will execute customers in strict rotation.
Hotel notice, Vienna:	In case of fire, do your utmost to alarm the head porter.
Hotel notice, Zurich:	Because of the impropriety of entertaining guests of the opposite sex in bedroom, it is suggested you use the lobby for this purpose.
Car rental firm brochure, Tokyo:	When passenger of foot in sight, tootle horn. Trumpet him melodiously first, but if he still obstacles, tootle him with vigour.
Hotel brochure, Italy:	This hotel is renowned for its peace and solitude. In fact, crowds from all over the world flock here to enjoy its solitude.
Hotel brochure, Switzerland:	We have nice bath and are very good in bed.
Notice on TV set in Belgrade hotel:	If set breaks, inform manager. Do not interfere with yourself.
Bar notice, Finnish ferry:	WERY STRONK BIER

Time zone warning Italian cruise ship:	The hour will be 60 minutes late today.
Hotel notice, Lisbon:	If you wish disinfection enacted on your presence please ring for chambermaid.
Hong Kong dress shop:	Ladies have fits upstairs.
Airline ticket office, Copenhagen:	We take your bags and send them in all directions.
Norwegian cocktail lounge:	Ladies are requested not to have children in the bar.
Ginza bar, Tokyo:	Special cocktails for ladies with nuts.
Roadworks sign, Tokyo:	Stop! Drive sideways.
Dry cleaners, Bangkok:	Drop your trousers here for best results.

═══ F5 ═══

FRENCH CROSSWORDS

Two people play against each other on two 5 × 5 grids. Each player has a blank grid at the outset and they call out a letter in turn. Both players enter the letters called, anywhere on their own grid.

The object of the game is to make 5, 4, 3 or 2 letter words in horizontal, vertical and the two corner-to-corner diagonal lines. One point is scored per letter for each word formed, but only one word can be scored on each line. The diagrams shown an example game.

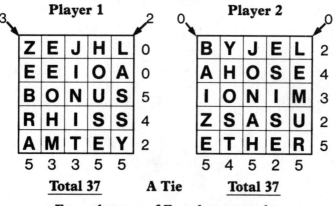

Example game of French crosswords

All scoring words must go from left to right or from top to bottom, only. In the diagonal lines, only words in the main corner-to-corner diagonals score, and they must travel from top to bottom.

GALLOPERS

This puzzle, which combines anagrams and synonym type clues, was invented by one of the authors in 1984 after he visited a Bradford hotel named 'The Gallopers' for a bar meal one lunchtime. The interior was designed like a roundabout and he learned that 'The Gallopers' was the old fairground name for the roundabout ride on horses, now better known as 'The Carousel'. An example of the puzzle for you to try is given in (a).

(a)   **GALLOPERS**

The object is to complete the words in each column, all of which end in the given letter 'G'. The scrambled letters in the section to the right of each column are an anagram of a word which will give you a clue to the word you are trying to find, to put in the column.

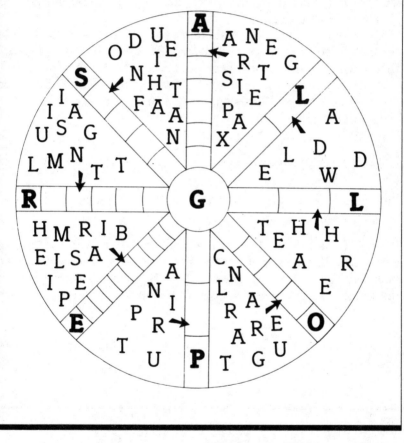

(Answers to G1 (a) on page 262)

125

GHOSTS

This is a word building game for two players. Player 1 thinks of a three-letter word and calls out the first letter of his word only. Player 2 then thinks of a four-letter word using the same initial letter and calls out the second letter only which continues, but does not complete, a word. Player 1 then thinks of a five-letter word beginning with the two letters already declared and calls out the third letter, making sure that he does not complete a three-letter word.

The game continues in this fashion until either someone is forced to complete a word or loses a challenge. At any time a player can be challenged to state what the next word is that he has in mind.

On losing a challenge, or completing a word, a player loses a life. After a player loses three lives, he is out of the game.

As an example, a game may progress like this.

Player 1	3-letter word	S O B	calls out S			
Player 2	4-letter word	S A N K	calls out	A		
Player 1	5-letter word	S A U C E	calls out		U	
Player 2	6-letter word	S A U C E R	calls out			C
Player 1	7-letter word	S A U C I L Y	calls out				I

Player 2 cannot think of an eight-letter word commencing SAUCI and loses a life. If, for example, at the five-letter word stage Player 1 had thought of the word SATIN and called out T, he would have lost a life and that game would have ended, because SAT is a word.

GRUESOMETTES

Gruesomette is the name coined by the authors for a short punning verse with a gruesome ending, for example:

> John and Ruth, side by side
> Went out for an auto ride;
> John hit a bump, the car hit a tree,
> And John drove on, Ruthlessly.

The most famous gruesomettes are Colonel Streamer's *Little Willie* verses:

> Little Willie, having fun,
> Tried to shoot his little sister –
> Said Mother, 'Mustn't cry so, son,
> Even Father might have missed her.'

> Willie, in a fit, insane
> Stuck his head beneath the train.
> And, you'd be surprised to find
> How that broadened Willie's mind.

> Little Willie, full of hell,
> Threw his sister down a well,
> Said his mother, drawing water,
> 'Gosh, it's hard to raise a daughter.'

=======================G4=======================

GUGGENHEIM

This game is played by selecting five categories which are written down the left-hand side of a sheet of paper; then a selected word of six letters is written across the top. Each player has to use each letter of the word written across the top as the initial letter for a word under each category. Here is a typical example:

Selected word: BRIDGE

	B	**R**	**I**	**D**	**G**	**E**
ANIMAL	Baboon	Rabbit	Ibex	Dog	Gerbil	Eland
FISH	Bass	Roach	Ide	Dace	Guppy	Eel
BIRD	Booby	Robin	Ibis	Drake	Gull	Emu
FLOWER	Begonia	Rose	Iris	Dahlia	Godetia	Edelweiss
TREES	Balsa	Rowan	Ilex	Deodar	Gum	Elm

The game can be played just for fun, or with a scoring system which you have devised. The 'official' version says that, either you score a point for a word that no one else has written or, you score a point for each of your opponents who has not written the same word. In this latter case, if ten people are playing and only one person writes 'Booby' for the bird beginning with 'B', this person scores nine points.

Why Guggenheim?

There are two version of how the game came to be called Guggenheim. The first is simply that it was played by the Guggenheim family. However, the second version is much more interesting. It has been said that P. G. Wodehouse, Jerome Kern and Howard Dietz were playing the game, then called Categories. One of the categories was 'Printers', against which Jerome Kern wrote 'Gutenberg'. 'Never heard of him,' said P. G. Wodehouse, and he refused to believe Kerr's explanation that Gutenberg was the German who actually invented printing with movable type. Sometime later, Howard Dietz suggested another game. Wodehouse agreed but said, 'No more of your Guggenheims.' This version is the one that we prefer to believe. It is certainly likely that Kern and Wodehouse would be involved in the same game as they were great friends, sometimes collaborating. For example, the song *Bill* was written by Wodehouse and used by Kern in his musical *Showboat*.

HANGMAN

This is a famous old game for two players which was popular when we were schoolboys. Each player in turn becomes the 'Hangman', and chooses a word, then writes in the blanks.

For example: CONDEMNED   (_ _ _ _ _ _ _ _ _).

The second player then selects a letter, say 'E', and the 'Hangman' writes in all the letter Es: (_ _ _ _ E _ _ E _).

The second player then selects another letter, say 'T' and, because there is no 'T', the 'Hangman' builds part 1 of the scaffold (see diagram).

The game progresses in this vein until the second player has found the word or has been 'hanged'. The sequence of wrong answers produces the scaffold as shown in the diagram.

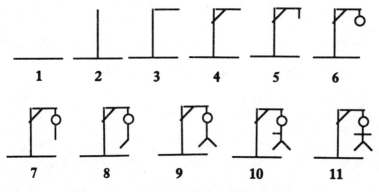

The sequence for building the scaffold

The 'Hangman' wins after the eleventh wrong guess. The game can be broadened to 'famous people', 'places', 'famous quotations', etc.

HELLO AND GOODBYE

The idea of this game is to invent appropriate 'hellos' and 'goodbyes' for various professions. It is another of those addictive games where it is difficult to stop once you have started. Here are some examples.

SALESMAN	–	Good buy
OIL DRILLER	–	Fair well
MOUNTAINEER	–	High there
FUNERAL DIRECTOR	–	Good mourning
BUTCHER	–	Nice to meat you
SKATER	–	Have an ice day
BAKER	–	Bun voyage
ACTOR	–	Be scene you
CARTOONIST	–	Doodle-loo
FISHMONGER	–	Sole long
SAILOR	–	Tar-ar

HERMANS

This is yet another punning game and is very similar to Tom Swifties (see page 228) but uses names only.

The following were submitted by *Word Ways* members after the idea was proposed a few years ago. The first example is the original.

'She's my woman,' said Herman.

which leads us into:

'Is that a window?' asked Isadore.

'That's quite a storm,' remarked Abigail.

'The cat scratched me,' complained Claude.

'Pass the butter,' said Pat.

'I can hear a horse,' said Winnie.

'Over and out,' remarked Roger.

'Step on it!' said Matt.

'On your knees,' said Neil.

'Pass me those binoculars,' said Seymour.

'I just got up,' said Rose.

'The moon is declining,' said Wayne.

'I'm the winner,' said Victor.

'I understand,' said Ken.

'That's given me quite a stimulus,' said Philip.

Hermonettes is a version that depends on the speaker's name to complete the overlapping thought:

'Out there it's a jungle,' Jim said.

'Hickory Dickory,' Doc said.

'How do you like your eggs?' Benedict asked.

'I collect fancy glass,' Crystal said.

Hermoine's complete the collection by taking the idea a stage further and using two names:

'We old farmers always order a big Mac,' Donald said.

'I keep having nightmares Doctor,' Jekyll complained.

'I need to use the John,' Wayne said.

'Listen, I'm a rock star, Ma,' Donna said.

'Cleopatra, I'm going to see my Aunt,' Tony said.

HETERONYMS

Heteronyms are two words or phrases with the same spelling but different pronunciations and meanings. For instance, the words gill and gill are heteronyms as gill (pronounced gil) is a breathing-organ and gill (pronounced jil) is a measure. Heteronyms lead to various puzzles and word play.

In (a) can you find the pairs of heteronyms for each of the clues? As an example to guide you, Remarkable / Incapable (7/3,4) leads to the heteronyms Notable / Not Able.

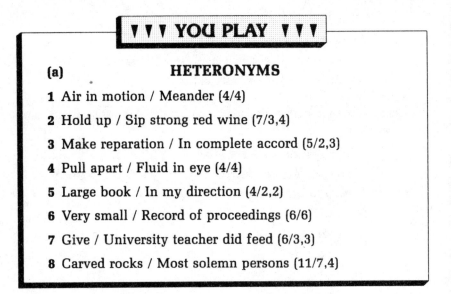

▼ ▼ ▼ YOU PLAY ▼ ▼ ▼

(a) **HETERONYMS**

1 Air in motion / Meander (4/4)

2 Hold up / Sip strong red wine (7/3,4)

3 Make reparation / In complete accord (5/2,3)

4 Pull apart / Fluid in eye (4/4)

5 Large book / In my direction (4/2,2)

6 Very small / Record of proceedings (6/6)

7 Give / University teacher did feed (6/3,3)

8 Carved rocks / Most solemn persons (11/7,4)

(Answers to H4 (a) on page 262)

HIDDEN WORDS

The hiding of words within other words in a sentence – for example, 'the man I accuse', hiding the word 'maniac' – is a well-known type of cryptic crossword puzzle clue.

The technique of hiding words and names has, however, led to other types of puzzles and games of which these are just a few examples.

Cuckoo in the nest

Invented by the authors in 1986 and first featured in their 1987 book *Take the IQ Challenge 2*, the idea is to hide within a sentence, in the correct order, the letters of a word that is opposite to the meaning of the sentence. For example C<u>L</u>OS<u>E</u> T<u>O</u> BOI<u>L</u>ING = COOL. Now try (a).

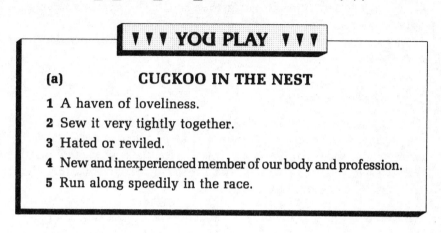

▼▼▼ YOU PLAY ▼▼▼

(a)   **CUCKOO IN THE NEST**

1 A haven of loveliness.
2 Sew it very tightly together.
3 Hated or reviled.
4 New and inexperienced member of our body and profession.
5 Run along speedily in the race.

Theme passages

The passage in (b) was compiled by J. Hyde for *Enigmasig* in April 1985.

▼▼▼ YOU PLAY ▼▼▼

(b)   **THEME PASSAGES**

Carefully hidden are 17 male Christian names. How many can you find?

... Wrestling is a 'con' and I knew it. My manager, an Asian, once called me into his large office and asked me to throw a bout. 'Not on your life,' I said. 'I don't know where your scruples lie, but I don't take such risks.'

I had a marvellous time though, I was never a heart throb. Indeed my face would out-do ugliness. I just bowled people over in the ring! I fought all and sundry and one day, top of the bill, met this man from Arkansas. This former ex-con looked mundane, was a rather pale colour and wrestled uncannily like a gorilla ...

Proverbs

In this game a proverb is selected and players compete to see who can find the most words of two or more letters hidden within it. The words must be verified in a previously agreed dictionary. As an example, 'A ROLLING STONE GATHERS NO MOSS' produces the words: roll, lin, ling, lings, in, ing, to, ton, tone, on, one, gat, gather, ers, the, he, her, hers, nom and oss, according to *The Shorter Oxford English Dictionary*.

Players score a point for each word, but two points are deducted for any non-words.

Kangaroo words

These are words that contain synonyms. If you remove some letters from the original word, you are left with a synonym of that word. Take, for example, the word CALUMNIES. If you delete the first, second, fourth, fifth and sixth letters, you are left with a synonym of the word, LIES. Here are a few more examples.

Catacomb	–	Tomb	Facetiousness	–	Fun
Chariot	–	Cart	Fatigue	–	Fag
Chocolate	–	Cocoa	Hurries	–	Hies
Deliberate	–	Debate	Illuminated	–	Lit
Destruction	–	Ruin	Instructor	–	Tutor
Encourage	–	Urge	Latest	–	Last
Evacuate	–	Vacate	Masculine	–	Male
Exhilaration	–	Elation	Pasteurized	–	Pure

You may now like to try the kangaroo words in (c) for yourself.

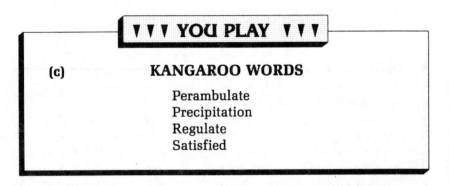

▼▼▼ YOU PLAY ▼▼▼

(c)   **KANGAROO WORDS**

Perambulate
Precipitation
Regulate
Satisfied

Can you find any more kangaroo words? There are many others, we can assure you. Now, try (d).

(d)   **BROKEN WORDS**

Can you find an easily broken word of nine letters? Remove the fourth and seventh letters and you are left with another easily broken word. Again remove the fourth and seventh letters and a further easily broken word will appear. What are the three words?

(Answers to H5 (a) to (d) on page 262)

H6

HOMONYMS

Homonyms (sometimes known as homophones) are words having the same sound as other words, but differing in meaning. Here are some examples of the many homonyms in the English language.

Aloud – allowed, alter – altar, beach – beech, beat – beet, bough – bow, build – billed, cell – sell, chaste – chased, climb – clime, coax – cokes, cord – chord

The following verse was included in *Foulsham's Fun Book of 1933:*

The Rite of Writing Right
by A. Playwright

Write we know is written right,
When we see it written write;
But when we see it written wright,
We know 'tis not then written right;
For write to have it written right,
Must not be written right nor wright,
Nor yet should it be written rite,
But write – for so 'tis written right.

In the 1960s, the American singer Perry Como recorded a number called *Delaware*. This became known as *The Homonym Song* as, in it, he sings his way through homonyms for most American States. For example: 'Della wear' for Delaware; 'Ah'l ask her' for Alaska; 'Taxes' for Texas; 'New brass key' for Nebraska; 'Misery' for Missouri; 'Mini-soda' for Minnesota; and so on.

Homonyms lead to several types of word play and puzzles, of which this, now, is a selection.

Pundromes

Introduced by David Morice in *Word Ways*, these are sentences in which the first half consists of homonyms of the second half.

> Find bee or be fined.
>
> Shoo gnats off Nat's shoe.
>
> No eye sees the seas I know.

Panvocalic homonyms

These are pairs of homonyms in which all five vowels occur within the pairs. For example, GORILLA – GUERILLA or ADIEU – ADO.

Alien homonyms

This is a rarity in which no letters that appear in one of the homonyms appears in the other. The two known pairs in the English language are YOU – EWE and I – EYE (or AYE – I).

Puzzles

This homonym puzzle was compiled by the authors in 1987. The answers to the clues are all homonyms of cities or countries. Example: Bashful girl in Wyoming – Cheyenne (Shy Anne). Now try the clues in (a).

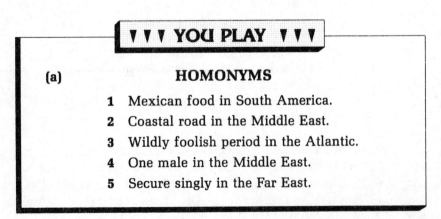

▼ ▼ ▼ YOU PLAY ▼ ▼ ▼

(a)   **HOMONYMS**

1 Mexican food in South America.
2 Coastal road in the Middle East.
3 Wildly foolish period in the Atlantic.
4 One male in the Middle East.
5 Secure singly in the Far East.

(Answers to H6 (a) on page 263)

HUMOROUS EPITAPHS

A tombstone would not be a place where you would expect to find examples of humorous and punning word play, yet there are a good many in existence which supply these qualities. Here are a few such examples taken from *Foulsham's Fun Book of 1933*.

An Edinburgh husband put this over his wife's grave:

> Here snug in grave my wife doth lie;
> Now she's at rest, and so am I.

This one is often quoted:

> Solomon Levy lies here in the ground,
> Don't jingle money while walking around.

A little homely tragedy is indicated in this one:

> Here lies the body of Margaret Crowther,
> Who died through drinking a Seidlitz powder.
> Oh! may her soul in Heaven be blessed;
> But she should have waited till it effervesced.

This is somewhat spiteful:

> Beneath this silent stone is laid
> A noisy, antiquated maid.
> Who from the cradle talk'd till death,
> And ne'er before was out of breath.

A sexton at Chester has this on his stone:

> Hurra! my brave boys,
> Let's rejoice at his fall!
> For if he had lived,
> He had buried us all.

And this one is on the stone of both his former wives in adjoining graves:

> Here lies the body of Sarah Sexton,
> She was a wife that never vexed one,
> I wish I could say the same for the one at the next stone.

INTELLIGENCE TESTING

It is said that to have a mastery of words is to have in one's possession the ability to produce order out of chaos and that command of vocabulary is a true measure of intelligence. As such, vocabulary tests are widely used in intelligence testing. The following are some typical examples of the type of vocabulary questions used in IQ tests.

CLASSIFICATION:

These are 'odd one out' questions where a list of words is given and you have to choose the odd one out.

Example: globe, orb, sphere, sceptre, ball

Answer: Sceptre is the odd one out since the others are all circular objects.

SYNONYMS:

A synonym is a word having the same meaning as another of the same language.

Example 1: Which word in the brackets means the same as the word in capital letters:

AVERAGE (poor, mean, public, weak, value)

Answer: mean.

Example 2: Which two words are the closest in meaning:

Walk, run, drive, stroll, fly, sit

Answer: walk and stroll.

ANTONYMS:

An antonym is a word having the opposite meaning to another of the same language.

Example 1: Which word in the brackets means the opposite of the word in capital letters?

CARELESS (exact, heedful, strict, anxious, dutiful)

Answer: heedful.

Example 2: Which two words are opposite in meaning?

    curved, long, big, small, broad, fat

Answer: big, small.

ANALOGY:

An analogy is similitude of relations, where it is necessary to reason the answer from a parallel case.

Example: OASIS is to sand as

           ISLAND is to (sea, river, water, waves, pond)?

The answer is 'water', because an oasis is surrounded by sand and an island is surrounded by water.

DOUBLE MEANINGS:

These are designed to test your ability to quickly find alternative meanings of words. You are looking for a word having the same meanings as the two definitions provided.

Example: Give account of _ _ _ _ _ _ noise from a gun.

Answer: Report.

DOUBLE-WORDS:

In this test you are given the first part of a word or phrase, and you have to find the second part. The same second part then becomes the first part of a second word or phrase.

Example: mean _ _ _ _ piece

Answer: Time; to make meantime and timepiece.

ANAGRAMS:

Example 1: Which of the these is not a vegetable?

                HRCYCOI
                CNSIAHP
                LCCEARO
                SPRIAPN

Answer: LCCEARO is an anagram of CORACLE. This is a boat. The vegetables are CHICORY, SPINACH, PARSNIP.

Example 2: Solve the anagram (one word): BARE MILES

Answer: MISERABLE.

CIRCLE WORDS:

Read clockwise to find a word. You have to provide the missing letters:

Example:

Answer: ADVOCATE

CODE WORDS:

Example: Which word goes in the brackets?

PILOT (LATE) PLACE
LIMIT (_ _ _ _) SPINE

Answer: MITE. The word in the brackets is formed in this way: the first letter is the third letter of the left-hand word. The second letter is the third letter of the right-hand word. The third letter is the fifth letter of the left-hand word; the fourth letter is the fifth letter of the right-hand word.

PRECEDING LETTERS:

Example: Find a four-letter word which forms a different word with each preceding letter or letters.

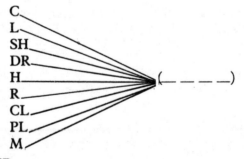

Answer: OVER.

IQ tests

The letters 'IQ' stand for 'Intelligence Quotient'. The definition of intelligence is the ability to 'comprehend quickly'; and quotient is the number of times that one number will divide into another. When measuring the IQ of a child, the child would attempt an intelligence test which had been given to thousands of children and the results correlated so that the average score had been assessed for each age group. Thus, a child who, at eight years of age, obtained a result expected of a ten-year-old, would score an IQ of 125 by the following simple calculation:

$$\frac{\text{Mental age}}{\text{Chronological Age}} \times 100 = IQ$$

Therefore: $\dfrac{10}{8} \times 100 = 125 \ IQ$

A child of eight years of age who successfully passed a test for a child of eight but failed a test for a child of nine years, would have an IQ of 8/8 × 100 = 100 IQ, which is the norm.

With adults this method of calculation would not apply. They would be judged on an 'IQ' test where the average score would be 100 and the results would be graded above and below this norm according to known test scores.

Readers interested in learning more about IQ testing may care to refer to the authors' book of IQ tests *Check Your IQ*, published by W. Foulsham.

KICKSELF

Kickself puzzles are those that usually have an 'obvious when you know it' answer. A good kickself is a puzzle that, if you cannot solve it, makes you want to kick yourself immediately you see the solution, because you cannot understand why you did not think of it. It is not a good kickself if you think 'Well, I would never have thought of that,' because the puzzle is either too obscure, complicated or involves specialist knowledge.

Kickself puzzles are said to have originated in 1980 at a lunch in Cambridge atttended by the Mensa President, Victor Serebriakoff, British Mensa Chairman, Sir Clive Sinclair, and Arthur C. Clarke, the renowned author of science fiction. Arthur C. Clarke asked, 'What was the first human artefact to break the sound barrier?' There was a brief pause before Clive Sinclair gave the answer 'The whip' – correct, of course, as the tip makes a small sonic boom (the crack) as it passes through Mach 1.

However, perhaps the first kickself puzzle was the one in Greek legend which was propounded by the Sphinx: 'What walks on four legs in the morning, two legs in the afternoon and three legs in the evening?' Scores of would-be solvers had been put to death by the Sphinx for their failure to solve the riddle. Then, Oedipus came to Thebes and won his throne by correctly answering the riddle. The answer is, of course, man, who crawls on all fours in early life, walks on two legs in mid-life, and walks with the aid of a stick in later life.

The authors have compiled many kickself word play puzzles. You may like to try a typical selection, in examples (a) to (d).

▼▼▼ YOU PLAY ▼▼▼

(a)   **KICKSELF**

All of these are place names in England. Which is the odd one out?

Witton-le-Wear
Alderley Edge
Warminster
Sherfield-on-Loddon
Winchester

▼▼▼ YOU PLAY ▼▼▼

(b)   **KICKSELF**

Arrange the fifteen letters of the phrase below into one familiar word.

LOWER   FAIR   DOMAIN

▼▼▼ YOU PLAY ▼▼▼

(c)   **KICKSELF**

In, or on, how many of the following might you find a date or dates?

A tree
A diary
A calender
A box
An appointment book
A newspaper
A digital watch

(d)   **KICKSELF**

Find the missing square. Choose from the squares 1 to 8.

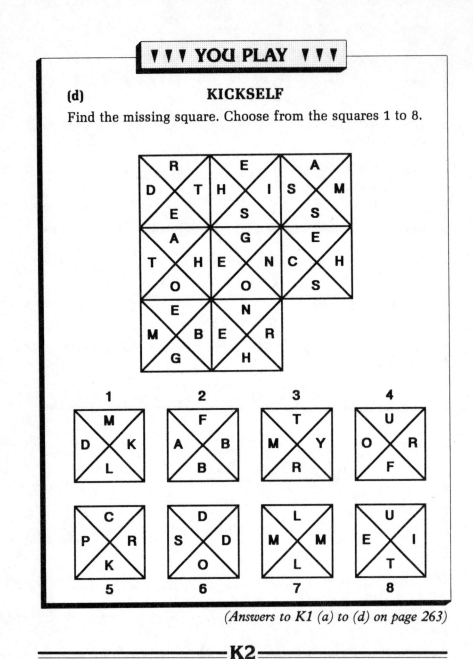

(Answers to K1 (a) to (d) on page 263)

═══════ **K2** ═══════

KNIGHT'S MOVE

This is a word game based on the knight's move in chess. it is a modern game but the originator is unknown. The authors have compiled several such puzzles for use in their puzzle books. They are fairly easy to compile but usually quite difficult to solve. You may like to try (a).

(a)   **KNIGHT'S MOVE**

Start at the letter 'T' in the bottom right-hand corner and by Knight's* moves spell out a quotation by Blaise Pascal.

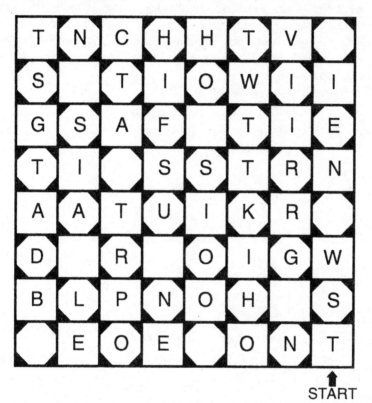

START

*In chess, the knight is the only piece allowed to jump over other pieces. It can move one square horizontally and two vertically or two horizontally and one vertically (as in the diagram). Usually represented by a horse's head, it is occasionally referred to as the horse (as in the Arabic version).

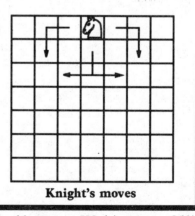

Knight's moves

(Answer to K2 (a) on page 263)

KNOCK-KNOCK

Knock-knock jokes are actually a very old children's punning game. They have been the subject of newspaper 'who-can-think-up-a-better-one' competitions. They were used in the 1940s and 1950s by the famous crossword compiler Torquemada as devious crossword puzzle clues. For example, 'Blank who? Blank you like a punch on the nose,' leads to the answer 'Howard'; and 'Blank who? Blank any more biscuits?' leads to the answer 'Arthur'.

Here are a few more examples:

Knock, knock. Who's there?
Ewan.
Ewan who?
No, just me.

Knock, knock. Who's there?
Mary.
Mary who?
Mary Christmas and a Happy New Year.

Knock, knock. Who's there?
Fred.
Fred who?
Fred I'm late.

Knock, knock. Who's there?
N.E.
N.E. who?
N.E. body you like, so long as you let me in.

LABYRINTHS

This is a type of anagram game where the object is to hide a word which has to be uncovered by tracking the way through a labyrinth. The authors use two versions in their puzzle books.

Pyramid

This version was not invented by the authors; it is several years old, but alas the inventor is unknown. It is possible to hide any 15-letter word or, if you require an easier version, a ten-letter word in a four-letter base pyramid. Example (a) gives the 15-letter word version.

▼ ▼ ▼ **YOU PLAY** ▼ ▼ ▼

(a)   **PYRAMID**

Spell out the 15-letter word by going into the pyramid, one room at a time. Go into each room once only. You may go into the passage as many times as you wish.

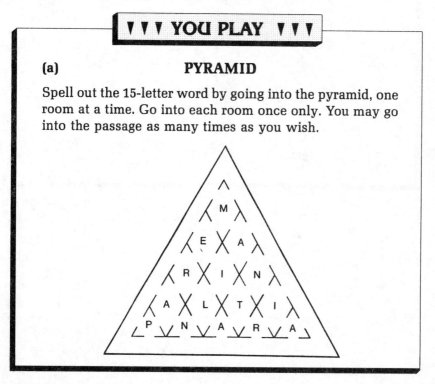

Network

This version was invented by the authors quite by accident a couple of years ago and involves the finding of a 14-letter word. The idea came when one of us was attempting to solve a puzzle which involved the planting of fourteen trees in rows of four.

You may like to try the example in (b). The word can be found by discovering the starting letter and travelling along the connecting lines in a continuous path to adjacent circles. You may visit each circle only once.

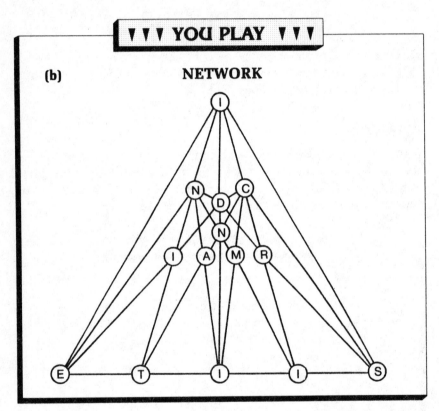

(Answers to L1 (a) and (b) on page 263)

LAPSUS LINGUAE

The idea of lapsus linguae is the overlapping of English with foreign languages to find amusing and outlandish definitions for foreign phrases. Here are a few examples.

Ad infinitum	–	This television commercial is too long.
Sub rosa	–	The Nautilus has surfaced.
Et cetera	–	He has chewed up the scenery.
Götterdämmerung	–	She's on the 'phone again.
Ad hoc	–	I've pawned the advertising agency.
Crêpe de Chine	–	Chinese propaganda.
Coup de grace	–	Cut the grass.
Faux pas	–	For father.
Mens rea	–	?

We leave the last one to your imagination.

LICENCE PLATES

In recent years, personalised car number plates have become quite in vogue. Many are collectors' items and fetch large sums; magazines such as *Exchange and Mart* carry long lists of them. Here is a selection of some interesting ones that we are aware really do exist – in Britain or overseas.

In the home town of one of the authors, a dentist has JAW5.

On a white VW Rabbit: IM LATE; also on a VW Rabbit: MOP5Y.

Jimmy Tarbuck, the Liverpool comedian, has COM1C.

Animals are very popular: DOG 1 on a Rover; EQUUS on a Mustang.

On a husband and wife team from Arizona: O2BNAZ and G2BNAZ.

FLAUNT on a new Mercedes.

XQQQME on a car owned by a polite old English gentleman.

6ULDV8 indicating, perhaps, unusual desires.

NEIN 24 on a Porsche 924.

THE CR8 on an old banger.

VEGAS 1 on a car owned by an unsuccessful gambler.

2FST4U on a sports car.

MRS PHD: this was on a doctoral gift to his wife.

Most of these are, in fact, ingenious forms of word play and very similar to rebuses, which are covered in greater detail on page 202.

There are other games involving car number plates which are ideal for relieving boredom whilst in traffic jams or on long tedious journeys.

One game is to make words out of the letters on the number plates. For instance, if you saw the car of one of the authors – B248 UVH, the challenge would be to find a word using the letters UVH in the correct order (or for advanced players, the letters BUVH in the correct order – which would not be easy).

The following are a few suggestions for unusual letter combinations:

WKW – awkward; ABC – abacus; FCN – confection

As can be seen, the letters must be in the correct order, but not necessarily adjacent.

L4

LIMERICKS

The limerick, it would appear,
Is a verse form we owe to Edward Lear.
Two long and two short
Lines rhymed, as was taught,
And a fifth to bring up the rear.

The limerick is a short form of comic and usually bawdy verse, having five lines of three or two feet, and usually rhyming AABBA, as in:

There was a young lady of Lynn,
Who was so uncommonly thin,
That when she essayed
To drink lemonade,
She slipped through the straw and fell in.

The form, the origin of which is uncertain, was popularised by the British artist and author, Edward Lear, who published his first book of nonsense verse, *The Book of Nonsense,* in 1846. This was written for the Earl of Derby's grandchildren. This example is taken from Lear's book.

> There was an Old Man with a nose,
> Who said, 'If you choose to suppose,
> That my nose is too long,
> You are certainly wrong!'
> That remarkable man with a nose.

Limericks are great fun to compose. Here are two further examples:

> There was an old fellow from Cosham,
> Who took out his false teeth to wash 'em,
> But his wife said 'Now Jack,
> If you don't put them back,
> I'll tread on your teeth and I'll squash 'em!'

> There was a young girl from Devizes,
> Whose eyes were two different sizes,
> The one that was small,
> Was of no use at all,
> But the other won several prizes!

L5

LIPOGRAMS

A lipogram is a text composed with the intentional omission of a particular letter of the alphabet throughout; that is, no words containing that particular letter are used in the text.

The word, lipogram, is from the Greek 'lipogrammatos', meaning 'wanting a letter' ('leipein', to leave; 'gramma-atos' letter).

The Greek poet, Tryphiodorus, of the 5th century BC, wrote an epic of 24 books on the voyages of Ulysses which, each in turn, omitted a different letter of the Greek alphabet.

One of the most famous lipograms is the 50 000-word novel by Ernest Vincent Wright, *Gadsby* (1939), which omits the most common letter of the English alphabet, E, throughout. Even later exponents of the art of lipograms are: the French author Georges Perec, who work, *La Disparition* (1969), also omits the letter E; and the American word play expert A. Ross Eckler, who in recent years has written several versions of the nursery rhyme, *Mary Had a Little Lamb*, in which each version omits a different letter of the alphabet.

In this example of a lipogram verse, author unknown, the letter E is omitted throughout:

> Bold Nassan quits his caravan,
> A hazy mountain just to scan;
> Climbs craggy rocks to spy his way,
> Doth tax his sight, but far doth stray.

=============================== L6 ===============================

LITERARY LAPSES

The object of this game is to select a well-known quotation and introduce an error which your opponent has to discover. For example, can you spot the error in the following?

> Laugh and the world laughs with you:
> Cry and you cry alone:
> For the sad old earth must borrow its mirth,
> But has trouble enough of its own.
>
> Ella Wheeler Wilcox (1855-1919)

We won't keep you guessing on that one. The correct line is: 'Weep and you weep alone'.

=============================== L7 ===============================

LOGOGRAMS

Cassell's Concise English Dictionary describes a logogram as, 'A puzzle in verse containing words synonymous with others formed from the transposition of the letters of an original word to be found out'.

Many words can be split up into several other smaller words. For example the word 'ANOTHER' is seven letters long: '1234567'. Within it are the following words: '12' = AN; '23' = NO; '234' = NOT; '34567' = OTHER: '456' = THE; '567' = HER; '56' = HE.

By taking this a stage further and jiggling the letters about, very many more words can be found such as: '2617' = NEAR; '457326' = THRONE; '45372' = THORN, etc.

We have compiled many such puzzles and examples (a) to (c) are typical.

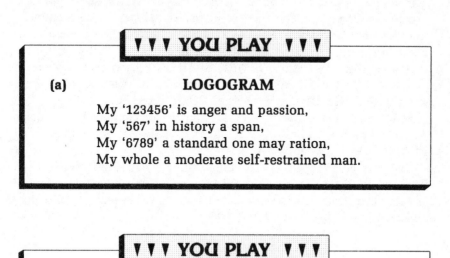

▼▼▼ YOU PLAY ▼▼▼

(a)   **LOGOGRAM**

My '123456' is anger and passion,
My '567' in history a span,
My '6789' a standard one may ration,
My whole a moderate self-restrained man.

▼▼▼ YOU PLAY ▼▼▼

(b)   **LOGOGRAM**

My '123' is amazing dread,
'2345' a point to go,
'56789's tyres have tread,
My all an overwhelming show.

▼▼▼ YOU PLAY ▼▼▼

(c)   **LOGOGRAM**

My one to four comes every way,
My four to six resort to play,
My six to eight will imitate,
My one to three bang up-to-date,
My five to nine is flat in sheets,
My all can be paid for in the streets.

(Answers to L7 (a) to (c) on page 264)

LOGOGRIPHS

The word 'logogriph' is a general term used to cover types of puzzles, usually in verse, such as beheadments, curtailments, syncopations, transpositions and reversals. The terms are fairly self-explanatory. A beheadment involves the removal of the first letter (TRAIN–RAIN); a curtailment, the last letter (SPARE–SPAR); a syncopation, any letter (TRACK–TACK); a transposition, a complete rearrangement or anagram (PARE–REAP); and a reversal (POOL–LOOP).

Sometimes a beheadment and a curtailment are combined. For example: SLATERS, SLATER, SLATE, LATE, ATE, AT, A; or FLASHY, FLASH, LASH, ASH, AS, A.

One very great expert in compiling such puzzles is our friend Mitzi Christiansen Kuehl. Her puzzles are a delight and the following examples are all taken from her 'Sphinx Winks' column (see page 221), which appeared in *Integra* from 1981 to 1986.

Transposition

> I laughed about the castle ghost,
> 'There's no such thing!' I said.
> But late that night a XXXXXXX seemed
> To hover near my bed.
> His XXXXXXX gleamed with ghostly gems,
> His crown with golden glow.
> He stirred in me a deep XXXXXXX –
> I guess my doubts must go.

Answer: SPECTRE – SCEPTRE – RESPECT.

Syncopation

> The little tin XXXXXXX that broke in two
> Was patched up with XXXXXX as good as new.

Answer: SOLDIER – SOLDER.

You may now like to try (a), a transposition.

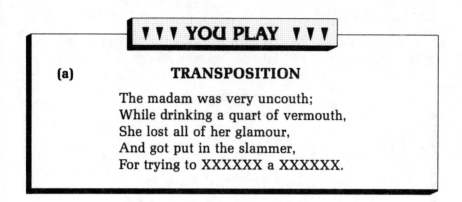

▼▼▼ YOU PLAY ▼▼▼

(a)   **TRANSPOSITION**

The madam was very uncouth;
While drinking a quart of vermouth,
She lost all of her glamour,
And got put in the slammer,
For trying to XXXXXX a XXXXXX.

Charade

In a charade, two or more words in sequence make up a long word; WOO–DEN (wooden), for instance.

This one, (b), is a charade / beheadment.

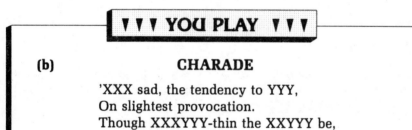

▼▼▼ YOU PLAY ▼▼▼

(b)   **CHARADE**

'XXX sad, the tendency to YYY,
On slightest provocation.
Though XXXYYY-thin the XXYYY be,
Or false the allegation.

And (c) is an example of syncopation.

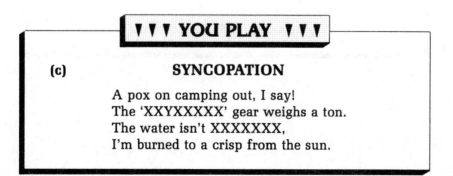

▼▼▼ YOU PLAY ▼▼▼

(c)   **SYNCOPATION**

A pox on camping out, I say!
The 'XXYXXXXX' gear weighs a ton.
The water isn't XXXXXXX,
I'm burned to a crisp from the sun.

Letter change

In a letter change, one single letter has been changed to make a new word – as in 'alter' and 'after' for instance. See how you get on with (d).

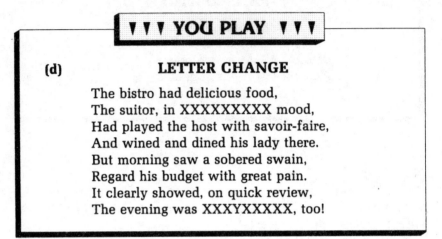

▼ ▼ ▼ YOU PLAY ▼ ▼ ▼

(d)   **LETTER CHANGE**

The bistro had delicious food,
The suitor, in XXXXXXXXX mood,
Had played the host with savoir-faire,
And wined and dined his lady there.
But morning saw a sobered swain,
Regard his budget with great pain.
It clearly showed, on quick review,
The evening was XXXYXXXXX, too!

Container

In a container, one or more short words is (are) contained within a longer word. The word SEAFARER, for example, contains the words SEER and AFAR – SE(AFAR)ER. Try container (e).

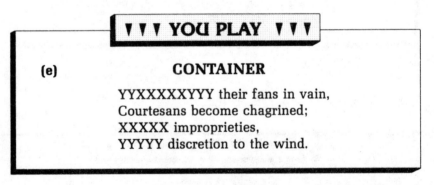

▼ ▼ ▼ YOU PLAY ▼ ▼ ▼

(e)   **CONTAINER**

YYXXXXXYYY their fans in vain,
Courtesans become chagrined;
XXXXX improprieties,
YYYYY discretion to the wind.

(Answers to L8 (a) to (e) on page 264)

LOONY LAWS

These are referred to as logical laws, sage statements, accurate axioms, profound principles, trusty truisms, homely homilies, colourful corollaries, quotable quotes and rambunctious ruminations.

The idea behind this clever game is to invent new laws, the more amusing the better.

The Cassell English Dictionary defines 'Sod's Law' as 'a wry maxim that anything which can possibly go wrong will do so', Sod being short for Sodomite.

Sod's is perhaps the most widely quoted of this type of maxim but there are many more similarly loony laws (or truisms?) which you can use either as mere amusement, talking points, or guides to your lifestyle. Here are a few examples from our collection.

> Nothing is as easy as it looks. Everything takes longer than you expect. If anything can go wrong it will do so; and always at the worst possible moment – *Murphy's Law*

> You can always find what you're not looking for – *Maryann's Law*

> If you're feeling good, don't worry. You'll soon get over it – *Boling's Postulate*

> Dimensions will always be expressed in the least usable terms. Velocity, for example, will always be expressed in furlongs per fortnight – *Percival's Observation*

> If you can tell the difference between good advice and bad advice, you don't need advice – *Van Troy's Truism*

> Smile, as it makes people wonder what you are thinking – *Hoffman's Rule*

> If mathematically you end up with the incorrect number, try multiplying by the page number – *Murphy's Ninth Law*

> Supersonic travel means that, although you can't be in two places at once, at least you can be heard trying over a wide area – *Allan's Axiom*

M1

MAGIC WORD SQUARES

A magic word square is a square of letters so constructed that, by using words of equal length, the same words can be read both horizontally and vertically, as in Example 1.

Another version is the double-word square (Example 2), where different words can be read horizontally and vertically, and a further version is shown in Example 3, which has the four words reading horizontally left, horizontally right and up and down.

Magic word square 1   Magic word square 2   Magic word square 3

Magic word squares become progressively more difficult to compile as the number of words increases. Several 8 × 8 word squares have been compiled, but it is only very recently, in America, that a 9 × 9 square has been achieved using known words from the same dictionary. The 10 × 10 breakthrough is still awaited.

Perhaps the easiest to compile are 4 × 4 squares and it is possible to quickly compile one beginning with each letter of the alphabet in turn, for example using: AWAY – WIRE – AREA – YEAR, or BASE – AWAY – SAME – EYES.

Squares using the more difficult letters Q and X are illustrated in Examples 4 and 5.

Q	U	A	Y
U	R	G	E
A	G	O	G
Y	E	G	G

Magic Word Square 4

X	M	A	S
M	I	S	T
A	S	H	Y
S	T	Y	E

Magic Word Square 5

The use of magic squares has led to the creation of several different types of puzzle. You may like to try some of them.

▼▼▼ YOU PLAY ▼▼▼

(a)   MAGIC SQUARE KICKSELF

This puzzle was submitted several years ago for *Enigmasig* by Tim Hazlewood.

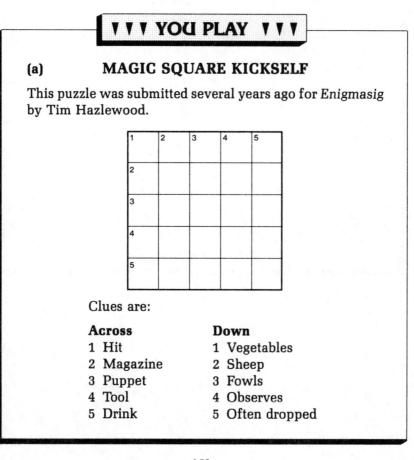

Clues are:

Across
1 Hit
2 Magazine
3 Puppet
4 Tool
5 Drink

Down
1 Vegetables
2 Sheep
3 Fowls
4 Observes
5 Often dropped

Around the turn of the century, the great English puzzle expert, Henry E. Dudeney, was responsible for a new innovation, that of magic word squares complete with clues. The puzzle, given in (b), was compiled by Dudeney in 1890, the clues being provided in the form of a verse entitled *The Abbey*.

▼▼▼ YOU PLAY ▼▼▼

(b)   **THE ABBEY**

The object is to replace the seven numerals in the verse with seven words which, when listed in their given order, form a magic word square where the seven words read the same both across and down.

'Twas spring. The abbey woods were filled with 'second'.
The abbot, with his 'fifth', no trouble reckoned;
But shared his meats and 'seventh' with every man,
Who loves to feast has 'first' since time began.
Then comes a stealthy 'sixth' across the wall,
Who 'fourths' the plate and jewels, cash and all,
And ere the abbot and the monks have dined;
He 'thirds', and leaves no trace or clue behind.

1	2	3	4	5	6	7
2						
3						
4						
5						
6						
7						

(c) ANAGRAM MAGIC SQUARE

This is from an idea by the authors. Using all 25 letters of the sentence below once each only, form five 5-letter words which, when placed correctly in the grid, will form a magic square where the same five words can be read both horizontally and vertically.

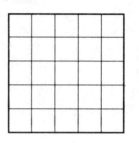

CARTER'S NORTHERN FACE SAFEST

(d) DIFFERENT WORDS

Also invented by the authors, this is a variation of (c).

Rearrange all 25 letters to find five different 5-letter words which, when placed correctly in the second grid, will form a magic word square.

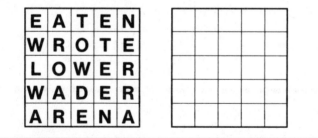

(e)   **MAGIC VERSE**

This puzzle was compiled by the authors for their 1991 book *Children's Challenging Brain Teasers* and they actually got the idea from H. E. Dudeney's puzzle, *The Abbey*. Each line of the verse gives a clue to a 4-letter word which should be entered in the grid. When all four clues have been solved correctly, a 4 × 4 magic word square will be produced.

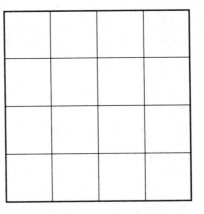

My first is to make a present of;
My second is the plan.
My third is to change direction;
And my fourth's a noble man.

Blended Squares

The first ever blended magic squares appeared in a women's magazine, *The People's Home Journal*, in September 1904 and a further ten examples appeared between 1904 and 1908. Some puzzle experts argue that these were the world's first crosswords. They consisted of five interlocked 3 × 3 magic squares, and at least eight more appeared in the companion magazine, *Good Literature*, starting in May 1905.

The example, (f), compiled by the authors, consists of five 5 × 5 magic squares.

(f)   **BLENDED SQUARES**

The diagram shows five connected 5 × 5 magic squares.
The answers are all 5-letter words, and each of the grids
reads the same across and down. The clues are given in sets
of five, which, in each set, are in no particular order.

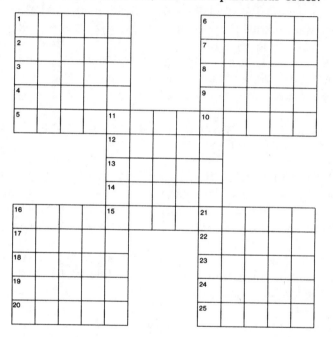

Clues 1–5
Diminish
Fence of bushes
Severe or cruel
Cause sharp pain
Swift

Clues 6–10
Nude
Finished
Religious dwelling
  place
Once more
Sift and strain

Clues 11–15
Eastern person
Horseman's spear
Huge person
Come into
Bird of prey

Clues 16–20
English royal house
Cosmetic red powder
Warehouse
Made a mistake
Smell

Clues 21–25
Love intensely
Regular arrangement
Large forest plants
Oven bake
Work for

(Answers to M1 (a) to (f) on pages 264-5)

MALAPROPISMS

A malapropism is a misuse of a word through confusion with a similar sounding word, sometimes deliberately for comic effect, for example, 'He's being used as a prawn in the game'.

The word was coined from a character in Sheridan's *The Rivals*, Mrs Malaprop, who was continually making such blunders. Modern day Mrs Malaprops have been the comedian Hilda Baker who carried on a continual conversation with her stooge, the silent Cynthia, and used the catchphrase, 'She knows ya know', and Jean Alexander's creation for *Coronation Street*, Hilda Ogden, who uttered a succession of beautifully delivered malapropisms while leaning on the bar of the Rover's Return.

Malapropisms are actually a wordsmith's delight and it is great fun trying to think up good ones. Here are a few.

Two children in a school playground were dragged into the headmaster's office by a school prefect who was carrying a heavy nail-studded board. He gasped out, 'Tommy was hitting Jimmy with this board. Look at this. It's a legal weapon!'

Hotel Notice in Ankara, Turkey: You are invited to visit our restaurant where you can eat the Middle East Foods in an European ambulance.

Your words fall off me like a duck's quack.

I'm on the horns of an enema.

The architect, Sir Edward Maufe, once arrived very late for a formal society dinner. Crouching down, he crept up behind the important host, sitting at the head of the vast table. 'I'm terribly sorry,' he apologised. 'I'm, Maufe.' The host spun around in surprise. 'But my dear chap,' he exclaimed. 'You've only just arrived!'

We talk about the fickle guy who 'wants his Kate and Edith too'.

A slap of the tongue.

Don't judge a boob by its cover.

Hoist by your own leotard.

Show business has stars such as Elephant Gerald, Daisy Doris and Gladys Knight and her Pimps.

The explorer, Thor Heyerdahl, once phoned for a taxi. The driver arrived at the hotel and the explorer said, 'I'm the one your looking for.' 'Not me,' said the driver, 'I'm supposed to pick up four Airdales.'

Other doggy ones are: Lavender Retriever and Doublemint Pinscher.

This smells to high herring.

They are not married but have been happily co-rabbiting for years.

Some of these out-malaprop Mrs Malaprop herself. Now try making up a few of your own. We hope your efforts reach the pineapple of success.

MANIAS

The term 'mania' was first used in the 17th century and indicated great enthusiasm. Later it was used as a suffix to Greek words indicating 'a mad passion'. A few unusual manias are:

BRUXOMANIA   – Compulsive and continual crunching of the teeth together with intermittent grinding.

GRAIOMANIA   – A passion for Greek things.

GRAPHOMANIA   – Excessive impulse to write.

KLAZOMANIA   – Compulsive shouting.

ONIOMANIA   – A compulsion to buy things.

TRICHOTILLOMANIA   – A morbid impulse to pull out one's own hair.

They do make good quizes. Example (a) was compiled by the authors for their 1993 book *Power Puzzles*.

▼▼▼ YOU PLAY ▼▼▼

(a)   MANIAS

In column (2) is a list of manias, and in column (1), a list of what they are an obsession with, or addiction to. However, they are all mixed up. Can you match them up correctly?

Column 1	Column 2
Alcohol	Hedonomania
Bridges	Logomania
Cats	Anthomania
Dogs	Dipsomania
Eating	Dromomania
Flowers	Plutomania
Pleasure	Gephyromania
Riches	Ailuromania
Talking	Phagomania
Travelling	Cynomania

(Answers to M3 (a) on page 266)

MISCHMASCH

Invented by Lewis Carroll in 1880, one player selects two or more letters. The other player then has to find a word which contains those letters in sequence.

Can you solve the words in (a)? They are all hyphenated words.

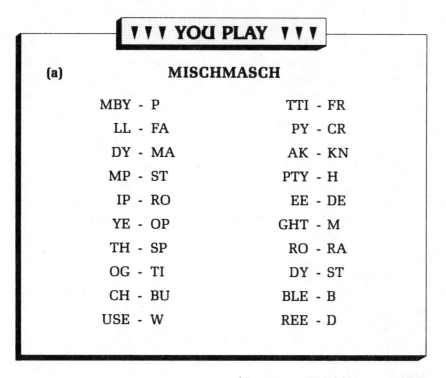

▼ ▼ ▼ YOU PLAY ▼ ▼ ▼

(a)   **MISCHMASCH**

MBY - P	TTI - FR
LL - FA	PY - CR
DY - MA	AK - KN
MP - ST	PTY - H
IP - RO	EE - DE
YE - OP	GHT - M
TH - SP	RO - RA
OG - TI	DY - ST
CH - BU	BLE - B
USE - W	REE - D

(Answers to M4 (a) on page 266)

MNEMONICS

Mnemonic devices and memory tricks,
Are fabulous helpers when nothing else sticks.
But then, to remember mnemonics I find,
They jam up the circuits in my addled mind.

Mitzi Christiansen Kuehl

A mnemonic is an aid to memory; the only problem we find, however, is that we can never remember them! The word mnemonic is derived from Mnemosyne who, in Greek mythology, was a Titaness, daughter of Earth and Heaven, and mother of all the Muses. Her name actually means 'Memory'.

Over the years we have formed quite a collection of these memory devices. The medical profession in particular would seem to almost entirely depend on them, for instance:

Bones of the wrist: – Never Lower Tillie's Pants; Mother Might Come Home: Navicular, Lunate, Triquetral, Pisiform, Greater Multangular, Lesser Multangular, Capitate, Hamate.

Of course, the reason for this is that medical students must commit to memory large amounts of information.

Take, for example, the names of the twelve sets of cranial nerves. These are: 1 The Olfactory Nerves, 2 The Optic Nerves, 3 The Occulomotor Nerves, 4 The Trochlear Nerves, 5 The Trigeminal Nerves, 6 The Abducens Nerves, 7 The Facial Nerves, 8 The Auditory Nerves, 9 The Glossopharyngeal Nerves, 10 The Vagus Nerves, 11 The Spinal Accessory Nerves, 12 The Hypoglossal Nerves.

During the 19th century, the recognised way of remembering these was by the following mnemonic: The **oil factory**'s **optic**ian **occupied** a **truck** in which **three gems** were **abducted** by a **face** with **ears**. A **glossy photograph** of them was **vague** and appeared **spineless** and **hypocritical**.

There is also a later mnemonic which gives the twelve initials: **On O**ld **O**lympic's **T**owering **T**ops, **A F**inn and **G**erman **V**end **S**ome **H**ops.

Still on a medical theme is PAIL for four types of skin wounds: **P**uncture, **A**brasion, **I**ncision and **L**aceration. There are also the five branches of the seventh cranial nerve (the facial nerve) remembered by: Tully Zucker's Bowels Move Constantly (**T**emporal, **Z**ygomatic, **B**uccal, **M**ental, **C**ervical). Then, to complete your medical education there is RICE (in the event of a sprain or strain): **R**est, **I**ce, **C**ompression, **E**levation.

Here, now, is a further miscellaneous selection from our collection:

WASPLEG – The seven deadly sins: **W**rath, **A**varice, **S**loth, **P**ride, **L**ust, **E**nvy, **G**luttony.

When it's **S**unday in **S**an Francisco, it's **M**onday in **M**anila.

Beer on whisky, mighty risky.
Whisky on beer, never fear.

And a German version which gives a similar warning:

Wein auf Bier, das rat ich dir;
Bier auf Wein, das lass seir.

If you munch a sprig of parsley,
You needn't eat your garlic sparsely.

To give possible solutions to a problem (or entertain, inform, get action, convince) or present evidence, SEDATE your audience:

> **S**tatistics
>
> **E**xhibit
>
> **D**emonstration
>
> **A**nalogy
>
> **T**estimony of an expert
>
> **E**xample

HOMES – The five great lakes: **H**uron, **O**ntario, **M**ichigan, **E**rie, **S**uperior.

The correct operation of a screw – Left loose, right turn; or
A turn to the right makes it tight; or
Clockwise is Lockwise.

Biological classification –

Kingdom	**K**ings
Phylum	**P**lay
Class	**C**hess
Order	**O**n
Family	**F**ine
Genus	**G**rain
Species	**S**and

Days in the months:

> 30 days hath September,
> April, June and November;
> All the rest have 31,
> Excepting February alone,
> Which has but 28 days clear,
> And 29 in each leap year.

Another way of remembering the number of days in each month is by your knuckles: raised knuckles, long months; valleys between, short months.

Pi – two mnemonics to enable you to recall pi to twenty decimal places (3.14159 26535 89793 23846). In both, the number of letters in each word coincide with the number in pi:

> Now I know a rhyme excelling,
> In hidden words and magic spelling,
> Wranglers perhaps deploring,
> For me its nonsense isn't boring.

or   Yes, I want a drink, alcholic of course, after the final gyration involving negative equations out of the semester exam sheets.

The names of the planets in order from the Sun: **Mother Very Easily Made Jam Sandwiches, Under No Protest. (Mars, Venus, Earth, Mer**cury, **Jupiter, Saturn, Uranus, Neptune, Pluto.)**

The colours of the rainbow: **Richard of York Gained Battle In Vain. (Red, Orange, Yellow, Green, Blue, Indigo, Violet).**

Trigonometry – **Tom Offered Anthony Some Of His Cattle And Horses. Tangent = O/A; Sine = O/H; Cosine = A/H** (H = Hypotenuse, O = Opposite side, A = Adjacent side).

Spelling of school subjects – Arithmetic: **A Rat In The Hat May Eat The Ice Cream;** Geography: **George Eliot's Old Grandmother Rode A Pig Home Yesterday.**

Henry VIII's wives – CAJACC: **C**atherine of Aragon, **A**nne Boleyn, **J**ane Seymour, **A**nne of Cleves, **C**atherine Howard, **C**atherine Parr. (The last 'C' is Catherine Parr, because she was 'par for the course'.)

The ruling houses of England – **No Point Letting Your Trousers Slip Half Way: Norman, Plantagenet, Lancaster, York, Tudor, Stuart, Hanover, Windsor.**

The order of operations in algebra – **Please Excuse My Dear Aunt Sally: Parenthesis, Exponents, Multiplication, Division, Addition, Subtraction.**

The difference between Stalactites and Stalagmites – **c** = ceiling; **g** = ground.

Types of camel –   A camel I am, it's plain to see,
                     But am I a Bactrian or Dromedary?
                     Lay down the ⋈ and then the ⌓ ,
                     And which I am is plain as can be.

We hope you might find some of these useful. Perhaps we should now invent some more mnemonics to enable us to remember the mnemonics.

MONOGRAMS

Invented by the authors, monograms are visual representations of a word or words formed by the circular arrangement of the letters of the alphabet in the grid shown.

The best examples form patterns which can, in some way, be related to the word or words represented.

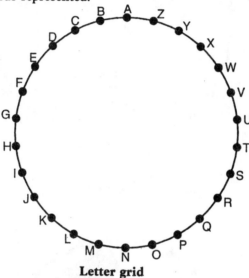

Letter grid

The patterns are formed by using the following rules. Let us take, as an example, the word 'HIGHWAYMAN'. The word is plotted out starting at the first letter 'H' and lines are drawn from letter to letter, that is, H to I, I to G, G to H, H to W, W to A, etc. When all the lines have been drawn, all triangular areas of the pattern so produced are: filled in if bounded by

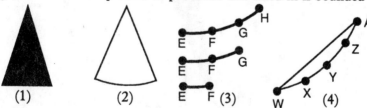

straight lines (1), but are not filled in if bounded by one or more curved lines (2). In the event of adjoining letters of up to three letters (3), then a thick line is drawn on the circumference. If, however, the move between letters exceeds three moves (4), then instead of the thick line on the circumference, a chord is drawn to link the first and last letters. In the event of double letters, just one of the double letters is visited.

Thus the word 'HIGHWAYMAN' is produced as in the diagram.

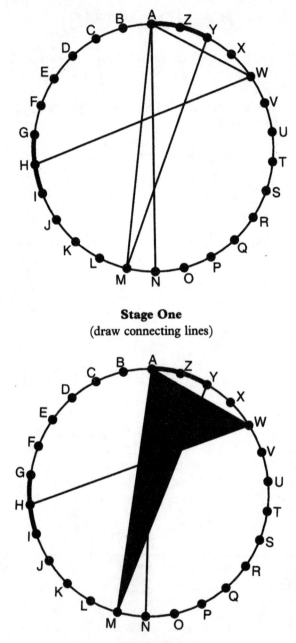

Stage One
(draw connecting lines)

Stage Two
(fill in all areas completely bounded by straight lines)

Representation of 'HIGHWAYMAN'

Monograms make good puzzles in their own right where solvers are asked to guess the word from the pattern, and cryptic or straight synonym clues can be provided. They are also very effective when presented as computer graphics.

A further selection is shown, together with suggested clues.

Monograms

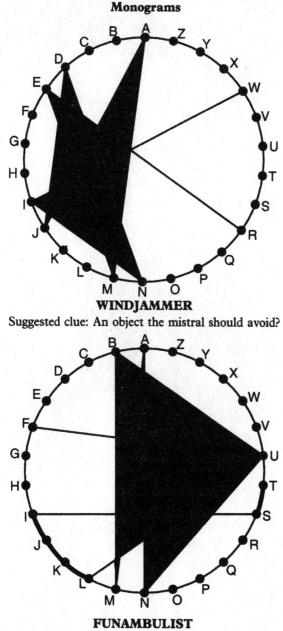

WINDJAMMER

Suggested clue: An object the mistral should avoid?

FUNAMBULIST

Suggested clue: Balanced circus performer.

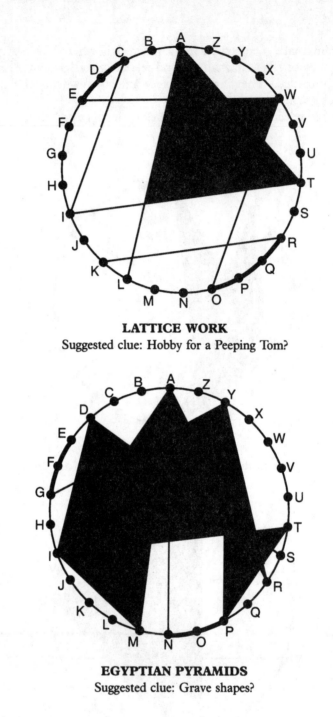

LATTICE WORK
Suggested clue: Hobby for a Peeping Tom?

EGYPTIAN PYRAMIDS
Suggested clue: Grave shapes?

NAME PLAY

In this game the object is to invent humorous names for authors and then attach them to appropriate book titles. It is an old game, several examples being included in *Fousham's Fun Book of 1933*. Some of these appear in the following list.

Cutting it Fine by Moses Lawn

The Corn by Honor Foote

Expelled from School by Millicent Holme

The Antique Shop by Fay Kingham

The Cliff Tragedy by Eileen Dover

Knighted by Watts E. Dunn

The Mother-in-Law by George Orr

Wine and Women by Rex Holmes

Stand and Deliver by Ann Dover

The Soprano by Topsy Sharpe

The Damaging Gale by Rufus Quick

The Song of the Shirt by Dryden Aird

Gossip by Liza Bound

The Dentist by Phil Macaffity

Damaged Windows by Eva Brick

Deep in the Forest by Theresa Green

The Parking Lot Attendant by Kara Parker

A Guide to Ornithology by Dicky Bird

Clear the Air by Nosmo King

My Land by Terry Tory

The Lion Tamer by Claud Bottom

THE NATIONAL PUZZLERS' LEAGUE

The Eastern Puzzlers' League, as the National Puzzlers' League was originally called, was launched on 4 July 1884 by 34 puzzle solving enthusiasts, and membership was restricted to men living east of the Mississippi. The original magazine, *The Eastern Enigma*, was circulated to members periodically and concerned itself with puzzle-related topics rather than puzzles themselves. In 1920, the Eastern Puzzlers' League changed its name to The National Puzzlers' League and, although some changes were made, the aim remained: 'To provide a pastime of mental relaxation for lovers of word puzzles, to raise the standard of puzzling to a higher intellectual level, and to establish and foster friendships among its widely scattered members'. Women had already been admitted in 1910, and after 1920 all geographical restrictions were eventually removed.

The league has continued to flourish and has played a major part in the construction and development of word puzzles in the 20th century. The magazine *The Enigma* is issued on a monthly basis and is now primarily concerned with the construction of puzzles.

The current editor is Judith E. Bagai, of Portland, Oregon, and the league issues a four-page mini sampler free of charge to prospective members. The league has kindly allowed us the use of their mini-sampler and this is reproduced on pages 177-180. The final page gives details of where to write should you be interested in membership.

This is a special introductory edition of The ENIGMA (just four pages instead of the usual twenty or more). It is also an invitation to you to participate in a pastime that will provide you with great enjoyment for very little expense.

The ENIGMA is the monthly publication of The National Puzzlers' League. The NPL, founded in 1883, is the oldest puzzle organization in the United States and the oldest continuously active one in the world. In 1987, we published our 1000th issue. We have a devoted membership of about 400, and all of us are IN THE GAME strictly to have fun and to perpetuate the puzzleistic art. The ENIGMA is our battleground where we challenge and entertain each other with ingenuity, wit, and humor.

Every issue of The ENIGMA contains a wide variety of puzzles, some easy and some tough. Beginner or experienced, you'll always get a good workout. About half the puzzles can be solved without reference books. (Some of our members collect dictionaries, specialized lists, even computer programs; many others have solved happily for years with no more than a college dictionary and thesaurus.) You'll also find stumpers to test the vocabulary, logic, and persistence of the most expert solvers.

The ENIGMA also contains performance records of those solvers (about a quarter of our members) who like to have their solutions checked and reported, votes for favorite puzzles, and news about puzzles and puzzlers. New members receive the guide to The ENIGMA, which explains the many types of puzzles. You'll also receive the NPL directory, giving names, addresses, and noms de plume of puzzlers. A member's nom serves as introduction to any other member. Our members do a lot of corresponding, and many lasting friendships have been made in the NPL. Each summer, we have a four-day convention filled with puzzles, games, and comradeship. For many, the annual convention is the best part of being an NPLer.

When you turn the page, you'll find puzzles that appeared a few years ago in The ENIGMA. Most of them were solved by about two-thirds of the members who sent in lists. (Few members solve everything—and at least some puzzles in every issue are supposed to be really challenging.) Most puzzles in The ENIGMA are in verse, but you don't have to be a poet to write them, or a scholar to solve them. In each verse, one or more words are missing, replaced by words like "ONE" and "TWO." Your job is to figure out the missing words. Look at this example:

> FIFTH-LETTER CHANGE (6)
> When Felix gets a whiff of ONE,
> You see him jump and run,
> But still, before the day is through,
> He's curled up for a TWO.

The title tells you what kind of answer you need. In this case, it's a letter change: a word becomes a new word when a designated letter is changed—like "design" to "resign," or "irritate" to "irrigate." The number in parentheses says you're looking for a six-letter word (ONE) that becomes a new word (TWO) when its fifth letter is changed. The context gives you your clues, and after some thought you hit on the answer: ONE is "catnip" and TWO is "catnap."

When you understand that example, you're ready to turn the page and tackle the rest of the puzzles. And if you enjoy this sample edition of The ENIGMA, we hope you'll join us in the NPL. Page 4 will tell you how.

BEHEADMENT: A word becomes a new one when its first letter is removed. Example: ONE = factor, TWO = actor.

1. BEHEADMENT (6, 5)
They followed the stream as it
  FIRST through the wood,
Staying as much in the shade as
  they could.
A splash, and a swimmer then came
  into sight.
"He's SECOND!" one Girl Scout cried
  out in delight.

CURTAILMENT: A word becomes a new one when its last letter is removed. Example: ONE = aspiring, TWO = aspirin. The asterisk indicates that the six-letter word is capitalized.

2. CURTAILMENT (7, *6)
"Cleopatra," if it's true
That opposites attract,
Could be called the ONE of "TWO"
By known historic fact.

DELETION: A word becomes a new one when an interior letter is removed. Example: ONE = simile, TWO = smile.

3. DELETION (9, 8)
So the jury finally TWO that czar of
  crime?
And a jury trial is ONE? High
  bloody time.

4. DELETION (5, 4)
One year fat, one year lean.
Never anywhere between.
Diet changes every day;
Either ONE or TWO, I say.

TERMINAL DELETION: A word is changed to a new one by removing its first and last letters. Example: ONE = foregone, TWO = Oregon.

5. TERMINAL DELETION (6, 4)
I knew my son would be a TALL
When he was very small,
For when I put him in his SMALL
He doodled on the wall.

WORD DELETION: A word removed from inside a longer one leaves a third word. Example: TOTAL = performance; ONE = man, TWO = perforce. The length is given only of the longest (TOTAL) word.

6. WORD DELETION (8)
I ate at seven, felt TOTAL by ten.
I doubt if I'll INSIDE eat OUTSIDE
  again.

7. WORD DELETION (10)
I TWO the praise of any soul
With knowledge of a ONE like this.
I've just an ALL—so on the whole
I'm glad that ignorance is bliss.

CHARADE: A word is broken into two or more shorter words. Example: TOTAL = scarcity; ONE = scar, TWO = city. The length is given only of the long word.

8. CHARADE (10)
My migraine was pounding; I needed
  some rest.
"There's WHOLE," said my FIRST, "in
  the medicine chest."
The SECOND on all of the labels
  looked blurred.
I took one at random and promptly
  got THIRD.

LETTER CHANGE: One letter is changed in a word to make a new one. Example: ONE = pastry, TWO = pantry (a third-letter change).

9. FIRST-LETTER CHANGE (8)
Our baby had colic, and ONE all the
  day.
No sound's ever TWO it, I'm happy to
  say.

10. THIRD-LETTER CHANGE (11)
His mood was indicative, her voice
  purely passive;
He grew more explicative, her
  boredom grew massive.
To his ONE, she said, "Somehow I
  feel it's not you
I'm looking for," ending their date
  with a TWO.

TRANSPOSAL: A word or phrase becomes a different one when its letters are rearranged. Example: ONE = sleuth, TWO = hustle.

11. TRANSPOSAL (6)
Listen, old fellow, my FIRST you may
  be,
But that gives you no right to pry.
You've plenty of crust, it is easy
  to see—
Why, you're even SECOND than I!

12. TRANSPOSAL (8, 5 3)
Their salad is Caesar,
But please hold the crouton—
They're the FIVE THREE.
Their fruit is the kiwi,
Their EIGHT is a futon—
They're the FIVE THREE.
They're as chic as you get,
SSTs, not the jet—
They're the FIVE THREE.

LETTER BANK: From the "bank" of letters contained in the short word, which has no repeated letters, a longer word is formed using all the letters at least once and as many more times as needed. Examples: ONE = lens, TWO = senselessness. ONE = field, TWO = fiddledeedee.

13. LETTER BANK (6, 9)
A SECOND broke a hundred knees
And FIRST along in her unease.

14. LETTER BANK (6, 10)
I work for an importing firm
That sells exotic birds.
Our president loves cockatiels
And tries to teach them words.
Our lawyers love the parrots—
How their talking gives them
  thrills.
But our LONGERs hate the SHORTERs:
They've no use for those big bills!

HETERONYM: Two words or phrases have the same spelling but different pronunciations and meanings. Example : ONE = notable, TWO = not able. Asterisks indicate capitalized words.

15. HETERONYM (2 9; 3, *3 5)
Adam said, "I'll take this film
  to FIRST," and off went he.
Jumping out of SECOND off to
  case the apple tree.

16. HETERONYM (3 5, *8)
In fourteen hundred ninety-two,
Columbus gasped, "I'm lost! I'm
  through!"
FIRST mounted as he turned quite
  green:
"What will I tell the SECOND queen?"

HOMONYM: Two unrelated words or phrases are pronounced the same but spelled differently. Example: ONE = hair, TWO = hare.

17. HOMONYM (6, 7)
Sweet to die for country?
The FIRST did not agree.
He SECOND in the bushes
Till it was safe to flee.

18. HOMONYM (6, 6)
Lambs who ONE on the green may get
  caught on a thorn;
Lambs who TWO on green tables get
  caught and then shorn.

SPOONERGRAM: A phrase becomes another phrase when the initial sounds in the words are swapped. Example: ONE = Morse code, TWO = course mowed.

19. SPOONERGRAM (6 6, 7 7)
His radio excitedly reported,
  "There's a sighting:
A UFO is just above and seems to be
  alighting!"
"Oh, dear, I'm all undressed and
  washed; this one last task, then
  bed.
I can't go out to see the FIRST,
  alas," the SECOND said.

20. SPOONERGRAM (6 3, 5 6)
No farce is Wagner's Ring; it is a
  ONE
Of music, drama. Fearful deeds are
  done.
The hero, Siegfried, battles mighty
  odds,
And TWO are played on dwarfs and men
  by gods.

REBUS: A word or phrase is represented by letters, numbers, or symbols. The word "abalone"—read as "a B alone"—might be represented by:

B

And the phrase "damper sand"—read as "D, ampersand"—might be represented by:

D&

21. REBUS (12)

$\overset{\cdot}{T} = T$

My holiday plans have been ruined
  this year;
I was going to go to the south.
But my ANSWER's bill took all my
  savings away;
Why should he, then, look down in
  the mouth?

22. REBUS (*6 *4 2 *3)

ⱂ T/IO

See Fred and Ginger southward wing—
In ANSWER they both dance and sing.

ENIGMA: A word or phrase is clued indirectly, as in a riddle.

23. ENIGMA (8)
My first half says I'm one alone,
My second that I'm many;
That's paradoxical, I own—
Makes little sense, if any.
But even worse is yet in store,
For when my halves combine,
Behold! not one, not two or more,
But everything is mine.

Not all ENIGMA puzzles are in verse. You may already be familiar with some of the following types from other puzzle publications.

ANAGRAMS: Apposite words or phrases composed of the same letters as the answer. For example, NAME FOR SHIP is an anagram of H.M.S. PINAFORE.

24. THEY SEE (3 4)

25. BEAR HIT DEN (10)

26. BENEATH CHOPIN (3 5 5)

27. TRUSS NEATLY TO BE SAFE (6 4 4 5)

ANAQUOTE: A quotation is divided into 3-letter chunks (ignoring punctuation and spaces). The chunks are alphabetized for you to rearrange. "Find the clues" would be: (4 3 5) DTH ECL FIN UES. Numbers in parentheses tell how many letters in each word of the quotation; asterisks represent capitalized words (in this case, the author's name).

28. ANAQUOTE (2 10, 2 2 4, 2 3 10 2 4 2 6 2 6. *5 *7)

AND ASI ATI AUR EAR EAS EDA ERS INL ISH ITE NBY NLO OIS OSE OTH RAT REM SCH TON TWH URE VEW

CRYPTOGRAM: A message in cipher. Each letter in the coded message stands for another letter wherever it appears; E might stand for N, R for W, and so on. (No letter stands for itself.) The asterisk marks a capitalized word.

29. CRYPTOGRAM

MVJRFKBR   *S   NJSVV   RMDP   M
XRFJFBLMXRSY   WPWFLT,   JRP   HSVW
XLFDSCPC   EFIMCMTN   SN   FH
ZKPNJSFEMOVP   ZKMVSJT!

FORMS: Puzzles similar to crosswords, but with regular geometric shapes and no black squares. The square and diamond look like this:

```
1. L A V A        1.              I
2. A V E R        2.           A  N  A
3. V E N T        3.        A  N  I  S  E
4. A R T Y        4.     A  N  O  T  H  E  R
                  5.  I  N  I  T  I  A  L  E  D
                  6.     A  S  H  A  M  E  D
                  7.        E  E  L  E  R
                  8.           R  E  D
                  9.              D
```

30. SQUARE (5-letter words)
1. A kind of puzzle in this minisample 2. Use one end of a pencil 3. Wash up 4. Theater employee 5. Mystics

31. DIAMOND
1. Last letter 2. Tell a lie 3. Jungle cat 4. Hissed, like soda 5. Went this way and that 6. Born in Brussels 7. Suitable for a king 8. Lair 9. Poor grade

SOLUTIONS

```
              D
            D E N
          R E G A L
        B E L G I A N
      Z I G Z A G G E D
        F I Z Z L E D
          T I G E R
          B A T H E
          E R A S E
            F I B
             Z
```

31.

30. R E B U S

1. s-naked 2. Antony-m 3. indic(a)-ted 4. f(e)ast 5. s(crib)e 6. f(ever)ish 7. s(matter)ing 8. pa-ink-iller 9. s/e-qualled 10. pr-o/e-position 11. senior, nosier 12. mattress, smart set 13. limped, milliped 14. toucan, accountant 15. be developed; bed, Eve loped 16. his panic, Hispanic 17. coward, cowered 18. gambol, gamble 19. flying saucer, sighting glosser 20. tragic mix, magic tricks 21. periodontist [period on "tist" is "t"] 22. flying Down to Rio [F lying down, "I," "or," "I O"] 23. monopoly 24. the eyes 25. hibernated 26. the piano bench 27. fasten your seat belts 28. In literature, as in love, we are astonished at what is chosen by others. André Maurois 29. Although I still have a photographic memory, the film provided nowadays is of questionable quality!

J O I N   U S

Membership in the National Puzzlers' League is $13 for the first year and $11 yearly thereafter (outside North America, add $9). Membership includes a subscription to The ENIGMA (12 monthly issues). For LARGE TYPE, add $9. Send your check, made out to the National Puzzlers' League, to the treasurer: Joseph J. Adamski (MERCURY), 2507 Almar, Jenison MI 49428.

The editor is SIBYL: Judith E. Bagai, Box 82289, Portland OR 97282.

NEOLOGISMS

A neologism is a newly-coined word or phrase, or a familiar word used in a new sense. It now seems to be the fashion to introduce such terms into the English language and some examples are:

CASH COW: A business which consistently produces large profits.

DONGLE: An electronic device which is plugged into a computer.

RED-EYE: An overnight journey from west to east.

The lastest fashion appears to be the mania for 'politically correct language'. Recently, there was quite a row because a supermarket was almost forced to change what was termed the sexist name 'Gingerbread Man' to 'Gingerbread Person'. Taking this to extremes, man-holes would become person-holes; Manchester would become Personchester, and its inhabitants Personcunians; and our friend Paul Chapman would become Paul Personperson (or even Paul Peroffspringperoffspring!).

Politically correct language is, unfortunately, taken very seriously in many quarters, and someone who is below the ordinary size is now 'vertically challenged'; someone who is bald should now be termed 'follicularly challenged'; while a boring person is now 'charm-free'. Someone who is clumsy is 'uniquely coordinated' and the deaf are 'aurally inconvenienced'. The new term for dishonest is 'morally different' and a husband or wife is now a 'partner'.

The old aren't elderly any more, they are 'chronologically gifted' (OK that one) and the plain stupid are 'differently logical'. If you are one of the unfortunate unemployed you are 'involuntarily leisured' and a person should no longer be described as white, but as a person of 'non-colour'.

Let us hope it is just a passing phase, or for amusement purposes only.

NORTH AND SOUTH

The authors of this book are both English, but one was born and bred in London and the other in West Yorkshire. There they both still reside, two hundred miles apart, at different ends of the M1 motorway. Two hundred miles does not seem too great a distance, but in terms of dialect it is a world apart, for London has its own second language, Cockney, and West Yorkshire has what is known as 'Broad Yorkshire'. Ask a Londoner to translate the first two lines of the Yorkshire anthem, *Ilkla Moor*, and he will be struggling; then ask a Yorkshireman to translate a piece of Cockney, and he will be equally lost. Consider these two examples.

Whear hast tha' bin sin ah saw thee?
On Ilkla Moor baht 'at.

(The first two lines of *Ilkla Moor*).

I'm goin' up the apples to change into my new whistle, then I'll go down the frog for a ball of chalk to the rub-a-dub for a glass of needle.

(Cockney)

Not so simple to decode, and almost worthy of the description cryptography, these are the two translations:

Where have you been since I saw you?
On Ilkley Moor without a hat.

I'm going upstairs to change into my new suit, then I'll go down the road for a walk to the pub for a glass of gin.

To the uninitiated it should be explained that Cockney is all in rhyme, 'Cockney rhyming slang', but just to confuse things they have the habit of leaving out the second word. For example, a Cockney might say he is going up the apples, and would mean that he was going up the stairs, because the Cockney rhyming slang for stairs is 'apples and pears'. Similarly, in the passage we gave, whistle is 'whistle and flute' (rhyming with suit), 'frog and toad' means road, 'ball of chalk' is walk, 'rub-a-dub' is pub (public house) and 'needle and pin' rhymes with gin.

Other examples of Cockney describe various parts of the anatomy: Barnet fair (hair); boat race (face); mince pies (eyes); I suppose (nose); north and south (mouth); Beau Geste (chest); Aunty Nellie (belly); Khyber Pass (a certain rear part of anatomy); and plates of meat (feet).

Of course, this is further complicated due to the fact that a Cockney does not exactly come out with these terms in the Queen's English. The letter 'h' does not really exist as far as a Cockney is concerned and he has a great reluctance to terminate words, for example 'put your hat on' might come out 'pu' your 'a' on'.

But, back again 200 miles up the M1. What of 'Broad Yorkshire'? Surely it can't be as difficult as that to decipher? Consider the following passage by retired journalist Mike Shaw, and reproduced from his column 'Bill O' Ben's', which appears weekly in *The Huddersfield Examiner*, the newspaper of a town deep in the heart of Broad Yorkshire dialect territory. How many of you can work out what it all means?

Thees days tha's a job ter fahnd wun o' th' owd-fasioned barbers wheer tha can catch up on awl t' latest gossip.

Mooast on 'em are wat they call unisex, sooa tha can be th' ooanly fella amang hauf a dozen women.

Well, Ah ask thee, aah can sich as me chew t' fat wi' a load o' women cacklin' away lahke battery 'ens abaat sooa an' sooa's new frock an' wat Bet Lynch is gettin' up to on *Coronation Street*?

We're lucky ter 'ave a men-ooanly barber i' t' village, an' tuthri on us meet up theer ivvery three or four weeks.

T' barber's been theer ommost a lahfetahme an' awl, an' t' other day 'e gate raand ter tellin' us abaat sum o' laffs 'e'd 'ad ovver t' yeears.

'Ah were varry friendly at wun tahme wi a chap fra t' valley 'at 'ad getten on reight weel as a musician,' 'e telled us. 'E used ter pop in naah an' ageean if 'e weer playin' t' violin 'i theese parts, usually t' Taan Hall i' 'Uddersfield.

'On this particular day 'e cums in wi' 'is violin case under 'is arm whahle Ah wer cuttin' owd Willie Haigh's 'air. "Ah thowt Ah'd jist let they 'ave a look at this," 'e sed. "Ah've been after wun o' thees for donkey's yeears."

'Wi that, 'e oppened up 'is case an' teks aat this reight grand violin 'at 'e 'andled lahke it wer a baby. Wille wer a bit upset wen Ah stopped cuttin' ter take a clooaser look. After a minnit or two 'e sed reight impatiently: "Wat's that tha's getten theer then, Bill?" "Na then, Willie," Ah replahd. "Tha'll nooan see monny o' thees. It's a Strad."

' "Well, Ah'll gooa ter yar haas," sed Willie. "Ah cud 'a sworn it wer a fiddle!" '

NOUGHTS AND CROSSWORDS

Although it uses the letters X and O, we have not included the well-known game of noughts and crosses in this collection of word games and puzzles, since by no stretch of the imagination could it be called a word game. This variation, however, was suggested by Ray Brooker in the July 1985 *Enigmasig*.

There are eight ways to win at noughts and crosses. To win this game you must get all eight lines. There are sixteen answers to solve: eight lines both forwards and backwards. The clues are in matching pairs; one clue fits three letters one way round and the other clue fits the same three letters the other way round. All the letters, exactly as they stand, form part of the answer to each clue. Unfortunately, you do not know if they begin the word, appear in the middle, or even end the word.

Try (a); to start you off we have provided the answers to the first pair of clues.

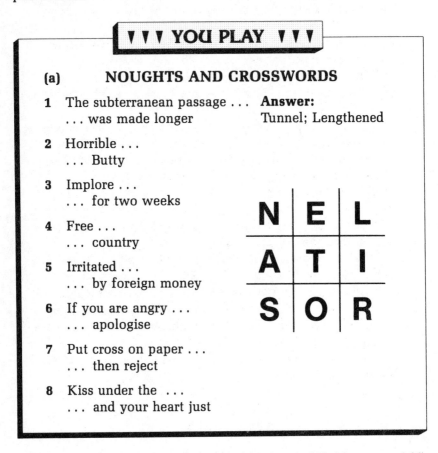

▼▼▼ YOU PLAY ▼▼▼

(a)   NOUGHTS AND CROSSWORDS

1   The subterranean passage . . .   **Answer:**
    . . . was made longer   Tunnel; Lengthened

2   Horrible . . .
    . . . Butty

3   Implore . . .
    . . . for two weeks

4   Free . . .
    . . . country

5   Irritated . . .
    . . . by foreign money

6   If you are angry . . .
    . . . apologise

7   Put cross on paper . . .
    . . . then reject

8   Kiss under the . . .
    . . . and your heart just

(Answers to N5 (a) on page 266)

═══ N6 ═══
NURSERY RHYME CROSSWORDS

Nursery rhymes are traditional jingles which are passed on from parent to child from generation to generation. Most date from the 18th century; some celebrate personalities, some are 'counting-out' rhymes and some celebrate events in history. The line from the rhyme, *Atishoo, atishoo, All fall down*, for example, has sinister implications and dates back to the time of the Great Plague when the first sign that someone had contracted the disease was a sneeze and, thus, soon he or she would die (fall down).

Some of the earliest rhymes, dating from 1744 to 1780, are *Little Tommy Tucker*, *Ba, Ba, Black Sheep*, *Sing a Song of Sixpence*, *Who Killed Cock Robin?*, *Jack and Jill*, *Ding Dong Bell* and *Hush-a-bye-Baby*.

The authors have developed a crossword-type puzzled based on nursery rhymes. A typical example is given in (a).

▼▼▼ YOU PLAY ▼▼▼

(a)   NURSERY RHYME CROSSWORD

Hidden in this passage are eight clues. Your task is to spot them, solve them and then place the answers (all seven-letter words) in the grid.

'I have a little nut tree with loose hanging threads. Nothing would it bear except a cultivated hazel, and a golden pear, and some fruit with reddish coloured skins.

'The King of Spain, who was a Commander in the Army and who had the soldiers punished with a whip, had a daughter who liked to eat profusely and who was a beginner. She came to visit me, her hair is less light through the addition of hair colouring, all for the sake of my little nut tree.'

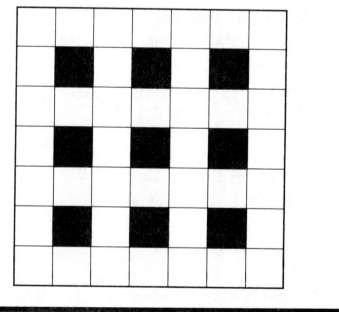

(Answers to N6 (a) on page 266)

OCCUPATIONAL FOOD

This is another of those infectious fun games, the idea being to select the favourite food for various occupations. Here are some suggestions to get you started.

BARBER – Hare

ELECTRICIAN – Currants

FINANCIER – Fortune cookie

MASTER OF CEREMONIES – Toast

MATHEMATICIAN – Pie

MODEL – Cheesecake

PHILOSOPHER – Sage

JEWELLER – Carrots

PHOTOGRAPHER – Cheese

PLUMBER – Leeks

POLITICIAN – Fudge

PSYCHIATRIST – Fruit cake with nuts

RETAILER – Turnover

WEIGHTLIFTER – Mussels

GARDENER – Potted meat

NANNY – Goat's milk

ACTOR – Ham

TAXI DRIVER – Cabbage

TAXIDERMIST – Stuffing

ONE LINERS

This was very popular in the 1930s, mainly because of the great interest in the Cinema. Parties would be held where the guests would go armed with the latest succinct, witty sayings, and a game would develop whereby the best one liners would win prizes. Here are some examples:

I once wanted to become an atheist but I gave it up – they have no holidays.

A doctor gave a man six months to live . . . he couldn't pay his bill . . . so the doctor gave him another six months.

I made a killing on the Stock Exchange; I shot my broker.

My wife is a light eater; as soon as it is light she starts to eat.

My wife has just had plastic surgery; I cut up her credit cards.

I wouldn't join a club that would take me as a member. (Groucho Marx)

Well, if I called the wrong number, why did you answer the phone. (James Thurber)

Let's get out of these wet clothes and into a dry Martini. (Robert Benchley)

OXYMORONS

'Make haste slowly' – Suetonius (69-130 AD)

An oxymoron is a linking of incongruous or contradictory terms as in 'The *wisest fool* in Christendom'.

The word oxymoron is formed from two Greek roots of opposite meaning: 'OXYS' meaning 'sharp, keen' and 'MOROS' meaning 'foolish' (the same root that gives us the word moron).

There are several one word oxymorons: PIANOFORTE (soft-loud), PREPOSTEROUS (before-after) and SUPERETTE (big-small). Others are actually two words fused together into one word as in ballpoint, speechwriting, someone, bridegroom and spendthrift.

Other familiar oxymorons are phrases such as these: small fortune, industrial park, open secret, loyal opposition, light heavyweight, final draft, random order, elevated subway, fresh frozen, recorded live, old boy, jumbo shrimp, baby grand, barely clothed, far nearer, accidentally on purpose, genuine imitation, at this time in history, skinny broad, bad goods, good grief, dry ice, advance to the rear, advanced beginner, feeling numb, loose fit, terribly nice, holy war, war games, thunderous silence, perfectly awful, guest host, and mandatory option.

Several oxymorons are a matter of opinion, such as: peacekeeper missile, business ethics, rock music, designer jeans, military intelligence, postal service and airline food.

There is also modern oxymoronology, including such as: metal wood (in golf), healthy tan, soviet union, criminal lawyer, paper table cloths, plastic glasses, friendly fire, and first repeat.

Several oxymorons have appeared in literature and the arts. These include: *hateful good* (Chaucer), *proud humility* (Spenser), *darkness visible* (Milton), *damn with faint praise* (Pope), *melancholy merriment* (Byron), *falsely true* (Tennyson), *Parting is such sweet sorrow* (Shakespeare), *Poor Little Rich Girl* (Coward) and *Bitter Sweet* (Coward).

Oxymorons which we have noted recently are: Christmas Day Night, old news, loose tights and tight slacks.

You may now like to try the little quiz in (a).

▼ ▼ ▼ YOU PLAY ▼ ▼ ▼

(a)   **OXYMORONS**

Here are 24 words. Can you match them up to form 12 oxymorons?

working, familiar, even, ill, again, pretty, idiot, never, non-dairy, homeless, light, holiday, miracle, living, strangely, odds, health, minor, death, ugly, night, creamer, shelter, perfect

(Answers to O3 (a) on page 267)

PAIR WORDS

This is a word association game invented by the authors. There are two sets of answers; the problem is that if you get answers, or just one answer, from one set mixed into the other set, then the solution will not work. Try the example in (a).

▼ ▼ ▼ YOU PLAY ▼ ▼ ▼

(a) **PAIR WORDS**

Pair a word from list 1 with a word from list 2 until you have ten pairs of words. Each word in list 1 can be paired with two words from list 2, and each word in list 2 can be paired with two words from list 1.

There are two sets of answers.

List 1	List 2
Proof	Moon
Racquet	Criminal
Sun	Alcohol
Race	Tennis
Dice	Evidence
Court	Ball
Russian	Spots
Moonshine	Speed
Cheetah	Roulette
Detective	Bear

(Answers to P1 (a) on page 267)

PALINDROMES

A palindrome is a word or phrase which reads the same backwards as forwards, such as 'madam', 'radar' and 'draw, o'coward'. Longer sequences are usually nonsensical, but there are exceptions. For example: 'Doc, note, I dissent, a fast never prevents a fatness, I diet on cod'.

One-word palindromes

Here are some common one-word palindromes: aga, bib, ere, gag, pep, deed, noon, toot, civic, kayak, refer, tenet, redder, rotator.

The claim for the longest one-word palindrome is 'detartrated', although there is some dispute whether or not this is an actual word. Tartrate is a salt of tartaric acid and tartrated is in the form of tartrate. Therefore, if the tartrate were removed, then there would be an argument in favour of it being 'detartrated', and we are inclined to give the word the benefit of the doubt.

Several words become palindromes when pluralised, for example SEX – SEXES, SHAH – SHAHS.

The longest palindrome in *Webster's Third Dictionary* is KINNIKIN-NIK, and the longest internal palindrome is (SENSUOUSNES)S.

Palindromic phrases

The earliest known palindrome was by John Taylor in 1614: 'Lewd did I live & evil I did dwel'. Another from history is 'Able was I ere I saw Elba', which is attributed to Napoleon.

Several more examples worthy of note are:

Tell a plateman on a morose dam-side by me to note my bed is made so Roman on a metal pallet.

Some men interpret nine memos.

No it's a bar of gold a bad log for a bastion.

Star comedy by Democrats.

Sex at noon taxes.

Sex at my gym taxes.

Pamela's Ale Map.

In a regal age ran I.

Are we not drawn onwards we jews, drawn onward to new era.

Ten animals I slam in a net.

If I had a hi-fi.

Dennis and Edna sinned.

Sit on a potato pan, Otis.

Notable palindromes

There is also an ancient Roman palindrome which is popular with lawyers: 'Si nummi immunis' (If you pay you will go free). Also of interest, is a forthcoming palindromic triennium in the years 1998, 1999, 2000 which, in Roman numerals are MIIM, MIM, MM; this will be the last time that palindromic years, Roman or Arabic, will occur consecutively.

One of the world's greatest experts in palindromic construction was an Englishman, Leigh Mercer (1893-1977), a word-play expert who, when he joined the National Puzzlers' League (see page 176) in 1952, took as his pseudonym Roger G. M'Gregor. Perhaps his most famous palindrome is: 'A man, a plan, a canal: Panama,' which honours George W. Goethals, chief engineer of the Panama Canal. The *London Times* characterised Mercer as: 'A king-pin of the game called *palindromes,* and whenever you pick up an American book on the subject you're likely to see his name indexed.'

Here is just a small selection from Leigh Mercer's collection of palindromes which were published in *Notes and Queries* between 1946 and 1953.

'Rats gnash teeth,' sang star.

Now Ned I am a maiden won.

In airy Sahara's level, Sarah a Syrian I.

Ban campus motto, 'Bottoms up, MacNab.'

'Reviled did I live,' said I, 'as evil I did deliver.'

'Tis Ivan, on a visit.

'Not New York,' Roy went on.

Won't lovers revolt now?

Never a foot too far, even.

'Not for Cecil?' asks Alice Crofton.

Pull a bat, I hit a ball up.

Tennis set won now Tess in net.

Draw pupil's lip upward.

Anne, I stay a day at Sienna.

Nurse, I spy gypsies run.

Niagara, O roar again.

Remit Rome cargo to Grace Mortimer.

Another game is the creation of antonym palindromes: words with opposite meanings appearing on opposite sides in reverse word order, for example:

Good men do women bad.

Fire! Fire! bring Water! Water!

Everybody, remember to forget nobody.

There are also many spin-off puzzles based on anagrams. The example in (a) was presented by Andrew Morton in the August 1986 *Enigmasig*.

▼ ▼ ▼ YOU PLAY ▼ ▼ ▼

(a)   **PALINDROMES**

Can you rewrite this sentence with the inclusion of seven 5-letter palindromes?

> One drop more and the citizen's authority will hand over the lady to be set adrift in a boat on the smooth sea until she disappears from the electronic screen.

(Answers to P2 (a) on page 267)

Foreign language palindromes

Also worthy of inclusion here are these foreign language palindromes.

Allar Munum ralla.
(We shall have a wild time.) – *Icelandic*

Ebro e Otel ma Amleto e orbe.
(Othello is drunk, but Hamlet is blind.) – *Italian*

Indul a pap aludni.
(The person is going to sleep.) – *Hungarian*

Et la marine va, papa, venir a Malte.
(And the navy, daddy, is going to come to Malte.) – *French*

Ein neger mit gazelle zagt im regen nie.
(A negro with a gazelle never falters in the rain.) – *German*

===================== P3 =====================

PANGRAMS

A pangram is a sentence that contains every letter of the alphabet, for example, the typists' test sentence: 'The quick brown fox jumps over the lazy dog'. Examples of well-known pangrams are:

Pack my box with five dozen liquor jugs.

Jackdaws love my big sphinx of quartz.

Quick waxy bugs jump the frozen veldt.

Jinxed KGB spy with qualms covers fez.

Foxy nymphs grab quick-jived waltz.

The five boxing wizards jump quickly.

The ultimate pangrams have just 26 letters, that is, every letter of the alphabet once each only; but such is a very rare phenomenon. The compiling of such a perfect pangram is a challenge well known to wordsmiths who have recently even enlisted the help of computers in their search. So far, only examples using very obscure words, proper names or abbreviations have been produced and include words such as cwm (a Welsh valley), kvutza (an Israeli settlement), jynx (a species of wryneck bird), qoph (a Hebrew letter) and crwth (a Welsh musical instrument).

In French, the shortest known pangram is: 'Whisky vert: jugez cinq fox d'aplomb', which has three duplications.

Panagram puzzles

The following is a selection of puzzles based on pangrams.

CROSS ALPHABET

The authors have compiled several hundred of these grids, in which all of the 26 letters of the alphabet have to be used, once each only, to form a crossword.

PANGRAM WORDS

You may like to try (a).

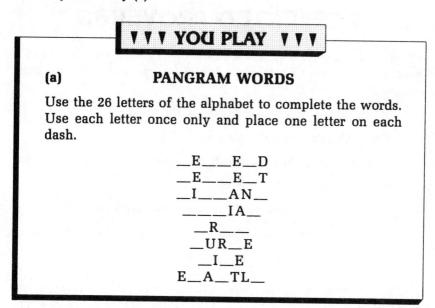

▼ ▼ ▼ YOU PLAY ▼ ▼ ▼

(a)   **PANGRAM WORDS**

Use the 26 letters of the alphabet to complete the words. Use each letter once only and place one letter on each dash.

_E___E_D
_E___E_T
_I___AN_
____IA_
_R___
_UR_E
_I_E
E_A_TL_

26-LETTER CROSSWORD

In *Enigmasig*, in 1985, we asked if it was possible to produce the ultimate 26-letter crossword using each letter once only in a 26-square grid. Member, Graham Ellis, succeeded – using a system of words running in different directions. Try his puzzle, in (b).

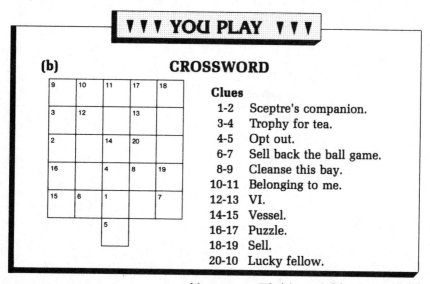

▼ ▼ ▼ YOU PLAY ▼ ▼ ▼

(b)   **CROSSWORD**

Clues

1-2	Sceptre's companion.
3-4	Trophy for tea.
4-5	Opt out.
6-7	Sell back the ball game.
8-9	Cleanse this bay.
10-11	Belonging to me.
12-13	VI.
14-15	Vessel.
16-17	Puzzle.
18-19	Sell.
20-10	Lucky fellow.

(Answers to P3 (a) and (b) on page 267)

PERVERTED PROVERBS

The idea of this game is to take a well-known proverb and alter it in the most amusing way. *Foulsham's Fun Book of 1933* contains these examples:

A hair on the head is worth two on the brush.

Where there's a frill, there's a fray.

To play cards is heavenly, to cheat divine.

While there's life, there's soap.

You never know what you can do without until you try.

A stitch in time saves a blush.

A friend in need is an awful nuisance.

In October 1993, the *Mensa Journal* ran a competition to complete the proverb: 'If at first you don't succeed, . . .' in the most amusing way. The following suggestions were submitted:

> . . . Delegate
>
> . . . Rephrase the motion
>
> . . . Become a legendary failure
>
> . . . Deny you were trying
>
> . . . Fudge
>
> . . . Try when sober
>
> . . . Revise the definition of success
>
> . . . Give up
>
> . . . Cheat

PROFESSIONAL DRUNKARDS

This game is to find ways in which various professions get inebriated. As examples:

BUILDERS	get	plastered
WAITERS	get	tipsy
SOLDIERS	get	tanked up
COOKS	get	stewed
MECHANICS	get	well oiled
DEMOLITION MEN	get	smashed
SAILORS	get	wrecked
PYSCHIATRIC DOCTORS	get	out of their heads
MUSICIANS	get	Brahms and Liszt
BOXERS	get	sloshed
TIN WORKERS	get	canned
BAKERS	get	pie-eyed
OPTICIANS	get	blind
STATIONERS	get	blotto
MATHEMATICIANS	have one over the eight	

PRINTERS' MISTAKES

This game is suggested in *Foulsham's Fun Book of 1933*.

Cut from a news article in a daily paper, an interesting paragraph of about fifteen lines. Then jumble up the lines and have the result copied, so that each player has a copy. Note that the words of a line are not, themselves, jumbled. The puzzle is to arrange the lines in their correct order. The first to write out the whole passage, as given in the newspaper, is the winner of the game.

For example, try (a).

▼▼▼ YOU PLAY ▼▼▼

(a)   **PRINTERS' MISTAKES**

be laid out by the amateur, whether
In fact, the way is here pointed out
the space at his disposal is large and
would have the satisfaction, after
which are given side by side throughout.
photogravure plates on numerous
This little volume is illustrated with
sunny or cramped or badly shaded.
diagrams. With its help gardens can
recognition, and the householder
Latin as well as more common names,
Leicester could be transformed beyond
whereby those unlovely backs in
alpine and rockery plants by their
close study, of being able to talk of his

(Answer to P6 (a) on page 268)

PSEUDODROMES

These are similar to Palindromes, but use words instead of letters. Here are two well-known examples.

You can cage a swallow, can't you, but you can't swallow a cage can you?

Girl, bathing on Bikini, eyeing boy, finds boy eyeing bikini on bathing girl.

PUNCTUATION

The use of punctuation has led to the creation of several classic puzzles. For example, try punctuating this:

Time flies I cant theyre too fast

At first glance it is just a simple matter of adding a few apostrophes, but it isn't quite so easy. The answer, in fact, is:

'Time flies.' 'I can't. They're too fast.'

Anyone solving that one has applied a bit of lateral thinking and put out of his or her mind the cliché 'time flies'. Instead of regarding time as the noun and flies as the verb, 'time' is used as the verb and 'flies' as the noun; and suddenly it all makes sense.

Now, try the examples in (a):

▼▼▼ YOU PLAY ▼▼▼

(a) PUNCTUATION

Every lady in the land has twenty nails upon each hand five and twenty on hands and feet all this is true without deceit

That that is is that that is not is not also that that is not is that that is nor is that that is that that is not

John where James had had had had had had had had had had the teachers approval.

Finally (b) gives a very famous old puzzle that you may like to try.

▼ ▼ ▼ **YOU PLAY** ▼ ▼ ▼

(b)   **PUNCTUATION**

An arab came to the river-side,
With a donkey bearing an obelisk.
But he did not venture to ford the tide.
For he had too good an *

* What is missing here?

(Answers to P8 (a) and (b) on page 268)

P9

PUNS

Puns are a play on words which have been described as both the lowest and highest form of wit. They follow Heisenberg's Uncertainty Principle: No one can be certain whether a pun will succeed until it is spoken. Only then is the punster either greeted with admiration and laughter, or derided as an idiot by stony silence.

We have included many variations on the theme of 'puns' in separate sections of this book; for example, in knock-knock jokes, Tom Swifties, feghoots and Spoonerisms.

In his book *Get thee to a Punnery*, Richard Lederer classifies most puns as homographic, homophonic or double sound. Examples of these are:

Homographic: The butcher backed into a meat grinder and got a little behind in his work.

Homophonic: 'My wife's gone to the West Indies.'
'Jamaica?'
'No, she went of her own accord.'

Double sound: The Brontë sisters engaged in scribbling rivalry.

In the title song of the film *Road to Morocco*, Hope and Crosby deliver a classic pun: 'Like *Webster's Dictionary*, I'm Morocco bound.' Other examples are:

The porpoises had settled down in their tents when the dinner gong was rung. Chow time for all in tents and porpoises!

The butcher was arranging his meat on the stall and didn't know where to put his 'Moose Steaks'. So he placed them under 'Mooselaneous'.

Parisian chefs obtain their rabbits from the hutch back of Notre Dame!

This is a famous pun from the poet, Thomas Hood:

They went and told the sexton, and
The sexton toll'd the bell.

As Lewis Carroll said in *The Hunting of the Snark*:

The third is its slowness in taking a jest,
Should you happen to venture on one,
It will sigh like a thing that is deeply distressed:
And it always looks grave at a pun.

REBUSES

A rebus is the enigmatic representation in visual form of the sounds of a name or word. Rebus is a Latin word meaning 'by things', indicating a coded text which can be deciphered by studying its visual display.

The types of rebuses illustrated in the diagram first became popular in the mid to late 1970s with various combinations of letter arrangements to suggest words or sayings. The answers to those illustrated are: 'Looking backward over the years', and 'The Andes'.

GNIKOOL 1978 1977 1976	THE & EEEEEE

1970s rebuses

More recently they have become popular features in newspapers and magazines and are the basis of the popular television quiz show *Catchphrase*.

Traditional rebuses such as that illustrated, use illustrations (Panda); whilst modern rebuses use letter arrangements as described above, further examples being DES/DES (despair) and 18U (I hate you).

A traditional rebus

Some rebuses have become part of everyday writing such as IOU (I owe you). Others are found in ancient means of communication such as hieroglyphics, ancient pictography, as in the early Minoan period in Crete, and modern pictography such as road signs.

Hieroglyphic rebus

Ancient pictograpy

Modern pictology

Rebuses were very much in vogue during the second half of the 19th century and many have been passed down to us from that time. Lewis Carroll compiled several and used them in letters to his friends. They seemed to go out of fashion during the middle part of the 20th century when they were seen only in children's books, but recently they have come very much back into fashion with more sophisticated types being invented and with the aid of computer graphics.

Some of the older rebuses, however, were very artistic and quite difficult to solve. Take, for instance, the rebus shown.

The answer is, in fact: 'Dishonesty ruins both fame and fortune'. It is fairly difficult to work out even when you know the solution:

(DISH)O(NEST)Y (RUINS) BOTH

F(HAM)E (HAND) FOR(4)(TUN)E

Perhaps the most difficult parts are the illustrated dish, the side of ham and the older word, tun, meaning large cask.

An older rebus

Now try the rebuses in (a), which were all drawn much more recently and appeared in *Enigmasig* in 1992.

Now try the examples in (b), which are modern rebuses and compiled by the authors between 1989 and 1993. Each answer is a well-known phrase or saying.

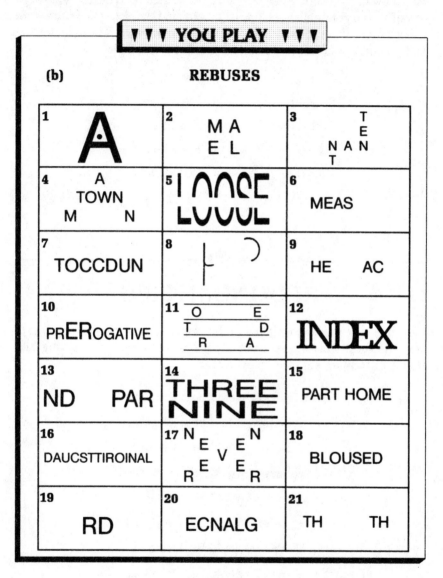

▼▼▼ YOU PLAY ▼▼▼

(b)   REBUSES

1 **A.**	2 M A E L	3 T E N A N T
4 A TOWN M N	5 I ∩∩CE L∪∪∪L	6 MEAS
7 TOCCDUN	8	9 HE AC
10 prERogative	11 O E / T D / R A	12 **INDEX**
13 ND PAR	14 **THREE NINE**	15 PART HOME
16 DAUCSTTIROINAL	17 N E E N E V E R E R	18 BLOUSED
19 RD	20 ECNALG	21 TH TH

(Answers to R1 (a) and (b) on page 268)

Qwaints

Readers may also be familiar with the 'qwaint', which is a type of rebus. In fact, nowadays, these would actually be termed as rebuses. The word 'qwaint' is an old English spelling of 'quaint' and the idea is to write a word in such a way that the meaning of the word is reinforced. The main feature of a qwaint is that only one word is used. For example:

JOY<	=	Joyless
XQQQ	=	Excuse
NNNNICK	=	Forensic
RE——— · · — ·	=	Remorse
.ICALLY	=	Periodically

=R2=

REDUNDANCIES

This is a very appropriate game in the current recession. The object is to find the most suitable word for a particular tradesman in giving him notice of termination of employment.

Train driver	would be	Derailed
Solicitor	would be	Debriefed
Sailor	would be	Debunked
Car salesman	would be	Declutched
Songwriter	would be	Decomposed
Tailor	would be	Decreased
Dictator	would be	Deduced
Tennis professional	would be	Defaulted
Office worker	would be	Defiled
Mannequin	would be	Defrocked
Electrician	would be	Defused
Butcher	would be	Delivered

Waiter	would be	Deserved
Politician	would be	Devoted
Steeplejack	would be	Descaled
Valet	would be	Depressed
Seamstress	would be	Depleted
Psychologist	would be	Detested
Fisherman	would be	Debated
Wine merchant	would be	Deported
Model	would be	Deposed
Heating engineer	would be	Deducted
Banker	would be	Denoted
Cyclist	would be	Detoured
Chiropodist	would be	Defeated
Jazz musician	would be	Defunct
Marriage Guidance Councillor	would be	Departed

The following might be the reactions of certain professions at being given the bad news:

A Steeplejack would feel brought down to earth

An Electrician would be shocked

A Car salesman would feel written off

A Sailor would feel all at sea

A Surgeon would be cut up about it

A Dentist would be gobsmacked

A Night Club bouncer would be put out

A Tiler would be floored

and A Psychiatrist would go mad.

RHOPALICS

In rhopalic verse, each word increases by one syllable, or each line contains words of one syllable, then two syllables, then three, etc.

In prose rhopalics, each word has one letter more than the preceding word. Here is an example compiled by the authors:

I do not like chefs making chopped kangaroo fricassee, masticable, unfailingly, disgustingly proteinaceous.

RHYMING PAIRS

These are otherwise known as 'nickel pickles', the idea being to invent rhyming descriptions of everyday objects. It is a very amusing game and almost unlimited.

What do you call:

a five cent gherkin	– a nickel pickle
a hobo in the rain	– a damp tramp
a very large Japanese	– a monumental oriental
a concerned fish	– a caring herring
a priest on a trampoline	– a gymnastic ecclesiastic
a spewing volcano	– a spouting mountain
an offbeat simian	– a funky monkey

Now try (a). All the answers to these clues are rhyming pairs of words.

▼▼▼ YOU PLAY ▼▼▼

(a) **RHYMING PAIRS**

Restrict lovemaking	Centre violin
Labyrinth mania	Cookhouse fungus
Fast deception	Chubby idiot
Humble European	Revoke alliance

(Answers to R4 (a) on page 269)

RIDDLES

The riddle does not exist,
If a question can be framed at all, it is also possible to answer it.

Ludwig Wittgenstein

A riddle is a linguistic guessing game, where a statement or verse is made with the intention of mystifying or misleading. Riddles are often in traditional form. In ancient Greece they had a serious purpose, and were used by judges and oracles to test a person's wisdom.

In biblical times, legend has it that two kings, Solomon and Hiram, took part in riddle contests for sums of money by each inventing riddles that the other could not solve. Concerning Solomon, it is reputed that the Queen of Sheba 'journeyed forth to meet him to prove him with hard questions' (1 *Kings* 10:1).

Here, now, is a selection of riddles for you to try your hand at.

William Cowper (1731-1800) was a British poet whose works include *Olney Hymns* (with John Newton in 1779); *John Gilpin's Ride* (1783); and *The Task* (1785). He was mentally unstable throughout his life and frequently attempted suicide. The riddle in (a) was compiled by him in July 1780.

▼▼▼ YOU PLAY ▼▼▼

(a)   **RIDDLE**

I am just two and two. I am warm. I am cold.
And the parent of numbers that cannot be told.
I am lawful, unlawful, a duty, a fault.
I am often sold dear, good for nothing when bought;
An extraordinary boon, and a matter of course,
And yielded with pleasure when taken by force.

William Bellamy was a composer of riddles who lived around the turn of the century in Dorchester, Massachusetts. His riddles are typically Victorian, full of puns and double meanings. He introduced an unusual element into his puzzles by not supplying an answer as such, but by providing a key by which the solver could check his solution and try again if it were incorrect. The authors had, therefore, to work out the answer to the following riddle themselves. The riddle and the key are given in (b) for you to try.

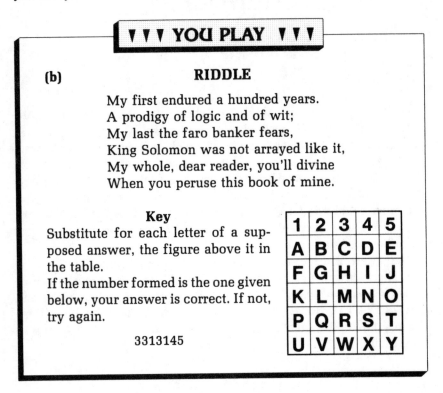

▼ ▼ ▼ YOU PLAY ▼ ▼ ▼

(b)   **RIDDLE**

My first endured a hundred years.
A prodigy of logic and of wit;
My last the faro banker fears,
King Solomon was not arrayed like it,
My whole, dear reader, you'll divine
When you peruse this book of mine.

Key

Substitute for each letter of a supposed answer, the figure above it in the table.
If the number formed is the one given below, your answer is correct. If not, try again.

3313145

1	2	3	4	5
A	B	C	D	E
F	G	H	I	J
K	L	M	N	O
P	Q	R	S	T
U	V	W	X	Y

Just to prove the authors like keeping things in the family, we present the riddle in (c) which was compiled by Barbara Carter in 1990.

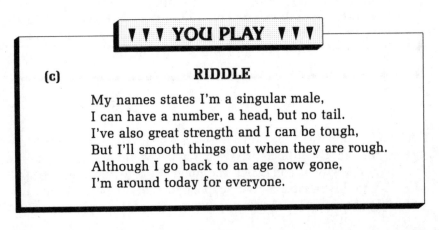

▼ ▼ ▼ YOU PLAY ▼ ▼ ▼

(c)   **RIDDLE**

My names states I'm a singular male,
I can have a number, a head, but no tail.
I've also great strength and I can be tough,
But I'll smooth things out when they are rough.
Although I go back to an age now gone,
I'm around today for everyone.

Charles James Fox (1749-1806) was a British Whig politician, who became Britain's first Foreign Secretary in 1782. He compiled several riddles including this one, (d).

▼▼▼ YOU PLAY ▼▼▼

(d)   **RIDDLE**

You eat me, you drink me, describe me who can,
For I'm sometimes a woman, and sometimes a man.

(Answers to R5 (a) to (d) on page 269)

AND ON THE INVOICE WE CALL
THIS ONE A 'TWIN-FLANGED,
SELF-SEATING, TAPPET HEAD
REGULATOR.'

SCRABBLE

Scrabble was invented in the 1930s by Alfred Butts, but not marketed until 1948. As most of you will be familiar with the game, it is the most famous of its type, and several books have been written on the subject, we shall not describe how it is played. Suffice it to say that it is mainly for two players, each having 7 tiles at the start. These are placed on the board to make words of 2 or more letters, which must connect with other words on the board, crossword style. Points are assigned based upon how many letters are used, with higher points for the rarer letters and, with certain squares in the grid more valuable than others, the double and triple squares.

The game has its own national championships and there is even a world championship.

There are a number of spin-off games and puzzles based on the game of *Scrabble*, three of which we shall describe.

(a)   **MAXIMUM SCORE**

Use all of these 25 letters to make five 5-letter words to score 200 or more in the boxes provided. The value of each letter is shown in brackets.

A (1)	G (2)	K (5)	O (1)	U (1)
A (1)	H (4)	L (1)	P (3)	X (8)
E (1)	I (1)	M (3)	Q (10)	Y (4)
E (1)	I (1)	M (3)	R (1)	Y (4)
E (1)	J (8)	O (1)	T (1)	Z (10)

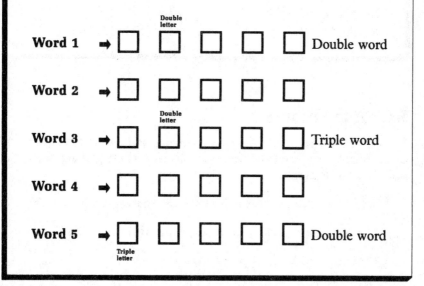

Double letter

Word 1 ➡ ☐ ☐ ☐ ☐ ☐ Double word

Word 2 ➡ ☐ ☐ ☐ ☐ ☐

Double letter

Word 3 ➡ ☐ ☐ ☐ ☐ ☐ Triple word

Word 4 ➡ ☐ ☐ ☐ ☐ ☐

Word 5 ➡ ☐ ☐ ☐ ☐ ☐ Double word

Triple letter

Radio Scrabble

This game was played on Saturday evenings on Great Yorkshire Radio and was won several times by one of the authors. The presenter, Peter Baker, drew out 10 tiles at random and listeners had to phone in with the largest word they could find. The first with the largest word possible won the prize on offer.

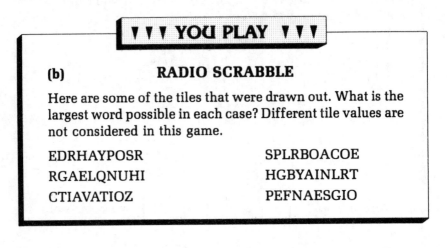

▼▼▼ YOU PLAY ▼▼▼

(b)   **RADIO SCRABBLE**

Here are some of the tiles that were drawn out. What is the largest word possible in each case? Different tile values are not considered in this game.

EDRHAYPOSR   SPLRBOACOE

RGAELQNUHI   HGBYAINLRT

CTIAVATIOZ   PEFNAESGIO

Scrabble Quotes

The idea of this game is to devise an amusing and appropriate quotation which might have been spoken by a celebrity whilst playing a game of *Scrabble*. For example:

Wild Bill Hickok: 'Let's draw to see who goes first.'

Michelangelo: 'I can't make anything with these tiles.'

King Edward VIII: 'I pass my turn.'

Groucho Marx: 'I wouldn't play in any *Scrabble* tournament agreeing to have me as an adjudicator.'

Jack Benny: 'All I get is Is, Os and Us.'

George Burns: 'I used to play *Scrabble* with Gracie. It was the only way I could get a word in edgeways.'

James Cagney (left with FBIFBIQ at the end of the game): 'You dirty rack!'

(Answers to S1 (a) and (b) on page 269)

SHOP NAMES

Appropriate shop names, apart from being an ingenious form of word play, can also be good for business since they attract people's attention. Here are some typical examples:

The Fryer Tuck-In	– A fish and chip shop in the Kirklees district of West Yorkshire, appropriately near to the reputed burial place of Robin Hood.
The Merchant of Venice	– On a store at Venice, California.
Yreka Bakery	– A famous palindromic name given to a bakery in Yreka, California.
Dukes of York	– A clothes shop in York, West Yorkshire.
The Strapped Jock	– At an athletics store in Tacoma, USA.
Hill and Dale	– Camping equipment suppliers, Huddersfield, West Yorkshire.

Also of interest are clever shop signs, such as these.

A cheese store at Lake Stockton, USA, near to the dam, has: 'Best Cheese in the World by a Damsite.'

'Mustard's Last Stand' – On a hot-dog stand.

'The Wizard of Ooze' – A septic-tank cleaning company.

On a car repair yard in America – 'U smash 'em, I fix 'em.'
'You holler, I haul 'er.'

The manager of a music store in Iowa City always hangs this note on the door when he closes for lunch: 'Back at 1.00, Offenbach at 1.30.'

SIDE BY SIDE

This game can be played by two or more players. One player flips open a dictionary and reads out two definitions of words that are adjacent in the dictionary. The other players must attempt to state what the two words are.

The following examples are taken from the *Cassell Concise English Dictionary*.

(i) To blotch.
(ii) A shorty pithy sentence.

Answer: mottle, motto

Now try the examples in (a), which are much more difficult.

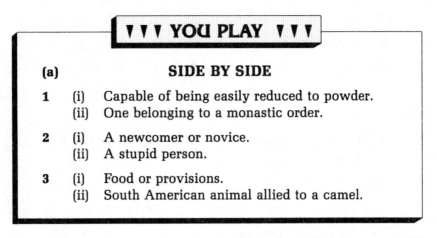

▼▼▼ YOU PLAY ▼▼▼

(a) **SIDE BY SIDE**

1 (i) Capable of being easily reduced to powder.
  (ii) One belonging to a monastic order.

2 (i) A newcomer or novice.
  (ii) A stupid person.

3 (i) Food or provisions.
  (ii) South American animal allied to a camel.

(Answers to S3 (a) on page 269)

SLANG

Slang is regarded as words or language used colloquially, but not regarded as correct English. Many different areas or groups have their own individual slang terms which are difficult to understand by outsiders and which often have their origins deep in folklore. For example, did you know that:

Alan Smithee is a fictitious director's name in TV credits.

George Spelvin or Harry Selby is a fictitious character on a playbill.

73 = best regards, and 95 = urgent message, in wire-service jargon.

A Marie Antoinette is a headless corpse in police jargon.

A rooster booster is a chicken-pox shot.

A Brandy Andy is a wine steward.

Modern slang

The language of the current teen generation reads like a foreign language to the 'crinkly crumblies' (anyone over 25). Expressions include: boyfs (boyfriends); babelicious (gorgeous); barfworthy (disgusting); dweeb (awkward male); hunktastic (a super-looking man); majorly (very, as in majorly irritating); and wibble (to quake at the knees when smitten).

The language of the businessman can be equally confusing, especially where 'buzzwords' abound. He may start to confide in you that his centrist philosophy is eroding as business declines, then leave your head spinning with talk of zero-sums, stagflation, golden handshakes, non-profit sectors, flex-time, followship (the opposite of leadership), profit centres, Fortress Europe, market mix, the corporate ladder, pro-active, competitive edge, cascade it, hands-on, the bottom-line, adverse possession and scenario.

Restaurant menus also lead to some creative language. Consider these:

Adam and Eve on a raft – Two eggs on toast.

Angels on horseback – Oysters rolled in bacon and served on toast.

Fry two, let the sun shine – Fry two eggs with the yolks unbroken.

Mama on the raft – Marmalade on toast.

One from the Alps – Swiss cheese sandwich.

Paint a bow-wow red – Hot dog with ketchup.

Throw it in the mud – Add chocolate syrup.

American slang

In America, slang is prevalent with certain groups. Take, for example, baseball lingo:

Cozy roller – A slowly batted ball.

Molly Putz – A player who performs badly.

Ukelele batter – A batter who hits weak balls to the infield.

Short leg – A player who lets his team-mates field balls that he should go after.

American carnival slang is equally colourful:

Break the ice   – To make the first money of the day.

Call them in   – To get people to play the game.

Deuce   – A twenty-dollar bill.

Gaff   – A rig in a game, or the rigged game itself.

Hollywood   – A fashionable or slick dresser.

Pink robber   – A game for small children.

Slough   – To disassemble the carnival.

Wrang   – A fight.

Yard   – A hundred dollars.

SPACE FILLER

Choose a word and write it down vertically, then reverse it and write this, also down vertically, spaced well to the right of the original, as here:

C	D
A	I
N	D
D	N
I	A
D	C

Now fill in the spaces to make six words using the first and last letters placed. One point is scored for each letter in the word thus formed. For example:

C	LAPPERBOAR	D	(scores 12 points)
A	LVEOL	I	(scores 7 points)
N	URSERYMAI	D	(scores 11 points)
D	ETERMINATIO	N	(scores 13 points)
I	GUAN	A	(scores 6 points)
D	IAMETRI	C	(scores 9 points)

The total score in this example is 58 points.

THE GREATEST PUZZLE OF THEM ALL

SPELLING BEES

Originating in America in the 1870s, Spelling Bees were competitions in which participants had to spell difficult words.

Spelling Bee is also the name of a cleverly designed word-trick puzzle.

Using the diagram shown, invite someone to choose one of the eight flowers, but not to reveal his choice. Now ask him to spell out the chosen word silently, saying one letter each time you tap a circle with your pencil. When he reaches the last letter of the chosen word, he stops you immediately, and finds that your pencil is on the flower of his choice.

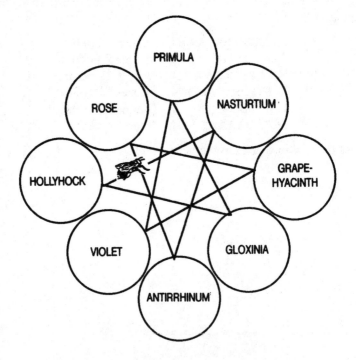

Spelling bee puzzle diagram

The secret of this trick is that you always make sure your first tap is on the word 'Hollyhock'. Then follow the bee's path as shown by the lines and you will always finish on the correct flower. You must make sure, however, that you follow the correct path after leaving Hollyhock, that is, to Nasturtium, to Antirrhinum, etc. If you travel from Hollyhock to Gloxinia, to Primula, etc., then it will not work.

SPHINX WINKS

'Sphinx Winks' was a monthly column compiled by Mitzi Christiansen Kuehl in *Integra*, the journal of the American based High-IQ Society, Intertel, from 1981 to 1986. Mitzi is a retired teacher who lives in Bakersfield, California, and she and husband Bill are great word play enthusiasts. Her column was a great delight and explored many items of word play which we have covered in this book including oxymorons, cryptograms, Spoonerisms, acrostics, tautology, rebuses and mnemonics.

It is a great pity that the column did not reach a wider audience, but the issues of *Integra* in which they appeared are a valued part of the library of one of the authors. Several examples of Mitzi Kuehl's work are reproduced in this book, with her blessing.

Intertel has around 2000 members worldwide. The qualifying level is a score in a supervised IQ test which puts the applicant in the top one per cent of the population. Anyone interested in receiving details should write to:

> Lourie Bell Davis,
> PO Box 1083,
> Tulsa,
> OK 74101
> USA

SPOONERISMS

The Spoonerism is a worm of ford play. Vincent Price on a radio mystery show once intoned, 'Do you mean to tell me you're going to kill us all in one swell foop?' – and yet another Spoonerism was born.

Some psychologists believe that Spoonerisms shed light on the way the brain processes information prior to articulation, but being psychologists they would say that, or something like it, wouldn't they?

William Archibald Spooner (1844–1930), Anglican clergyman, Dean (1876–89) and Warden (1903–24) of New College, Oxford, was an albino who suffered from weak eyesight. The story goes that after turning on a light in order to escort a guest down a dark stairway, he extinguished the light and accompanied his guest in the dark. He thus committed Spoonerisms in deed as well as word. Some of his originals are:

> 'I remember your name perfectly, but I just can't think of your face.'
>
> 'We all know what it is to have a half-warmed fish in our bosoms.'
>
> 'Yes, indeed, the Lord is a shoving leopard.'
>
> 'For real enjoyment give me a well-boiled icicle.'
>
> 'I know only two lines – "God save the weasel" and "Pop goes the Queen".'
>
> 'Let us drink to the queer old Dean.'
>
> 'I have just received a blushing crow.'
>
> 'We shall now sing Kinquering Kongs their Titles Take.'

The following may be a Spooner original, but this is doubtful:

> 'Sir, you have deliberately tasted two whole worms; you have hissed all my mystery lectures and have been caught fighting a liar in the quad; you will leave Oxford by the next town drain.'

Deliberate Spoonerisms are greatly treasured by punsters. For example, 'Boyfoot Bear' and 'Time wounds all heels'.

Several Spoonerism competitions have been run, including a Mary Ann Madden *New York Magazine* competition in which the following was received from a reader, Marjorie Friedman:

Poor Susan, you're really undone,
You tell me that now you've begun,
   To think that the sister,
   Is hiding your mister?
There's nothing, Sue, under the nun!

=S9=

SPORTMANTEAUX

The object of this game is to change the ending of a town, state or country and so describe the citizens.

Vernon D. Maclaren, of Augusta, Georgia, has devised these. They are for fun only, and no offence is intended.

Antwerps	Belfasteroids
Baltimorons	Buffellows
Bermutants	Spartisans
Lebananas	Waterloonies
Woodstockings	

And here are few more devised by the authors:

Georgiants	Wisconsinners
Alabamammies	Fort Worthies
Clevelandlubbers	Dallassies

=S10=

SYNONYM CHAINS

Synonym chains were invented by Dmitri Borgmann in 1967. They are based on Lewis Carroll's doublets, but whole words are changed, instead of letters, using synonyms.

For example, Dmitri Borgmann changed BLACK into WHITE using synonyms, as follows:

BLACK – DARK – OBSCURE – HIDDEN – CONCEALED
– SNUG – COMFORTABLE – EASY – SIMPLE – PURE
– WHITE

SYZYGIES

On 12 December 1879, Lewis Carroll wrote in his diary: 'Invented a new way of working one word into another. I think of calling the puzzle "Syzygies".'

The syzygy is in fact a development of, and more complicated version of, doublets. As with doublets, the idea is to change one word into another; but instead of changing one letter only at each link, the solver may change a series of adjacent letters.

This example was proposed by Carroll: Change CONSERVATIVE to LIBERAL. We shall, in 1995, resist the temptation to answer 'hold a bye-election'!

Carroll's solution is:

```
C O N S E R V A T I V E
   ( S E R V A T I )
R E S E R V A T I O N S
         ( A T I O N )
D E L I B E R A T I O N
   ( L I B E R A )
   L I B E R A L
```

The game never won the popular and lasting appeal of doublets and was, in fact, rejected by *Vanity Fair* who had, earlier, welcomed the doublet puzzle. However, the puzzles were eventually published in *The Lady* on 30 July 1891. This is one of the puzzles:

Make BULLETS out of LEAD:

```
          L E A D
        ( L E A )
          P L E A
        ( P L E )
      S A M P L E
        ( S A M )
    J E T S A M
        ( E T S )
B U L L E T S
```

Now try the two examples in (a).

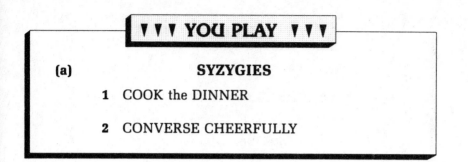

(a)   **SYZYGIES**

   1 COOK the DINNER

   2 CONVERSE CHEERFULLY

The shared letters constitute the 'syzygy' or 'yoke', the whole set is a 'chain' and the intermediate words are 'links'.

Several rules were laid down and a complicated scoring system. We do not propose to go into this since we believe it complicates the puzzle to such an extent that it detracts from its appeal. Perhaps the complicated mathematical mind of Carroll had overspilled into what should have been a fairly simple word game.

Variation of the game

This is an even more simple variation of the game, devised by the authors. Start with a word, then change to another word in steps, each new word having some letters in common with the previous word, until the required end word is reached.

Example: Change from PAINT-BOX to IRON-GREY in five steps.

                    PAINT-BOX

1 Containing material   . . . .

2 Boring insect   . . . .

3 Voided mass of earth   . . . .

4 Iron melted into moulds   . . . .

5   IRON-GREY

Answer: PAINT-BOX, BOXWOOD, WOOD-WORM, WORM-CAST, CAST-IRON, IRON-GREY.

Now try the example in (b).

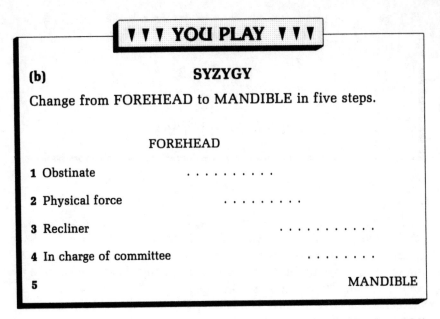

(Answers to S11 (a) and (b) on page 270)

Incidentally, the word 'syzygy' actually means the conjunction or opposition of any two of the heavenly bodies, especially of a planet with the Sun and, in biology, a conjunction or union.

TARGET

This is a word game, also called Words within words, which has been featured in the *Daily Express* for many years. The object is to find as many words as possible made up from any of the nine letters in the grid, used once only, for any word. Each word must contain the central letter, and one word must consist of all nine letters. Try the example in (a).

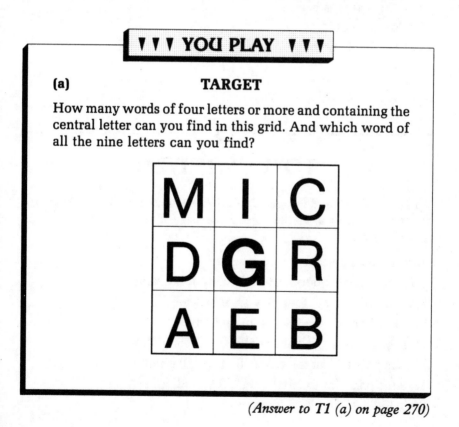

▼▼▼ YOU PLAY ▼▼▼

(a)   **TARGET**

How many words of four letters or more and containing the central letter can you find in this grid. And which word of all the nine letters can you find?

M	I	C
D	G	R
A	E	B

(Answer to T1 (a) on page 270)

TAUTOLOGY

Tautology is the repetition of an idea by needless or emphatic use of words as in 'Reverse backwards and do a U-turn to face the other way.'

The game is to try and spot such examples. A few that we have collected are:

Narcissus fell in love his own reflected image in a pool.
Hollow tubes
Full quart
Irregardless
Real meaning
True facts
We heard some terrible horror stories.
The rescue team was searching for living survivors.
In my opinion, I think ...
The reason is because ...
Revert back
Absolutely nothing

TOM SWIFTIES

This is another punning game. It was first suggested in a book by Edward Stratemeyer and was all the rage 25 years ago. The idea is to make a pun on an adverb:

'Turn on the light,' Tom said, brightly.

'L-L-Look before your l-l-leap,' Tom said, hesitatingly.

'I've got the cramp,' Tom said, spasmodically.

'My shorts are on the line,' Tom said, briefly.

'I'll help you into the railway carriage,' Tom said, tenderly.

'I'm sorry that I lost the fight,' Tom said, bashfully.

'Take the plane up to 30 000 feet,' Tom said, loftily.

'I'm on a diet,' Tom said, fatuously.

'I can run a mile in five minutes,' Tom said, fitfully.

'I've given this project up for dead,' Tom said, gravely.

'Not guilty, my lud,' Tom said, defensively.

'Ouch! I've cut myself,' Tom said, sharply.

There are also adjectival swifties:

'Straighten out this room at once,' Tom hollered, upset.

And verbal swifties:

'Oil made me rich,' Tom gushed.

'The water's all turned on,' Tom piped up.

And preposition swifties:

'I'll be darned,' Tom laughed, in stitches.

'He's guilty,' Tom said, with conviction.

=== T4 ===

TONGUE TWISTERS

This is one of the few word games that relates purely to the spoken medium. There are many examples which will be familiar, such as:

The Leith police dismisseth us.

The sixth sheik's sixth sheep's sick.

She sells sea shells on the sea-shore.

One game, which is good fun, is to make up a phrase of your own and your opponent has to repeat this six times without making a mistake. Here are some suggestions:

Sister Susie's sewing shirts for sixty-six sick seamen.

Ken Dodd's dad's dog's dead.

They threw three thousand free thistles this Thursday.

Freddy freely fried freshly fleshy frozen fish.

Sixty-six thick things and sixty-six thin things.

The witch switched the switch that the Ipswich witch had switched.

TRANSDELETIONS

In transdeletions, one letter is deleted from a word and the remaining letters are rearranged to form a new word. This process is continued until only one letter is left. The opposite of this is called word building. Here are some examples of transdeletions.

Ashamed, mashed, shame, hams, has, as, a

Braised, rabies, raise, rise, sir, is, I

Steamed, teased, sated, teas, sat, at, a

Blister, tilers, stile, tile, lit, it, I

A variation of transdeletions is to delete, in turn, each letter of a word and to transpose the remainder. The maximum length of word for which this appears possible is nine letters. There are several of these:

MALINGERERS: aligners, minglers, smearing, manglers, gremials, marlines, marlings, measling, malinger.

RETINULAS: alunites, lunarist, lunaries, neutrals, uralites, latrines, urinates, insulter, tenurial.

IDOLATERS: delators, soterial, dilaters, asteroid, stolider, soredial, dilators, diastole, tailored.

All the words can be found in *Chambers Twentieth Century Dictionary*. Now try (a).

▼ ▼ ▼ YOU PLAY ▼ ▼ ▼

(a)   **TRANSDELETIONS**

Can you find another example of nine letters, where all the words can be found in *Chambers* and, in fact, are rather more familiar words?

(*Answers to T5 (a) on page 270*)

TRIGRAMS

A trigram is similar to a bigram except that, instead of a run of two consecutive letters in a word, it is any run of three consecutive letters. Try the examples in (a).

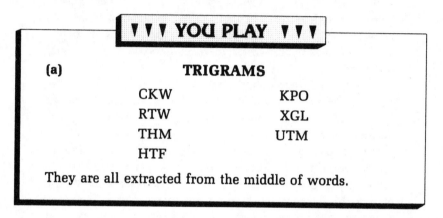

▼▼▼ YOU PLAY ▼▼▼

(a)   TRIGRAMS

CKW	KPO
RTW	XGL
THM	UTM
HTF	

They are all extracted from the middle of words.

(Answers to T6 (a) on page 270)

TRIPLE (PLUS) CHOICE

There are several popular games based on triple choice. One is the game *Call My Bluff* which has appeared on television both in America and Britain. This was devised by Americans, Mark Goodson and Bill Todman. The game is played by two teams of three, and each team takes a turn in devising amusing definitions for an obscure word. Two of the definitions are always false and the opposing team has, then, to try to identify the other, true, definition.

Enriching your word power

An extension of the game has, for many years, appeared in *The Readers' Digest* under the heading *It Pays to Enrich Your Word Power*. *The Readers' Digest* is the longest selling publication in the world, with 28 million copies in 16 languages each month. The compiler, Peter Funk, has provided us with a fascinating insight into how the feature originally came about. Peter Funk writes:

'In 1942, may father, Wilfred Funk, published a book titled *30 Days to a More Powerful Vocabulary*. The book in its own way was a pioneering effort, for he was virtually the first person to stress that increasing your vocabulary could be an enjoyable experience.

'As a writer, poet and lexicographer, my father carried on a love affair with words. They astonished and intrigued him and he was able to convey this enthusiasm to millions of people. The book was a best seller then, and today it is still sold and read.

'In 1945, he approached DeWitt Wallace, founder of *The Readers' Digest*, with an idea for a vocabulary development feature. Mr Wallace immediately saw the possibilities and decided to try it.

'The first few tests listed only 10 words. There was no answer page, for the answers were in one of the alternative choices. The games became an immediate success and by the end of the year the 10 words were increased to 20 with a separate page giving answers, an illustration for usage, and the origins.

'In 1960 my father became quite ill. I also am a writer and a trained lexical semanticist and I wrote the feature *sub rosa* until his death in 1965. It was a great experience for me, for I had the pleasure of being so closely associated with my father in the work we both enjoyed so much. It's not often that a son has such a privilege.

'Upon his death I notified my father's editor that I'd been doing the feature for several years. He talked to Mr Wallace and I was asked to attend a meeting with the editor-in-chief, managing editor, Mr Wallace and four or five other leading members. The question put before me was: "Just what are your qualifications?" I gave my background and we talked for several hours. Having just been through a most debilitating illness I'm afraid I did not look very robust and wondered what the decision would be.

I received a letter from Mr Wallace stating that he knew of no reason why I should not continue. I was delighted. The feature was continuing to grow in popularity and it gave me what I call "the largest classroom in the world". Over the years I've received a myriad of letters telling me how the feature has helped the correspondents to pass entrance examinations to schools as well as being a help in their professional work.

'I'm continually amazed and heartened by the millions of people that show such interest in their language. It's a joy. If you read the various issues, you will see that the chosen words are always based on a different theme.'

The examples in (a), which he has kindly provided for inclusion in this book, are typical of Peter Funk's work.

▼▼▼ **YOU PLAY** ▼▼▼

(a)   **ENRICH YOUR WORD POWER**

Just as a propeller drives a ship ahead, the 'fy' ending on a word impels it forward. 'Fy' comes from the Latin *facere* (to make). Choose the correct meaning in each case.

1 **certify** – A: to verify. B: claim. C: issue a licence. D: list.

2 **vilify** – A: to shame. B: to slander. C: confront. D: lie.

3 **amplify** – A: to satisfy. B: round off. C: increase. D: prolong.

4 **quantify** – A: to measure. B: empower. C: excuse oneself. D: add to.

5 **sanctify** – A: to consecrate. B: become quiet. C: be in seclusion. D: grow in religious fervour.

6 **stultify** – A: to be stubborn. B: make ineffective. C: harden. D: shrink to unusable size.

7 **codify** – A: to translate. B: make firm. C: systematise. D: explain.

8 **transmogrify** (trans MOG rih fy) – A: to transform. B: be in a hypnotic sleep. C: disintegrate. D: be in distress.

9 **reify** (REE ih fy) – A: to make louder. B: reinforce continually. C: treat an abstract as a tangible. D: become more elegant.

10 **gentrify** – A: to impoverish. B: farm as a hobby. C: upgrade. D: be excessively polite.

(Answers to T7 (a) on page 271)

233

TWISTED TRUISMS

The idea is to take a well-known trite saying and change it to give it a 'sting in the tail'. Here are some examples.

If you can keep your head when all about you are losing theirs, then you don't fully understand the problem!

If you cast your bread upon the waters, it will return soggy.

To go to bed late and get up early, makes a man cross, mean and surly.

If things appear to be getting better, then you have probably overlooked something.

If at first you don't succeed, then find someone who knows what he is doing.

All work and no play means that you make money hand over fist.

The difficult is easy and the impossible is a little bit harder.

The only person who got everything done by Friday was Robinson Crusoe.

If you see the light at the end of a tunnel, it may be an oncoming train.

If it were not for the last minute rush, nothing would ever get done.

UNIVOCALICS

A univocalic is any written work which includes only one of the five vowels. The earliest works date back several thousand years and were very popular with the Greek poets. The 19th century Spanish and French playwrights also used univocalics.

The opening couplet from a 16-line poem by C. C. Brombaugh, written in 1890, illustrates the nature of the task.

> No monk too good to rob, or cog, or plot,
> No fool so gross to bolt Scotch collops hot . . .

The puzzle in (a), compiled by the authors, uses univocalics in the answers and is a popular type often found in puzzle books and magazines.

(a)   **UNIVOCALICS**

Each horizontal and vertical line contains the consonants of a word, not necessarily in order. The word can be completed by adding a number of 'E' vowels. The number 33 at the end of each line indicates that each word you are looking for has 3 consonants and 3 'E' vowels.

Each letter in the grid may be used only once and all letters must be used.

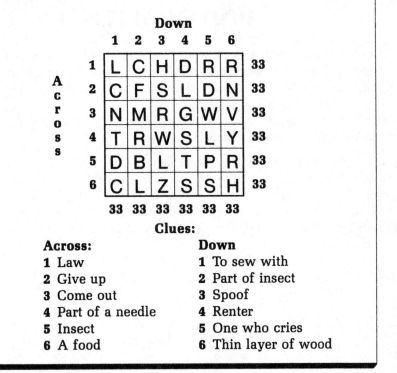

Down

	1	2	3	4	5	6	
1	L	C	H	D	R	R	33
2	C	F	S	L	D	N	33
3	N	M	R	G	W	V	33
4	T	R	W	S	L	Y	33
5	D	B	L	T	P	R	33
6	C	L	Z	S	S	H	33

Across

33 33 33 33 33 33

Clues:

Across:
1 Law
2 Give up
3 Come out
4 Part of a needle
5 Insect
6 A food

Down
1 To sew with
2 Part of insect
3 Spoof
4 Renter
5 One who cries
6 Thin layer of wood

(Answers to U1 (a) on page 272)

VOWELS

The use of vowels leads to several forms of word play and word searches. Here are some examples.

Word play

According to *Webster's Third New International Dictionary* (1961):

> The shortest word which uses each vowel once is SEQUOIA. (And, counting Y as a vowel, FACETIOUSLY.)
>
> The shortest word with all vowels in order is CAESIOUS.
>
> The longest word with all vowels in order is ABSTEMIOUSLY.
>
> The longest two-vowel word is LATCHSPRINGS.
>
> The longest word using only vowels is EAU.

Despite this, *Enigmasig* members have found even shorter words using all five vowels, namely MIAOUE, a variant spelling of MIAOW, and, perhaps the ultimate in vowel words, IOUEA, a cretaceous fossil sponge genus, which was unearthed from *The Encyclopedia of Paleontology* by Dr Susan Thorpe in 1993.

Sequences

There are several sequences of letters in which all the five vowels, A, E, I, O, U, can be inserted in turn to form words. For example:

> BALL, BELL, BILL, BOLL, BULL
> PACK, PECK, PICK, POCK, PUCK
> LAST, LEST, LIST, LOST, LUST
> MASS, MESS, MISS, MOSS, MUSS
> BAND, BEND, BIND, BOND, BUND
> RACK, RECK, RICK, ROCK, RUCK

The challenge, however, is to find the longest sequence of letters where this is possible. This is believed to be two 7-letter word sequences as follows:

BLANDER, BLENDER, BLINDER, BLONDER, BLUNDER
PATTING, PETTING, PITTING, POTTING, PUTTING

Now see if you can find the words in (a).

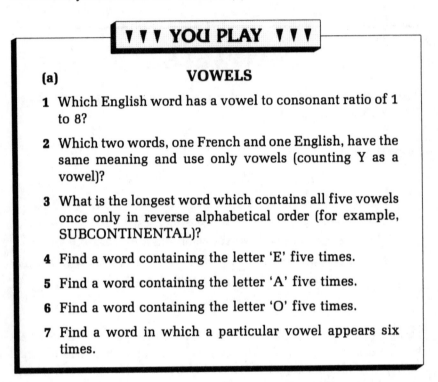

▼ ▼ ▼ YOU PLAY ▼ ▼ ▼

(a)   **VOWELS**

1 Which English word has a vowel to consonant ratio of 1 to 8?

2 Which two words, one French and one English, have the same meaning and use only vowels (counting Y as a vowel)?

3 What is the longest word which contains all five vowels once only in reverse alphabetical order (for example, SUBCONTINENTAL)?

4 Find a word containing the letter 'E' five times.

5 Find a word containing the letter 'A' five times.

6 Find a word containing the letter 'O' five times.

7 Find a word in which a particular vowel appears six times.

The puzzle in (b) was devised by the authors and is actually a 'Y' vowel puzzle and excludes the five recognised vowels A, E, I, O and U.

(b)   **'Y' VOWELS**

Find 22 words of three letters or more. Words can be found in any direction, reading forwards or backwards, but only in a straight line. Letters may be used more than once.

L	T	R	Y	S	T	P	L
Y	Y	Y	H	R	R	Y	M
Y	L	M	S	Y	N	X	P
T	Y	P	P	C	F	R	Y
P	H	R	H	H	X	S	G
Y	S	C	D	N	T	P	M
R	G	L	Y	P	H	Y	Y
C	F	L	Y	L	Y	L	S

(Answers to V1 (a) and (b) on page 272)

THE MOST PROFITABLE WORDGAME

WORD CHAIN

This is a game for two players in which the first player selects two words which have a connection and which have the same number of letters. The aim is to get from the first word to the second word in the fewest steps.

The second player takes the last two letters of the first word and they must form the first two letters of the next word. This continues until the last word is reached.

As an example: PURPLE to ORANGE. This can be achieved in three links, thus: PURPLE – LEAPER – ERODED – EDITOR – ORANGE.

Word circle

The authors have invented this puzzle, on similar lines. Several examples have been included in their publications, and (a) is typical.

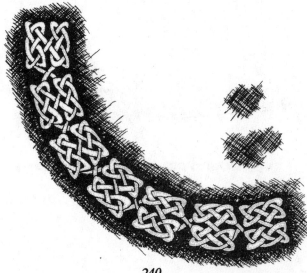

▼ ▼ ▼ YOU PLAY ▼ ▼ ▼

(a)   **WORD CIRCLE**

Complete these eight words, so that two letters are common
to each word. That is, the two letters that end the first word
also start the second word, and the two letters that end the
second word also start the third word, etc. The two letters
that end the eighth word are also the first two letters of the
first word, completing the circle.

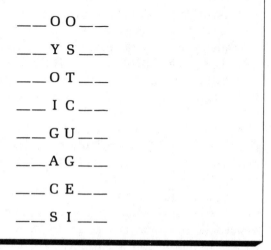

```
__ O O __ __

__ Y S __ __

__ O T __ __

__ I C __ __

__ G U __ __

__ A G __ __

__ C E __ __

__ S I __ __
```

(Answers to W1 (a) on page 272)

WORD CURIOSITIES

6 **3** Although the number on the right seems larger, that on the left is actually twice as big.

This is a clever play on words that cannot be disputed and there are many more types of word play and word curiosities which you can unearth should you have the time and patience.

The best-selling author of science fiction, the late Isaac Asimov, once posed a similarly clever question in a Mensa publication. 'What word in the English language changes its pronunciation when it is capitalised?' We won't keep you guessing on that one; try 'polish'.

Another trick question is based on calculator words. For example, if GEESE, EGG and BIBLE make LIBEL, what am I? If you don't understand that question, try punching in the numbers 35336 + 663 + 37818 = 73817 on your calculator, and then looking at each number upside-down.

Once you start getting into such aspects of word play the possibilities are almost endless. Can you find, for instance, a word which is a plural of a word which is also a plural? Try OPERAS, the plural of OPERA which is, in turn, the plural of OPUS.

Or what about roller coaster words? These are words in which, after the first letter, each successive letter alternates between going 'down' in the alphabet (in the direction of A) and up in the alphabet (in the direction of Z). An example of a 14-letter roller coaster word is MILITARISATION, found by David Morice of Iowa in 1989 *Word Ways*. Other roller coaster words are SYSTEMISATION (13 letters) and PROVINCIALISATION (17 letters).

Another curiosity involves suffixes, many of which convert masculine nouns to female, such as HOST – HOSTESS and HERO – HEROINE. But is there a suffix which works in reverse and coverts a feminine noun to masculine? Try WIDOW – WIDOWER, to solve that particular teaser.

And what are Contronyms? Well, these are words that are actually homonyms which have directly contrary meanings. The best example is RAISED / RAZED, but there is also a transatlantic contronym, CLINKER, which in Britain means 'something first rate' and in American slang, 'an utter failure'.

There is also the BEST/WORST curiosity, two words which are synonyms when used as verbs but antonyms when used as adjectives, adverbs or nouns. Another unusual feature is words that consist of two antonyms. Take, for example, the words NOOK (NO–OK) and NOYES (NO–YES). We know of no others, but you may be more successful if you search.

And, there is the feature of words with no repeated letters. The longest we know are UNCOPYRIGHTABLE and DERMATOGLYPHICS. We also know of three 13-letter English villages with no repeated letters: BUSLINGTHORPE, BUCKFASTLEIGH and RUMBOLTSWHYKE.

Record breakers

The English language to us is a bottomless treasure chest and it is possible to go on, seemingly endlessly, uncovering more curiosities, and topping those already discovered. The following is a list of various record breakers, all uncovered by Chris Cole for *Word Ways* in May 1990 and sourced from *Webster's Third International Dictionary* (1961) and *A Supplement to Webster's Third International Dictionary* (1986). We would be interested to hear from any of our readers who can top any of these.

- Longest non-trivial charade (words within words): IN-DISC-RIM-IN-A-TI-ON (16 letters, 7 words) or IN-DISC-RIM-IN-AT-IONS (17 letters, 6 words).

- Most consecutive double-letters: BOOKKEEPER (4, if SUB-BOOKKEEPER allowed).

- Most repeated letters in a word: POSSESSIONLESSNESSES.

- Longest pair isogram: SCINTILLESCENT (2 × S, 2 × C, 2 × I, 2 × N, 2 × T, 2 × L, 2 × E).

- Longest polygram (all letters repeated): UNPROSPEROUSNESSES.

- Longest alternating vowel consonant word: SUPEREROGATORILY (counting Y as a vowel).

- Longest word with one consonant: ASSESSES.

- Longest word with horizontal symmetry letters: CHECKBOOK.

- Longest charitable word (subtract a letter anywhere): PLEATS (LEATS, PEATS, PLATS, PLEAS, PLEAT).

- Longest hospitable word (insert a letter anywhere): CARES (SCARES, CHARES, CADRES, CARIES, CARETS, CARESS).

- Shortest isolano (no substitution possible): ECRU.

There are, of course, many more examples. We hope that those we have given have whetted your appetite for this type of word play.

WORD MATCH

This game is for two or more players and starts with any word selected at random. The first player uses the end of the chosen word to start another word. For example, if the word 'DECREE' were chosen, he could select the word 'edit' for one point, 'eerie' for two points, 'reed' for three points or 'creed' for four points.

The next player must now use the last letters of the new word selected to form a word of his own. For example, if the word selected were 'eerie' he could select the word 'riesling' for three points.

Players take turns to form words in this manner and the first to reach an agreed total is the winner.

WORD SCORE

The object of this challenge is, by allocating each letter of the alphabet a score: $A = 1, B = 2$, etc., down to $Z = 26$, to find the highest scoring words for 4-, 5-, 6-, 7-, 8-letter words, etc. Examples are:

5-letters:	WHIZZ	= 23, 8, 9, 26, 26	= 92 points
6-letters:	SYZYGY	= 19, 25, 26, 25, 7, 25	= 127 points
7-letters:	PIZZAZZ	= 16, 9, 26, 26, 1, 26, 26	= 130 points

A spin-off game, investigated by Dr Susan Thorpe after a suggestion by the authors in *Enigmasig*, was to find the longest and shortest words in the English language to total 100, using the same system. Dr Thorpe found several obscure words, including:

BATRACHOIDIDAE - A family of marine fishes.

BIDDUPHIACEAE - A large genus of rectangular diatoms abundant in marine plankton.

She also found, from *The Oxford English Dictionary*:

ADIABATICALLY - Pertaining to a condition where no heat leaves or enters a system.

HAEMOPHILIAC - A person with a tendency to bleeding.

The shortest words possible, totalling 100, were five letters long: BUZZY; NUTTY; PUSSY; STRUV (dialect: past tense of strive); STUTT (A form of stut; obsolete, to stutter or stumble); TOTTY (unsteady); TOUSY (dishevelled); TUTTS (plural of TUTT; alternative spelling of TUT); YOUST (obsolete form of joust; to join).

====================== **W5** ======================

WORD WAYS

Word Ways, The Journal of Recreational Linguistics, is a magazine published and edited by A. Ross Eckler and distributed to subscribers from his home in Morristown, New Jersey. The authors would recommend it as a publication not to be missed for anyone remotely interested in word play. It has been described as:

'A lively journal of recreational linguistics.' – Martin Gardner

and 'A merry magazine.' – Willard Espy

The authors have found it interesting, informative, amusing, relaxing, stimulating, rude, challenging, engrossing and often mind-blowing. Former editors have included the famous wordsmith, the late Dmitri A. Borgmann in 1968, and Howard W. Bergerson in 1969.

Word Ways is unlike any other magazine in the recreational linguistics field. In publication longer than any of its competitors, it has created a dedicated readership which renews its subscriptions year after year. The field of the magazine includes all aspects of word play. Words are examined as combinations of letters which can be manipulated in myriad ways. The sight and sound of language is looked at, foremost, with meaning as a secondary property. The magazine instructs, amuses, and sometimes frustrates. It may contain the results of serious research, but these results are always presented in a highly readable vein. Articles promote word study as pure enjoyment and it will certainly make you more alert to the curiosities and ambiguities of the language we use every day. Subjects covered include lipograms, palindromes, word squares and cubes, anagrams, pangrams and new types of word play not yet given names.

A. Ross Eckler once wrote to one of the authors to ask what type of word play might be of interest. 'Over 25 years,' he said, '*Word Ways* has published a vast amount of material and has introduced many newer topics of word play such as the eodermdrome (no matter how you place the letters E, O, D, R and M on a sheet of paper, you cannot trace out the spelling of 'eodermdrome' by drawing a pencilled line from one letter to the next, without somewhere crossing a previously-drawn part of the line). I think that *Word Ways* has published "surprising" and "unusual" material, but this is, of course, in the eye of the beholder. Are you interested in such real-life logology as the fact that Stanley Kimbrough of Chattanooga or Julie Schwarzkopf of Toledo are real people with 16-letter names with no repeats? Or that a nine-square has been found in which all the words can be found in a single dictionary? Or a 19 × 22 rectangle containing all 37 different US presidential surnames?' If ever there was a letter designed to whet the appetite, this was it and we found it irresistible.

Word Ways is published quarterly with 64 pages per issue. If you are interested, write to:

A. Ross Eckler,
Spring Valley Road,
Morristown,
New Jersey 07960,
USA

246

Z1

ZOETROPE

A zoetrope is an old-fashioned toy with a revolving cylinder which shows a series of pictures as if the subject were alive and moving, and it is this toy which is the inspiration for this game.

In the diagram on page 248, the letter 'A' on the inner wheel is set against the letter 'D' on the outer wheel. This means that the word 'FOB' on the inner circle produces the word 'IRE' on the outer circle. This is done by taking the letters F–O–B on the inner circle, then finding their corresponding letters, I–R–E, in the same order on the outer circle. You may, now, like to try (a).

▼ ▼ ▼ YOU PLAY ▼ ▼ ▼

(a)   **ZOETROPE**

The game is simply that, by setting the 'A' on the inner wheel against any desired letter on the outer wheel, it is possible to find 3-letter, 4-letter and in almost all cases, 5-letter, words.

There are, therefore, $25 \times 3 = 75$ separate puzzles for you to solve. Proper nouns are allowed.

When you have exhausted your searches you can check with the list in the Answers on page 273. Of course, you may have found other words, besides.

You will see that four solutions (all 5-letter words) have eluded the originators of the zoetrope puzzle.

Longer words

You may also wish to search for words of 6 letters or more. These are possible; however, a full search has not yet been undertaken. Examples of these (all setting 'A' on the inner wheel against the letter listed on the outer wheel) are:

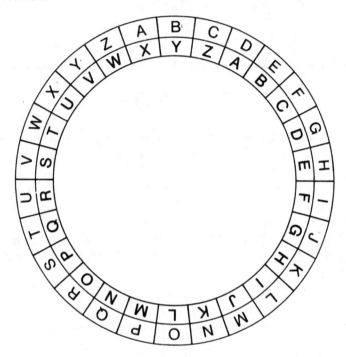

6-letter words

B outer:	STEEDS – TUFFET
E outer:	LALLAN – PEPPER
G outer:	FUSION – LAYOUT
H outer:	MANFUL – THUMBS
K outer:	MUU-MUU – WEE-WEE

7-letter words

N outer:	PURPURA – CHECHEN
	and ABJURER – NOWHERE
D outer:	PRIMERO – SULPHUR

8-letter words

G outer:	WILIWILI – COROCORO

ANSWERS

ANSWERS

A1 Abbreviations

(a)

13 Months in a Lunar Year
60 Nautical Miles in a Degree of Latitude
5 Events in the Modern Pentathlon
3600 Seconds in an Hour
39 Steps of John Buchan
60 Years for a Diamond Jubilee
2 Atoms of Hydrogen in a Water Molecule

(b)

The Quality Of Mercy Is Not Strained *(Portia)*
My Little Chickadee *(W. C. Fields)*
Not Tonight Josephine *(Napoleon Bonaparte)*
Elementary My Dear Watson *(Sherlock Holmes)*

(c)

Birds Of A Feather Flock Together
Curiosity Killed The Cat
To Flog A Dead Horse
To Roar Like A Bull

(d)

The Taj Mahal at Agra in India
The Wailing Wall in Jerusalem
Stonehenge on Salisbury Plain
Table Mountain in Cape Town

(e)

The Trojan War
Magna Carta Sealed by King John
Sir Francis Drake Sailed Round the World
George Washington Became First President of the United States
Invasion of Russia by Napoleon

(f)

page/pages = p/pp

A2 Acronyms

(a)

It sounds like the punctuation of GP.

(b)

He reversed his initials GR, i.e. RG, which is a homophone of Hergé.

(c)

A suggested answer is:

> Keen
> Necessary
> Implement
> For
> Eating

(d)

Double employed with kids; dual income no kids; disillusioned relatively ordinary professionals; downwardly mobile middle-aged professionals; formerly radical upwardly-mobile professionals; grown-up mature professionals; middle-aged affluent folk; frequenters of malls; middle-aged urban professionals; those who went to prep schools; poor urban professionals; school kids with incomes; two income couples with kids; well-off over-50 persons; well-off older people; young urban failures.

(e)

BASIC:	Beginners All-Purpose Symbolic Instruction Code
ERNIE:	Electronic Random Number Indicator Equipment
PIN:	Personal Identification Number
RADA:	Royal Academy of Dramatic Art
RAM:	Random Access Memory
VAT:	Value Added Tax

A3 Acrostics

(a)

> M   inut   E
> E xclamatio N
> N   avigat   E
> T   ea   R
> A   spirin   G
> L   ibert   Y

(b)

> A do R in G
> M usk E tee R
> B an D ag E
> E con O mis E
> R eite R atio N

(c)

The question is actually the answer. The first letters of the acrostic spell 'WHAT'.

(d)

Like as the waves towards the pebbled shore,
So do our minutes hasten to their end.

W. Shakespeare

1 With, 2 Sweeten, 3 Hour, 4 Abbots, 5 Kith, 6 Esteem, 7 Shoot, 8 Paviors, 9 Endless, 10 Add, 11 Round, 12 Ethereal

A5 Alphametics

(a)	2147	(b)	423) 8037 (19	(c)	102263	(d)	4027
	2147		423		983703		4027
	418		———		120341		5057
	———		3807		———		797275
	4712		3807		1206307		———
	———		———				810386
			————				

A7 Anagrams

(a)

The theme is vessels: Gondola (dog, loan); Galleon (lean, log); Cruiser (cure, sir); Steamer (stare, me); Coaster (cat, sore); Tanker (ark, ten); Frigate (fit, rage).

(b)

Rot – Corrode; Novel – Original; Due – Payable; Skip – Gambol

(c)

Enthral; Breathless; Recreant; Glucose; Radiant

(d)

Vibraphone

(e)

The Adventures of Sherlock Holmes; Agatha Christie's Poirot; Father Dowling Investigates; A Man Called Ironside

(f)

Alerts
Laster
Estral
Resalt
Talers
Staler

(g)

Fragmentary

A8 Australian Crossword Club

(a)

The Shakespearian play is Romeo and Juliet; the hero's friend is Mercutio. (Note that: MELINITE, No. 15 can be entered in two ways. MURIFORM, No. 19 can be entered in two ways. ARMOURED, No. 17 can be entered in two ways.)

B2 Bigrams

(a)

Hippopotamus; Remember; Balalaika; Convivial; Entities; Asinine; Banana; Prototype

B4 Boggles

(a)

jay, magpie, cormorant, cuckoo, robin, oriole, mallard, linnet, lapwing, wren, partridge, redwing, lark, sparrow, dove, reeve, swan, parrot, rook, roc, lanner, tercel, ka, sora, gannet, gowk, loon, rail, reedling, ringtail, serin, cob

(b)
CHIVALROUS

C1 Carrollian Word Play

(a)
LIAM (the reverse of MAIL)

C2 Categories

(a)
Peace, Physics, Chemistry (Nobel Prizes)
Amity, Harmony, Concord (Peace)
Shackleton, Harrier, Comet (Aircraft)
Astronomy, Star, Planet (Astronomy)

C5 Charades

(a)
Breakfast

C6 Chronograms

(a)
42 = Exploitation (XLII), 59 = Helix (LIX), 62 = Luxuriation (LXII), 52 = Liaison (LII), 97 = Excavationist (XCVII). (There are alternative answers.)

(b)
Substitute letters for the Roman numerals. Thus the words become LYNX, CEDAR, ELAND, CAMEL, LLAMA and BULL. Cedar is a tree, whereas all the others are animals.

(c)
Two thousand nine hundred and forty - MMCMXL

C8 Collective Nouns

(a)
coven (of witches); hover (of crows); rafter (of turkeys); rake (of colts); span (of mules); sloth (of bears); building (of rooks); covey (of partridge); rout (of wolves); charm (of finches); down (of sheep); fall (of woodcock); gang (of elk); husk (of hares); gam (of whales); earth (of foxes); nide (of pheasant); wisp (of snipe); blush (of boys); kennel (of dogs); drift (of wild pigs); clamour (of rooks); glean (of herrings); hover (of crows); cry (of hounds); observance (of hermits); rayful (of knaves); troop (of foxes).

C9 Colourful Language

(a)
Where there's smoke there's fire.
(b)
A bird in the hand is worth two in the bush.

(c)

A rolling stone gathers no moss.

(d)

Don't put off until tomorrow what you can do today.

(e)

A stitch in time saves nine.

(f)

Early to bed, early to rise, makes a man healthy, wealthy and wise.

(g)

Look before you leap.

(h)

Through a piece of music – character = clef; wooden strip = stave; several apartments = flats; whimsical fancies = crochets; array of glossary = notes; tremble = quaver; keen edges = sharps; siestas = rests; places of refreshment = bars.

C13 Conundrums

(a)

His son's photograph.

C15 The Crossword Club

18 CT GOLD

(a)
Puzzle by 'Pidghins'
The hidden phrase is 'Blood ran down the stairs' from W. H. Auden's poem *Victor*. VI-CT.-OR suggests 6 carat gold; with the instruction 'add an extra dozen carats' gives 18 CARAT GOLD.

Across:
Redundant words (in *italics*).
1 H + SIP + SAW, rev; *(ale)*
6 MA(J)OR + IS; *(Dutch)*
12 Three mngs; *(dealer)*
13 T(R)O - OP; *(attend)*
16 anag; *(number)*
17 RAN(CE) + DAN; (elder)
18 DAG in Bone; *(xenophobe)*
19 C(U)R in SEED; *(tough)*
21 R + IN + SE(A); *(recruit)*
22 anag; *(arch)*
23 PAW + (MA)N'S; *(destitute)*
25 'T + USK; *(oyster)*
27 PAVI(D) + N *(Zulu)*
29 anag; *(Espresso)*
30 MAN rev + EAST anag; *(never)*
31 (A)LE + S + SEE; *(cold)*
33 RAPER in DIES; *(almost)*
36 A + FIRE; *(rousing)*
37 anag L, GOES, NO I + M(ajor);
  (absent)
38 GALE + NA; *(traders)*
39 T in SAYERS; *(swearing)*

Down:
1 anag
2 anag
3 RED rev under PLOD
4 Two mngs
5 HE(R)N
7 NOM rev in A DISH
8 (B)OFF
9 RA's + TAS(H)
10 KEEP'ER in STREETS
11 R in BEACH
14 A + ROC rev + N
15 URGE(NT)
18 BOW(L) + NE
20 S(L)IPE rev + E(A)MON
24 hidden
25 TEST + FLY (fly = flee, run = flee)
26 SNEE + R + S
27 R in PAD
28 MAT in (K)AOL(IN)
31 A in LES + T
32 SA(P) + ICE
34 IRIS(H)
35 (R)ULE

C16 Crosswords

(a)
Across: 2 Man, 4 Begot, 6 Paraded, 8 Hare, 9 Elan, 11 Role, 12 Lies, 14 Beta, 15 Reed, 16 Deck, 18 Side, 19 Leaf, 21 Apes, 22 Sleeves, 24 Elbow, 25 Low
Down: 1 Saga, 2 Mere, 3 Node, 4 Bare, 5 Tell, 6 Palaces, 7 Dairies, 8 Hotel, 10 Needs, 11 Red, 13 See, 17 Kale, 18 Spew, 20 Fell, 21 Avow, 23 Ebon

(b)

¹L	²I	³S	⁴P	⁵S		⁶H	⁷A	⁸R	⁹P	¹⁰P	¹¹S	¹²T
¹³A	N	T	L	E	R		¹⁴C	O	A	T	E	E
¹⁵S	L	O	O	P		¹⁶S	H	O	W	E	R	S
¹⁷T	E	N	T	A	¹⁸C	L	E	D		¹⁹R	E	T
²⁰S	T	Y		²¹R	O	A	D		²²M	A	N	E
	S		²³L	A	D	Y		²⁴C	A	T	E	R
²⁵C		²⁶D	O	T	E		²⁷S	A	T	E		S
²⁸A	²⁹S	I	D	E		³⁰F	I	V	E		³¹D	
³²R	A	V	E		³³T	I	R	O		³⁴T	O	³⁵O
³⁶A	L	E		³⁷D	E	T	E	R	³⁸R	I	N	G
³⁹M	I	S	⁴⁰H	A	P	S		⁴¹T	E	N	O	R
⁴²E	N	T	I	R	E		⁴³M	E	A	G	R	E
⁴⁴L	E	S	S	E	E	S		⁴⁵D	R	E	S	S

(c)

Across: 1 Parole, 3 Bogus, 6 Charred, 9 Loose, 10 Nitro, 11 Prime, 12 Scars, 14 Steal, 19 Bench, 20 Romeo, 21 Evade, 22 Plotter, 23 Tongs, 24 Usurer
Down: 1 Pacino, 2 Largo, 3 Bullitt, 4 Glove, 5 Sleuth, 7 Attic, 8 Dupe, 13 Rangers, 15 Admit, 16 Covert, 17 Shop, 18 Horror, 19 Brain, 20 Roofs

C17 Crossword Variations

(a) Clueless crossword

(b) Hexagon

(c) Word Power

1 HONEYCOMB
2 TAXIMETER
3 PHRENETIC
4 NOVENNIAL
5 SEQUESTER
6 PROMINENT
7 TRIMESTER
8 MEDITATED
9 PELMANISM

(d) Target

GARDEN, GOSPEL, GUITAR, IMBRUE, ORRERY, OUTFIT, OODLES, KENNEL, KIDNAP, LEGUME, KIMONO, SALINE, PLENTY, SHEATH, SHIVER, POTATO

(e) Quotation Pyramid

```
        O
       H E
      B E T
     T E S T
    L I M I T
   P L I N T H
  A P P A R E L
 S H A R E O U T
```

(f) Directional crossword

¹C	⁵R	E	L	G	G	U	M	⁴S
¹⁰S	O	E	¹³P	I	R	¹²T	S	⁷C
H	N	N	V	E	N	E	O	I
I	¹⁷Y	E	D	E	N	U	¹⁵D	T
N	E	P	M	I	R	A	A	A
G	¹⁸W	E	S	A	M	S	¹⁴L	N
L	L	I	¹⁶G	E	T	E	A	U
¹¹E	O	⁸E	P	I	C	⁹S	N	⁶L
³N	E	M	S	E	D	A	R	²T

(g) No blanks

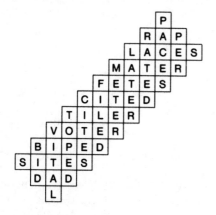

(h) Blank out crossword

P	E	R	M	I	T	■	O	R	A	N	G	E
E	■	A	R	R	I	V	A	L	■	■	■	N
A	■	A	R	I	A	■	E	N	I	T	■	G
R	E	D	■	S	P	E	N	T	■	E	R	A
L	A	Z	E	■	C	■	■	B	R	I	G	■
S	T	E	M	■	A	L	E	■	O	N	C	E
■	A	■	B	O	N	A	N	Z	A	■	K	■
A	B	L	E	■	D	I	D	■	R	E	E	D
B	L	U	R	■	■	R	■	D	A	T	E	■
L	E	T	■	C	A	S	T	E	■	R	Y	E
A	■	E	W	E	R	■	U	P	O	N	■	M
Z	■	E	R	U	P	T	E	D	■	■	■	E
E	S	T	E	E	M	■	S	E	E	D	E	D

(i) Niners

S	H	O	W	P	I	E	C	E
O	A	■	■	E	■	■	T	X
C	■	C	■	N	■	A	■	P
I	■	R	S	N	■	■	■	L
A	M	P	L	I	T	U	D	E
L	■	H	■	O	F	■	■	T
I	■	C	■	N	■	I	■	I
S	A	■	E	■	■	C	■	V
M	I	S	E	R	A	B	L	E

C18 Cryptic elimination

(a)

A Trappist monk, B Principal boy, C Drill sergeant, D Jury-rigged, E Basking shark, F Spoonbill, G Stonewall, H Freelance, I Roadrunner, J Snapdragon, K Red Admiral, L Filing cabinet

Odd word: Squash

C19 Cryptics

(a) London underground stations quiz

1 Victoria
2 Angel
3 Oval
4 Paddington
5 Waterloo
6 St Paul's
7 Parsons Green

8 Knightsbridge
9 Bond Street
10 Elephant and Castle
11 Covent Garden
12 Baker Street
13 Charing Cross
14 Burnt Oak

15 Piccadilly Circus
16 Bank
17 Chalk Farm
18 Fairlop
19 Kensington Olympia
20 Hampstead
21 Golders Green

22 Holland Park	31 Sloane Square	41 Cannon Street
23 Tower Hill	32 Notting Hill Gate	42 Marble Arch
24 Ladbroke Grove	33 Pimlico	43 Westminster
25 Barbican	34 Swiss Cottage	44 Earl's Court
26 Wood Green	35 Wimbledon	45 Whitechapel
27 Euston	36 Moorgate	46 Hammersmith
28 Bethnal Green	37 Clapham Common	47 Mansion House
29 King's Cross/	38 Temple	48 Green Park
St Pancras	39 Heathrow Central	49 Shepherd's Bush
30 Russell Square	40 Monument	50 Oxford Circus

C20 Cryptography

(a)

It is known to many that we need solitude to find ourselves. Perhaps it is not so well known that we need solitude to find our fellows. Even the Saviour is described as reaching mankind through the wilderness.

Havelock Ellis

Message, keyed (HIDEANSK): HIDE AND SEEK

(b)

Bates, if I choose, be in or about Hawkeye Creek at dark tomorrow. Wednesday evening, could you without inconvenience meet me and pass an hour or two with me. – A. Lincoln, Burnside, Falmouth, Virginia

D2 Devilry

(a)

1 charMED LARge	11 HoW A TERM ELONgated at Eton
2 reSULT AN Agent	12 shun PLAN TAINted
3 loansharK – I WIsh	13 Smith wailed miserabLY, 'CHEEr up the Left'
4 jUG 'LIar!'	14 seQUIN CEasing
5 sHIPped	15 ManaGUA VAndals
6 sHAWl – I'm	16 hipPO MEG RAN A TEa shop
7 airPUMP KINship	17 sailS HAD DOCKed
8 dRAM BUT A Nice	18 glasseS, LO Each
9 heM ANGOra	19 men, NECTAR IN Edelweiss
10 anyone's PA PAY A printer	20 Emmen talCUM QUATercentenary

D4 Doublets

(a)

Smith, smite, spite, spits, spats, seats, beats, beads, bends, bonds, bones, Jones

E1 Enigmagrams

(a)

Linnet, Parrot, Gannet, Thrush. Key anagram: Pheasant

E2 Enigmas

(a)
Cares; Caress

(b)
A fan

(c)
A pen

(d)
Today

E3 Enigmasig

(a)
hijacked, pasqueflowers, kleptomania, flamingo, flagship, deflating, monopoly, rostrum, brocade, abscond, spaceflight, squarest

(b)
Dell. (The 'short' letters – those without ascenders or descenders – spell maroon, cream and rose.)

G1 Gallopers

(a)
ANNOYING (Exasperating); LAG (Dawdle); LING (Heather); OBLONG (Rectangular); PRIG (Puritan); EVERLASTING (Imperishable); ROUSING (Stimulating); SPRING (Fountainhead)

H4 Heteronyms

(a)
1 Wind / Wind, 2 Support / Sup Port, 3 Atone / At One, 4 Tear / Tear, 5 Tome / To Me, 6 Minute / Minute, 7 Donate / Don Ate, 8 Gravestones /Gravest Ones

H5 Hidden Words

(a)
1 hell, 2 sever, 3 adored, 4 doyen, 5 loiter

(b)
Conan, Sian, Geoff, Tony, Leslie, Chris, Lou, Robin, Doug, Leo, Allan, Bill, Mark, Rex, Edmund, Alec, Duncan

(c)
Ramble and amble; Rain; Rule; Sated

(d)
Frangible, Fragile, Frail.

H6 Homonyms

(a)
1 Chile (chilli), 2 Beirut (bay route), 3 Madeira (mad era), 4 Amman (a man), 5 Taiwan (tie one)

K1 Kickself

(a)
Sherfield-on-Loddon. The others contain parts of the body: Witton-le-W(ear), Alderl(ey E)dge, W(arm)inster, Win(chest)er

(b)
ONE FAMILIAR WORD

(c)
All except a calender which is a machine used to smooth paper or cloth, etc. A calendar is a tabulation of days.

(d)
The missing square is 8. A message can be read across each horizontal line: READ THIS MESSAGE THEN CHOOSE NUMBER EIGHT.

K2 Knight's move

(a)
'The last thing one discovers in writing a book is what to put first.'

(Blaise Pascal)

7	32	19	42	9	30	21	X
18	X	8	31	20	41	10	29
33	6	43	50	X	54	39	22
44	17	X	53	40	49	28	11
5	34	45	48	51	38	23	X
16	X	52	X	46	25	12	27
35	4	47	14	37	2	X	24
X	15	36	3	X	13	26	1

L1 Labyrinths

(a)
PARLIAMENTARIAN

(b)
INDISCRIMINATE

L7 Logograms

(a)
TEMPERATE

(b)
AWESTRUCK

(c)
NEWSPAPER

L8 Logogriphs

(a)
Hustle / Sleuth

(b)
Tis / Sue / Tissue / Issue

(c)
Portable / Potable

(d)
Expansive / Expensive

(e)
Fluttering / Utter / Fling

M1 Magic word squares

(a)

P	U	N	C	H
P	U	N	C	H
P	U	N	C	H
P	U	N	C	H
P	U	N	C	H

(b)

P	A	L	A	T	E	D
A	N	E	M	O	N	E
L	E	V	A	N	T	S
A	M	A	S	S	E	S
T	O	N	S	U	R	E
E	N	T	E	R	E	R
D	E	S	S	E	R	T

(c)

S	C	A	R	F
C	A	T	E	R
A	T	O	N	E
R	E	N	T	S
F	R	E	S	H

(d)

W	A	T	E	R
A	W	A	R	E
T	A	L	O	N
E	R	O	D	E
R	E	N	E	W

(e)

G	I	V	E
I	D	E	A
V	E	E	R
E	A	R	L

(f)

1 H	A	R	S	H		6 M	A	N	S	E
2 A	B	A	T	E		7 A	G	A	I	N
3 R	A	P	I	D		8 N	A	K	E	D
4 S	T	I	N	G		9 S	I	E	V	E
5 H	E	D	G	E	11 A	G	L	10 E	N	D	E	D

12 A	S	I	A	N
13 G	I	A	N	T
14 L	A	N	C	E

16 S	T	O	R	15 E	N	T	E	21 R	O	A	S	T
17 T	U	D	O	R				22 O	R	D	E	R
18 O	D	O	U	R				23 A	D	O	R	E
19 R	O	U	G	E				24 S	E	R	V	E
20 E	R	R	E	D				25 T	R	E	E	S

M3 Manias

(a)

Alcohol	– Dipsomania	Flowers	– Anthomania
Bridges	– Gephyromania	Pleasure	– Hedonomania
Cats	– Ailuromania	Riches	– Plutomania
Dogs	– Cynomania	Talking	– Logomania
Eating	– Phagomania	Travelling	– Dromomania

M4 Mischmasch

(a)

Namby-pamby

Ill-fated

Ready-made

Jump-start

Rip-roaring

Eye-opener

Smooth-spoken

Dog-tired

Coach-built

House-warming

Tutti-frutti

Creeply-crawly

Weak-kneed

Empty-handed

Knee-deep

Right-minded

Zero-rated

Body-stocking

Double-barrelled

Three-dimensional

(You may have found other possible solutions.)

N5 Noughts and crosswords

(a)

1 Tunnel, Lengthened; 2 Nasty, Sandwich; 3 Entreat, Fortnight; 4 Gratis, Italy;
5 Riled, Lira; 6 Cross, Sorry; 7 Vote, Veto; 8 Mistletoe, Melts

N6 Nursery rhyme crosswords

(a)

O3 Oxymorons

(a)

Working holiday, minor miracle, never again, living death, strangely familiar, pretty ugly, non-dairy creamer, homeless shelter, night light, even odds, perfect idiot, ill heath

P1 Pair words

(a)

Russian	–	Bear	–	Cheetah
Cheetah	–	Speed	–	Race
Race	–	Ball	–	Racquet
Racquet	–	Tennis	–	Court
Court	–	Criminal	–	Detective
Detective	–	Evidence	–	Proof
Proof	–	Alcohol	–	Moonshine
Moonshine	–	Moon	–	Sun
Sun	–	Spots	–	Dice
Dice	–	Roulette	–	Russian

Solution A

Solution B

P2 Palindromes

(a)

One *minim* more and the *civic* authority will *refer* the *madam* to be set adrift in a *kayak* on the *level* sea until she disappears from the *radar* screen.

P3 Pangrams

(a)

Weekend, request, timpani, jovial, brag, furze, hide, exactly

(b)

P6 Printers' mistakes

(a)
This little volume is illustrated with
photogravure plates and numerous
diagrams. With its help gardens can
be laid out by the amateur, whether
the space at his disposal is large and
sunny or cramped or badly shaded.
In fact, the way is here pointed out
whereby those unlovely backs in
Leicester could be transformed beyond
recognition, and the householder
would have the satisfaction, after
close study, of being able to talk of his
alpine and rockery plants by their
Latin as well as more common names,
which are given side by side throughout.

P8 Punctuation

(a)
Every lady in the land has twenty nails; upon each hand, five; and twenty on
hands and feet; all this is true without deceit.

That that is, is. That that is not, is not. Also that that is not, is that that is. Nor is
that that is, that that is not.

John, where James had had had, had had had had. Had had had had the
teacher's approval.

or: John, where James had had had had, had had had. Had had had the
teacher's approval.

(b)
Ass to risk (asterisk).

R1 Rebuses

(a)
A place in the sun; The Iron Curtain; Great minds think alike.

(b)
1 In a spot, 2 A square meal, 3 Sitting tenant, 4 Man about town, 5 Breaking
loose, 6 Short measure, 7 Disorderly conduct, 8 Split pea, 9 A piece of the action,
10 Royal prerogative, 11 To read between the lines, 12 Index linked, 13 Part and
parcel, 14 Long odds, 15 Mixed metaphor, 16 Industrial action, 17 Never a cross
word, 18 Mixed doubles, 19 Garden centre, 20 Backward glance, 21 The ends of
the earth.

R4 Rhyming pairs

(a)

Ration passion; maze craze; quick trick; meek Greek; middle fiddle; kitchen lichen; plump chump; retract pact

R5 Riddles

(a)

Although compiled in July 1780, the riddle was not published until December 1806 in *The Gentleman's Magazine,* some six years after Cowper's death. The following solution was received from one of its readers, giving the answer as 'Kiss'.

> A riddle by Cowper,
> Made me swear like a trooper:
> But my anger alas was in vain;
> For remembering the bliss
> of beauty's soft kiss,
> I now long for such riddles again.

(b)
Charade

(c)
Iron

(d)
Toast

S1 Scrabble

(a)
AXIOM = 44
THYME = 13
EQUIP = 78
JOKER = 16
ZYGAL = 76
Total = 227

(b)
Drayhorse; Harlequin; Viatica; Baroscope; Labyrinth; Espionage

S3 Side by side

(a)
1 friable, friar; 2 jackaroo, jackass; 3 victual, vicuna

S11 Syzygies

(a)

```
1    C O O K              2 C O N V E R S E
     ( C O O )                ( E R S E )
     S C O O P I N G        P E R S E V E R I N G
         ( P I N )                    ( E R I N )
         P I N N E D              M E R I N O
         ( I N N E )                  ( M E R )
         D I N N E R          P E R F U M E R Y
                                      ( E R F U )
                              C H E E R F U L L Y
```

(Well done, if you found other solutions.)

(b)
FOREHEAD, HEADSTRONG, STRONG-ARM, ARMCHAIR,
CHAIRMAN, MANDIBLE

T1 Target

(a)
The 9-letter word is CAMBRIDGE. Other words are:

BRIDGE	RIDGE	BADGER	CRAG
IMAGE	GAME	BRIG	GIRD
GARB	GRAB	GRACE	GEAR
CIGAR	GRADE	RAGE	GRIM
BADGE	CAGE	DRAG	MIRAGE
DIRGE	GRID	BARGE	BRAG
RAGED	CAGED	MAGI	EGAD
MAGIC	GRIME	GRIMED	BRIGADE
MIDGE	MARGE	BEGAD	CADGE
CADGER	MADGE	GERM	GRACED
AGED			

T5 Transdeletions

(a)
TRIANGLES: realigns, stealing, strangle, tinglers, glariest, latrines, astringe, starling, relating.

T6 Trigrams

(a)
BACKWARD; CARTWHEEL; ASTHMA; STRAIGHTFORWARD;
JACKPOT; FOXGLOVE; NUTMEG
(You may have found other words.)

T7 Triple (Plus) Choice

(a)

1 certify – A: To verify; confirm as true and accurate; guarantee; as, to have a bank teller *certify* that the signature is yours. Latin *certus* (certain).

2 vilify – B: To slander; make vicious statements about; blacken a good name; as, The surprise witness lied and *vilified* the two defendants. Latin *vilis* (cheap, base).

3 amplify – C: To increase or make stronger; as, The floods *amplified* the earthquake's devastation. Also, to add details or illustrations for clarity. Latin *amplus* (large).

4 quantify – A: To measure; determine or indicate the extent of; as, to try to *quantify* the amount of pollution in the air. Latin *quantus* (how much).

5 sanctify – A: To consecrate; set apart as holy; as, to *sanctify* a burial ground. Also, to give religious sanction to, as in marriage vows. Latin *sanctus* (holy).

6 stultify – B: To make ineffective; impair, reduce to futility; as, Over-reliance on rote drill can *stultify* a student's ability to learn. Latin *stultus* (foolish).

7 codify – C: To systematise laws, rules or regulations into a collection or code; as, to *codify* a town's building regulations. Latin *codex* (tablet on which laws were written.

8 transmogrify – A: To transform; change completely in a fantastic or grotesque way; as, Dr Jekyll was *transmogrified* into the monstrous Mr Hyde. Origin unknown.

9 reify – C: To treat an abstraction as if it had a concrete or tangible existence; as, Some physicists *reify* the concept of space-time. Latin *res* (thing).

10 gentrify – C: To upgrade a neighbourhood by renovating homes; as, to *gentrify* the Independence Hall area of Philadelphia. English *gentry*.

Vocabulary ratings: 5-7 correct . . . good
                       8-9 correct . . . excellent
                    10 correct . . . exceptional

U1 Univocals

(a)

Across		Down	
1	DECREE	1	NEEDLE
2	SECEDE	2	FEELER
3	EMERGE	3	WHEEZE
4	EYELET	4	LESSEE
5	BEETLE	5	WEEPER
6	CHEESE	6	VENEER

V1 Vowels

(a)

1 Strengths; 2 Aye and oui; 3 Uncomplimentary; 4 Defencelessnesses (the longest univocalic word); 5 Abracadabra; 6 Protozoological; 7 Indivisibility

(b)

GLYPH	FRY	SLYLY
PYX	FLY	THY
PYGMY	LYNX	PRY
CRYPT	LYNCH	SPY
TRYST	LYMPH	PLY
TRY	MYRRH	SHYLY
CRY	SLY	
DRY	SHY	

Readers may have found other, more obscure words, such as LYN and LYM. The 22 words listed are considered by the authors to be the most widely recognised words to be found in the grid.

W1 Word chain

(a)

Stooge, Geyser, Erotic, Icicle, Legume, Meagre, Recede, Desist

Z1 Zoetrope

(a)

This list of words was found, setting 'A' on the inner wheel against the letter shown, on the outer wheel.

Outer Wheel	3 letters	4 letters	5 letters
B	NEE – OFF	STAR – TUBS	SHEER – TIFFS
C	DYE – FAG	CAPS – ECRU	– – –
D	FOB – IRE	CROP – FURS	COBRA – FREUD
E	OAT – SEX	HARE – LEVI	PECAN – TIGER
F	NOT – STY	ODIN – TINS	FIZZY – KNEED
G	GIN – MOT	BUFF – HALL	GUMMY – MASSE
H	ATE – HAL	IBEX – PILE	CHEER – JOLLY
I	FAD – NIL	TALK – BITS	HALLS – PITTA
J	RIB – ARK	SIRE – BRAN	RIVER – ARENA
K	FEN – POX	DEED – NOON	CUBED – MELON
L	APE – LAP	HATS – SLED	SPITS – DATED
M	FIB – RUN	BOAS – NAME	TOUCH – FAGOT
N	ANT – NAG	REEF – ERRS	CREEL – PERRY
O	TUB – HIP	TAPE – HODS	HULAD – VIZOR
P	LIP – AXE	CLAD – RAPS	DAZED – SPOTS
Q	TOG – JEW	BOON – REED	XENON – NUDED
R	RAN – IRE	CRAN – TIRE	BUNNY – SLEEP
S	LIE – DAW	EMIT – WEAL	– – –
T	ALL – TEE	SPUN – LING	SHALY – LATER
U	LOT – FIN	MALL – GUFF	POSSE – JIMMY
V	ANE – VIZ	KNEE – FIZZ	KNEED – FIZZY
W	FIX – BET	STIR – OPEN	– – –
X	ORE – LOB	JUDE – GRAB	FLOOD – CILLA
Y	KEG – ICE	URGE – SPEC	– – –
Z	BEE – ADD	BEET – ADDS	BEEFS – ADDER

ACKNOWLEDGEMENTS

We are indebted to our wives, both named Barbara, for their continued enthusiastic support for all our projects.

Thanks are also due to the following:

The staff of Kirklees and Bexleyheath libraries for their courtesy and helpfulness. Peter Funk for supplying details of the feature 'It Pays to Enrich Your Word Power'. The *Huddersfield Examiner* and Mike Shaw for the feature 'Bill O' Ben's'. Mitzi Christiansen Kuehl for permission to reproduce material from her column 'Sphinx Winks' which appeared in *Integra* between 1981 to 1986. Audrey Austin for providing material from 'The Australian Crossword Club'. Brian Head for providing material from 'The Crossword Club'. Marjorie B. Friedman and Judith E. Bagai for providing material from 'The National Puzzlers' League'. A. Ross Eckler for permission to use selected material from *Word Ways*. Members of Enigmasig for their various contributions which have been selected for inclusion. Tony Sharrock for permission to reproduce material from *Whodunnit*. British Mensa for support given to us in our various projects.

The authors are grateful to all the above, without whose support this book would not have been possible.

INDEX